The Unbreakable Thread

Non-Racialism in South Africa

It is you, the reader, that catches the cannon breath and drum beat off the written page. I am no more, no less, than your clerk that writes it down, like a debt always owed and partly paid. This book of debt and part payment.

Woody Guthrie, 'People I Owe'
Coney Island, USA, 1946

Born to Win, Harmony Music Ltd, MacMillan Publishing Co., New York

The Unbreakable Thread
Non-Racialism in South Africa

Julie Frederikse

Indiana University Press

BLOOMINGTON AND INDIANAPOLIS

The Unbreakable Thread: Non-Racialism in South Africa was first published in 1990 by:

In the UK
Zed Books Ltd, 57 Caledonian Road, London N1 9BU

In the USA
Indiana University Press, Tenth and Morton Streets, Bloomington,
IN 47405

Copyright © The Popular History Trust

Cover design by Andrew Corbett
Typeset by Opus 43, Cumbria
Printed and bound in the UK by Dotesios Printers Ltd,
Kennet House, Kennet Way, Trowbridge, Wiltshire

British Library Cataloguing in Publication Data
Frederikse, Julie
 The unbreakable thread : non-racialism in South Africa
 1. South Africa, 1910-
 I. Title
 968.05

 ISBN 0-86232-970-1
 ISBN 0-86232-971-X pbk

Library of Congress Cataloging-in-Publication Data

Frederikse Julie.
 The unbreakable thread : non-racialism in South Africa / by Julie
 Frederikse.
  p. cm.
 ISBN 0-253-32473-4–ISBN 0-253-20619 7 (pbk.)
 1. South Africa–Race relations. 2. African National Congress.
 I. Title.
 DT1756.F73 1990
305.8′00968–dc20

90-33708
CIP

CONTENTS

PICTURE CREDITS

*   *International Defence and Aid Fund*

ABBREVIATIONS AND ACRONYMS

ABRECSA	Alliance of Black Reformed Churches in South Africa
ANC	African National Congress
ANC (WP)	African National Congress (Western Cape)
Anti-CAD	Anti-Coloured Affairs Department
Anti-PC	Anti-President's Council
Anti-SAIC	Anti-South African Indian Council (Campaign)
ARM	African Resistance Movement
APDUSA	African People's Democratic Union of South Africa
AZACTU	Azanian Council of Trade Unions
AZAPO	Azanian People's Organization
AZASM	Azanian Students Movement
AZASO	Azanian Students Organization
AZAYO	Azanian Youth Organization
BAMCWU	Black Allied Miners and Construction Workers Union
BC	Black Consciousness
BCM	Black Consciousness Movement
BCP	Black Community Programmes
BOSS	Bureau of State Security
BPC	Black People's Convention
BSS	Black Students Society
CAD	Coloured Affairs Department
CAHAC	Cape Areas Housing Action Committee
CAL	Cape Action League
Cathsoc	Catholic Students Society
CAYCO	Cape Youth Congress
CCB	Civil Cooperation Bureau
CI	Christian Institute of Southern Africa
COD	Congress of Democrats
Comintern	Communist International
Contralesa	Congress of Traditional Leaders of South Africa
COSAS	Congress of South African Students
COSATU	Congress of South African Trade Unions
COSG	Conscientious Objectors Support Group
CP	Communist Party
CPC	Coloured People's Congress
CPSA	Communist Party of South Africa
CUSA	Council of Unions of South Africa
CWIU	Chemical Workers Industrial Union
DEFA	Defence and Aid Fund
Descom	Detainees Support Committee

DEW	Detainees Education and Welfare
DPSC	Detainees' Parents Support Committee
EATWOT	Ecumenical Association of Third World Theologians
ECC	End Conscription Campaign
FAWU	Food and Allied Workers Union
FBWU	Food and Beverage Workers Union
FedSAW	Federation of South African Women
FedTraw	Federation of Transvaal Women
FOSATU	Federation of South African Trade Unions
FSU	Friends of the Soviet Union
GAWU	General and Allied Workers Union
GCD	Grahamstown Committee of Democrats
Gradac	Grahamstown Democratic Action Committee
GWU	General Workers Union
IANC	Independent African National Congress
ICFTU	International Confederation of Free Trade Unions
ICT	Institute for Contextual Theology
ICU	Industrial and Commercial Workers Union
IDAF	International Defence and Aid Fund
IDASA	Institute for Democratic Alternatives in South Africa
IUEF	International University Exchange Fund
IIE	Institute of Industrial Education
ISL	International Socialist League
IWA	Industrial Workers of Africa
IYY	International Youth Year
JORAC	Joint Rent Action Committee
MAWU	Metal and Allied Workers Union
MDM	Mass Democratic Movement
Milcom	Military Committee
MK	Umkhonto we Sizwe
MWASA	Media Workers Association of SA
NAC	National Action Council
NACTU	National Council of Trade Unions
NADEL	National Association of Democratic Lawyers
NAFCOC	National African Chamber of Commerce
NAMDA	National Medical and Dental Association

NCFS	National Catholic Federation of Students
NEC	National Executive Committee
NECC	National Education Crisis Committee
NFC	National Forum Committee
NGK	Nederduitse Gereformeerde Kerk (Dutch Reformed Church)
NIC	Natal Indian Congress
NIS	National Intelligence Services
NLL	National Liberation League
NOW	Natal Organization of Women
NP	Nationalist Party
NUM	National Union of Mineworkers
NUMSA	National Union of Metalworkers of South Africa
NUSAS	National Union of South African Students
OAU	Organization for African Unity
OB	Ossewa Brandwag (Oxwagon Sentinel)
PAC	Pan-Africanist Congress
PC	President's Council
PEYCO	Port Elizabeth Youth Congress
PFP	Progressive Federal Party
PMC	Political-Military Council (ANC
POPCRU	Police and Prisons Civil Rights Union
RDM	Rand Daily Mail
SAAWU	South African Allied Workers Union
SACC	South African Council of Churches
Sached	South African Council on Higher Education
SACOS	South African Council on Sport
SACPO	South African Coloured People's Organization
SACP	South African Communist Party
SACTU	South African Congress of Trade Unions
SACTWU	South African Clothing and Textile Workers Union
SADF	South African Defence Force
SADWU	South African Domestic Workers Union
SAIC	South African Indian Council
SAIC	South African Indian Congress
SAIRR	South African Institute of Race Relations
SANNC	South African National Natives Congress
SANROC	South African Non-racial Olympic Committee
SAP	South African Party
SARHWU	South African Railways and Harbour Workers Union
SASM	South African Students Movement
SASO	South African Students Organization
SASPU	South African Students Press Union
SAYCO	South African Youth Congress
SAYRCO	South African Youth Revolutionary Council
SOMAFCO	Solomon Mahlangu Freedom College
SOYCO	Soweto Youth Congress
Spro-cas	Special Programme for Christian Action in Society, Study Project on Christianity in Apartheid Society
SRC	Students Representative Council
SSRC	Soweto Students Representative Council
TIC	Transvaal Indian Congress
TLSA	Teachers League of South Africa
TUACC	Trade Union Advisory and Coordinating Conference
TUCSA	Trade Union Council of South Africa
UBJ	Union of Black Journalists
UCC	United Committee of Concern
UCT	University of Cape Town
UDF	United Democratic Front
UDW	University of Durban-Westville
UN	United Nations
UNISA	University of South Africa
UWC	University of the Western Cape
UWCO	United Women's Congress
UWO	United Women's Organization
VAT	Victims Against Terrorism
Wits	University of the Witwatersrand
YCS	Young Christian Students
YCW	Young Christian Workers
ZANLA	Zimbabwe African National Liberation Army
ZANU	Zimbabwe African National Union
ZAPU	Zimbabwe African People's Union
ZIPRA	Zimbabwe People's Revolutionary Army

AUTHOR'S NOTE

This book is the product of a collective process. The work of organizing and transcribing the interviews that form its core, the research and collection of documents and pictures, and the editing of the manuscript was all coordinated by a collective in Harare, the Popular History Trust. Sue Godt developed a computerized oral history database which was not only invaluable for writing the book, but will make these and other interviews accessible to future writers and researchers. Sukthi Naidoo, Luisa Potenza, Harriet Bolton, Hilary Brown, Benny Graves, Imogene Rider and Jenny Ruckelshaus transcribed the interview material and entered it into the database. Kerry Nelson helped with research. Derek Hanekom administered the project. The Popular History Trust is using royalties from the sale of this book to make it available at the lowest possible cover price and to assist in its distribution in South Africa.

Research inside South Africa was coordinated by the South African History Archive of Johannesburg, with the assistance of Michael Westcott, Chris Mathabe and Mike Aldrich. Professors Thomas Karis and Gail Gerhart supplied various documents from their collection in New York. Two Dutch development agencies, ICCO and NOVIB, funded the research, writing and production.

The book was considerably strengthened by Mike Kirkwood's work as editor and production coordinator. Many others offered advice and criticism, from the initial outline through to the final draft. I am especially grateful to André Proctor of the Popular History Trust, Frank Meintjes and Junaid Ahmed of the Congress of South African Writers, Rob Davies of the Centre of African Studies in Maputo, Mongezi Stofile, Alice Dinerman, Colin Darch and Chris Giffard.

For assistance in arranging interviews I am indebted to Gavin Evans, Gary Cullen, Fiona Dove and Richard Goode in South Africa, and Margaret Ling in Britain. John Daniel exhorted me to research and write this book many years before he became involved in its publication. As for my family, Stelios, Nikki and Alex Comninos, they have lived with this book for five years; I thank them for their support and understanding.

My greatest debt is to the people I interviewed, who gave of their time and of themselves. Most of these interviews took several hours, and required that people reflect on both their personal background and their political development. I conducted more than 200 interviews in the course of researching this book; excerpts from 118 interviews appear in these pages.

Some 75 interviews were conducted inside South Africa in 1985. Thereafter I was not granted a visa to enter South Africa, so the rest of the interviews, conducted between 1986 and 1989, were with South Africans living in or visiting Zimbabwe, Zambia, Tanzania, Britain, Canada and the US. Nearly all the interviews were conducted in English, although for the majority of people this was not their first language.

Many writings about South Africa include a justification of the use of racial terminology, i.e., the labels 'African', 'coloured', 'Indian' and 'white'. No such apology appears here. This book is inspired by the conviction that to acknowledge and explore the divisions of colour and class is an important step in empowering people to build an undivided, non-racial society.

Julie Frederikse
Harare, Zimbabwe
August 1990

PART ONE
1652—1950

Tens of thousands of people celebrated on Cape Town's Parade on 11 February 1990 while waiting for their first glimpse of ANC leader Nelson Mandela.

1 Our Fathers Dwelt Together in Peace

'Message from the Youth Leadership', issued from underground by the South African Youth Congress:

The resilience of our people and their determination to be free defies all odds: it is an unshakeable belief in democracy and non-racialism which motivates them to forge ahead.

Titus Mafolo, a spokesperson for the Mass Democratic Movement:

What is the unifying perspective of the Mass Democratic Movement? It is, simply, to turn our country into a non-racial, democratic and united South Africa.

Frederik van Zyl Slabbert, director of policy and planning for the Institute for a Democratic Alternative for South Africa:

The '70s saw the collapse of the partition state, the '80s saw the shift to the integrated state — the '90s will see the battle for the non-racial democratic state.

Ahmed Kathrada, member of the African National Congress, the South African Communist Party and the High Command of the ANC's military wing, Umkhonto we Sizwe:

In the face of the severest persecution and repression imaginable — banning, torture, imprisonment, maiming, killing — the ANC has a proud and incomparable record of consistently maintaining its policy of non-racialism.

Nelson Mandela, in his first public address upon his release from prison: [1]

We call upon our white compatriots to join us in the shaping of a new South Africa — the freedom movement is a political home for you, too. Universal suffrage on a common voters' roll in a united, democratic and non-racial South Africa is the only way to peace and racial harmony.

When the people of South Africa make their demands for justice, there is one word they use again and again: 'non-racialism'. In an era of pat slogans, sung and shouted at mass meetings and headlined in leaflets and banners, this word stands out precisely because it is not glib. The demand for a non-racial South Africa is the common ground that unites a wide range of forces for change. The primary goal is a completely restructured society, a democracy in which people are not differentiated according to racial criteria, but enjoy rights as equal citizens in one united country. To be democratic, the future South Africa must be non-racial: that premise is fundamental.

This book traces the development of the theory and practice of non-racialism in South Africa through the words and writings of its people. The focus is on their lived experience in a struggle for change that defines the enemy as a system — not as members of particular racial or cultural groups.

To understand non-racialism, one must first understand the racialism it seeks to displace. From the first settlement at the Cape of Good Hope in 1652 and for the next two centuries, an ideology based on racial prejudice came to sustain the trading interests of Dutch, and later British, merchants. Inequality between blacks and whites stemmed from the pressing need of European settlers producing agricultural products for the world market to exploit the labour of the indigenous population.

At first the settlers imported labour from the slave markets of Asia and West Africa, for the indigenous people saw no need to leave their viable and independent societies to work for others. But as soon as the settlers were powerful enough, they began attacking these hunter-gatherer and herder communities with their horses and guns, taking land and livestock by force. Those unable to escape beyond the frontier became the settlers' slaves.

In the seventeenth, eighteenth and early nineteenth centuries, the Boers (descendants of the Dutch settlers who spoke a dialect that came to be called Afrikaans) swallowed up more and more land. Only the larger and more powerful Bantu-speaking societies later encountered by Boer and British settlers were able to mount effective resistance. Xhosa society, relentlessly driven eastwards in a series of frontier wars, nonetheless retained its political independence well into the nineteenth century, by which time many other African societies were beginning to assert control over traditional domains now penetrated by 'Voortrekkers'[2] and other settlers. This led to increasing interdependence between black and white: settler farmers often paid tribute to chiefs, and cohabitation was not uncommon.

There was no inherent racism in traditional African society. In early contacts, shipwrecked Portuguese sailors were integrated into Xhosa communities and English traders became Zulu chiefs. Without the means to exploit, whites embraced blacks as equals; when not threatened with dispossession, blacks welcomed whites.

It took the large-scale investment of international capital in the late nineteenth century, and the destruction of independent African societies in order to provide a workforce for the mines, to create a single racially-stratified society in South Africa. Such accommodation as had existed on the frontier was shattered by rapid industrialization. Whites, who mainly owned the means to produce wealth, needed blacks to work for them at wage levels well below the rate required to support workers and their families. Whites needed an ideology to defend this exploitative labour form. A philosophy of racial superiority justified the system and a battery of racial laws enforced it.

Life on the frontier was not so rigidly segregated: mutual dependence and respect cut across racial and social distinctions, as shown by this mid-nineteenth century painting of Boers with their Khoi servants. The racial division between master and servant was institutionalized in the more advanced economy of settler society.

Independent African societies resisted conquest and colonization in the only way they could, by force of arms. Still, the desire for cooperation and the preference for peaceful coexistence were continually expressed.

Xhosa chiefs to the British forces which invaded their land, 1818:

The war, British chiefs, is an unjust one. When our fathers and the fathers of the Boers first settled in the Zuurveld [far eastern Cape Colony] they dwelt together in peace. Their flocks grazed on the same hills, their herdsmen smoked together out of the same pipes — they were brothers.

Then the Boers made commando [raids] on our fathers. What those covetous men could not get from our fathers for old buttons they took by force. Our fathers began to hate the colonists, and aimed at their destruction. The white men hated us, but could not drive us away. When there was war we plundered you. When there was peace some of our bad people stole, but our chiefs forbade it. You came at last like locusts. We stood — we could do no more.

You sent a commando, you took our last cow. Without milk, our corn destroyed, we saw our wives and children perish. We saw that we must ourselves perish. We followed, therefore, the tracks of our cattle into the Colony. We plundered and we fought for our lives. We found you weak — we destroyed your soldiers. We saw that we were strong and we attacked your headquarters. And if we had succeeded, our right was good, for you began the war. We failed, and you are here.

We wish for peace. We wish to rest in our huts, we wish to get milk for our children, our wives wish to till the land. But your troops cover the plains and swarm in the thickets, where they cannot distinguish the man from the woman and shoot all.

Faced with aggressive armies fuelled by the industrial power of Britain, Africans lost their freedom but not their spirit of resistance. A tradition of defiance existed from the earliest slave revolts and continued into the industrial age. Agricultural communities resisted relocation, preferring even sharecropping to wage labour. Squatting, illicit liquor brewing, industrial sabotage, desertion, strikes: defiance had many faces.

New conditions gave rise to new forms of resistance, and new generations no longer yearned for a return to a traditional autonomy. The consciousness that developed in the early twentieth century aspired towards equality in the modern industrial society and inspired new forms of organization to achieve this goal. This evolving resistance to racial oppression never took the form of a single homogeneous ideology, but has always been as varied and complex as the society that engendered it. A key distinction to emerge was that between the liberal tradition, rooted in nineteenth-century British missionary culture, and a popular democratic tradition that emerged with black working-class organizations.

The main concern of the liberal tradition was to draw a small minority of the oppressed into an alliance with the elites, with change to come from the top down. Characterized by reformism and paternalism, liberalism never challenged the basic features of exploitation, seeking merely to make the unjust system more humane. As will be shown, the liberal tradition has proved to be a minority trend.

The popular democratic tradition is rooted in an alliance of all the oppressed. As workers began to organize against the racial system that took from them the means of controlling their lives and the wealth they produced, they joined forces with others of all races and social backgrounds committed to change 'from below'. This popular democratic — and non-racial — tradition gave rise to a mass movement that has dominated South African resistance politics. Non-racialism runs like an unbreakable thread throughout the movement's history.

Notes

1. The first four quotations date from 1989. Mandela was speaking in 1990.
2. The Afrikaans word for pioneers is commonly applied to burghers who joined the 'Great Trek' of the 1830s. Mythologized by twentieth-century nationalists as a single event — a rite of passage giving birth to the Afrikaner nation — this migration was made up of several different (sometimes feuding) parties of burghers who trekked north to escape British rule at the Cape, and later founded the republics of the Orange Free State and the Transvaal.

2 White Workers! On Which Side Are You?

It was mining — mainly of gold — that catapulted South Africa into the industrial age. But the gold-bearing 'reef' of the Witwatersrand was of very poor quality, so high profits depended on low production costs. The cheapest way for the mine-owners to get the gold required vast numbers of unskilled workers using labour-intensive methods. Britain obliged by sending its armies to destroy the independent African societies, invade the Boer republics, and create a Union of South Africa largely beholden to the powerful Chamber of Mines. The supply of African labour was assured by imposing taxes on peasants, restricting their access to land and markets, instituting pass laws and housing workers in compounds.[1]

White workers, in contrast, had far more clout: most skilled labour on the mines was performed by immigrants with a militant tradition of West European craft unionism, which won them a relatively high standard of living and protection from undercutting by cheaper black labour. Early on, white workers formed a kind of alliance with capital — both profits and higher wages deriving from the extreme exploitation of black workers.

But relations were not always harmonious. Attempts by the mining houses to cut costs and increase profits by replacing white workers with blacks whom they paid much less led to bitter strikes that climaxed in 1922. A miners' strike which the state helped the Chamber of Mines to smash saw white workers attack scabbing black workers and is remembered for the slogan, 'Workers of the World, Fight and Unite for a White South Africa!' Once it had put down the 'Rand Revolt' the state acceded to the white workers' racist demands, thus buying fifty years of relative peace on the white labour front.[2]

Black workers also organized on the mines: widespread job actions for better wages and conditions culminated in the 1920 miners' strike, involving 70,000 workers over a period of twelve days. Most of the strikes were spontaneous and workers lacked the leverage to sustain their actions. Still, it was the fear of this growing black worker militancy that had prompted the government to put long-term security before short-term profits and concede the demands of the Rand Revolt.

Prime Minister Jan Smuts, 21 March 1922, addressing parliament after the white miners' strike was brutally crushed with the aid of bomber aircraft and tanks, resulting in some 250 deaths, 1,000 arrests, and the execution of four strike leaders:

The fear that obsessed me above all things was that owing to the wanton provocation of the revolutionaries, there might be a wild, uncontrollable outbreak among the natives.

Not all white workers embraced the racial division of labour. A section of white labour broke with the mainstream and demanded a unity of the working class that transcended racial barriers. Some of these whites were West European artisans attracted by the mining boom, others were less skilled refugees from anti-Jewish repression in Eastern Europe, and a few were British Army veterans who had stayed on in South Africa[3] after the Boer War. In 1915 they broke from the racist South African Labour Party and formed the International Socialist League (ISL), the first political group to attempt to organize non-racially and build a mass base among the oppressed.

ISL leaflet issued during the black miners' strike of 1920:

White Workers! Do you hear the new Army of Labour coming? The native workers are beginning to wake up. They are finding out that they are slaves to the big capitalists. But they want to rise. Why not? They want better housing and better clothes, better education and a higher standard of life.

White Workers! On which side are you? Your interests and theirs are the same as against the Boss. Back them up! The Chamber of Mines will be asking you to take up the rifle to dragoon the Native strikers. Don't do it!

The ISL had already begun working with the newly established South African Native National Congress (SANNC, later renamed the African National Congress). The attempts of the white radicals at organizing black workers led to the founding of South Africa's first black trade union in 1917, the Industrial Workers of Africa (IWA). In 1919 the new Industrial and Commercial Workers Union (ICU) led a strike on the Cape Town docks that involved both African and coloured workers.[4] Those arrested that same year after a strike wave on the Rand included blacks and whites, and the 'public violence' trial that followed was the first in South African history in which blacks and whites were charged together for political offences.

This glimmer of non-racialism in the early twentieth century was overshadowed by the firmly established, if not always stable, political alliance between white labour and capital. The promotion of whites as supervisors of less skilled black labour facilitated the emergence of a 'labour aristocracy' in league with industry and government against the blacks below them. Members of the ISL who formed the Communist Party of South Africa (CPSA) in 1921 began to realize that the country's problems could not be understood solely as conflict between social classes: evidently, relations between the races were also vitally important.

Jack Simons, Communist Party member active from the 1930s to the present:

I remember in 1930 or '31, during the Depression, seeing a mixed white and black procession demonstrating for jobs and wages and bread, and this

The capitalization of agriculture spawned a new class of landless Afrikaners who flooded the cities in search of work in the 1930s and 1940s. This cartoon shows the fears of white railways (spoorwee) workers that Smuts's South African Party (SAP) would replace them with cheaper black labour. The white government worried that poor whites might one day stop fearing blacks as competitors and instead join forces to demand change.[5]

impressed me greatly. You might say I had a romantic idea, but then I think people with a radical outlook who reject the existing social system are romantics — some people call them mad. You have to have a great deal of confidence and faith, you have to look for little things like that as beginnings. Now I was shaping the ideological framework at that time, and this gave me evidence of a non-racial class approach. But that had to mature, though it was difficult to mature it in the South African situation at that time.

You see, the Communist Party of South Africa had a theoretical platform, which is important. As far back as 1928, Sidney Bunting and Eddie Roux,[6] the two leaders, had gone to Moscow and they'd been ticked off by the Communist International. At that time there was a group of American negroes who were very vocal in the Comintern, and they were represented by a couple of very voluble fellows who criticized the communists of South Africa very savagely for being a white supremacist party,[7] and insisted that the correct policy for the communists to adopt was to launch a programme in support of the national democratic revolution, in terms of resolutions adopted by the Communist International as far back as 1920 and '21.

There's a whole history of this, communism and the national liberation movement — this was before my time. Basically the communists had been oriented towards white workers, thinking the white workers would be revolutionary. Now by 1928 that optimism had ebbed, died away, and I think the visit to Moscow had opened their eyes that their true function was to work with the African working class, and they thereupon proceeded to do it.

It wasn't easy to make this shift. The white communists who had led the party since its inception and even before that had to turn right round and reject their former colleagues and make an approach to blacks, whom they had no real contact with or experience of. You see, the communists had launched this — we were pioneers in that respect. Nobody else had ever come forward with this notion of a black republic and a black majority.

The South African communists returned home from Moscow having pledged to implement the Comintern's call for 'an independent native South African republic as a stage towards a workers' and peasants' republic, with full, equal rights for all races'. The 'Black Republic' thesis caused strife within party ranks for the next decade, but it also generated a transformation of both the membership and then the leadership, from mainly white to overwhelmingly black.

Letter from Moses Kotane, CPSA member who became general-secretary in 1939 and served until his death in 1978, writing from Cradock to the Johannesburg District Committee, 1934:

Dear Comrades,

Our party has and is suffering owing to being too Europeanized. The European language is not blindly applicable for South Africa. In Europe class-consciousness has developed immensely whilst here national oppression, discrimination and exploitation confuses the class war, and the majority of the African working population are more national-conscious than class-conscious.

My first suggestion is that the party become more Africanized, that the CPSA must pay special attention to South Africa, study the conditions in this country, and concretize the demands of the toiling masses from first-hand information, that we must speak the language of the Native masses, and must know their demands. That while it must not lose its international allegiance, the party must be Bolshevized, become South African not only theoretically, but in reality. It should be a party working in the interests and for the toiling people in South Africa, and not a party of a group of Europeans who are merely interested in European affairs.

With revolutionary greetings,

Yours fraternally,

Moses M. Kotane

While increasing numbers of blacks endorsed the non-racialism of the CPSA, others joined the growing non-racial trade union movement, along with whites who had embraced the goal of a 'Black Republic'.

Ray Alexander, who came to South Africa as a young refugee from Latvia and helped organize non-racial trade unions from the 1930s to the 1950s:

I came to South Africa on 6 November 1929, when I was 15 years old, going on for 16, and the very next few days I was introduced to people who were supporters of the Communist Party. I went to do shopping for my sister, so when I was buying the vegetables I saw workers coming out from the factory. I asked them whether they have a union and if they are members of the union. One of them said they have a union but they are not members of the union, and the others said they have no union. And I walked off with the idea that here in South Africa is virgin soil!

The fact that these workers were black didn't bother you?

Being Jewish, I knew of the oppression that the Jewish people had in the ghettos, and also the fact that they were discriminated against in Tsarist Russia from entering universities and from learning professions, trades. There was a kind of apartheid. Therefore race discrimination and job reservation in South Africa was very close to me because it is part of my upbringing. I got to know about the white 'civilized labour policy',[8] so that all fitted in with the anti-semitism that was present in Tsarist Russia and in Poland and even in Latvia, particularly in the ghettos.

I never felt — honestly, on my word of honour — I never felt odd working among African or coloured people, working with them together. We were one. I never felt when I was with Comrade Moses Kotane that he's African and I'm white, and he never felt that I'm white. He used to say to me, 'With you I feel one.'

I remember the first holiday I had in Cape Town, my mother took me to introduce me to her relatives, and my cousin saying to me that I'll never be able to marry, you know. I was still going on for 17 years and he's telling me there won't be a Jewish boy: it's already known that I walk about with coloureds and blacks and no Jewish boy will marry me. I just looked at him — to me this was completely nonsense that he was speaking to me. I wasn't going to alter my lifestyle.

On 16 December 1929 a demonstration was going through Adderley Street, coming up from Plein Street, led by Eddie Roux and others, Africans. I quickly go to the manager's desk and I say, 'May I take an hour off — my lunch hour — or I'll work it off later on?' and she said yes, and I just quickly went and joined the demonstration. So there were only two whites, Eddie and myself. However, when I came back from the demonstration an hour later — I looked at my watch so that I shouldn't be late — I was called into the office and told that I can't work there any more because I participated in this demonstration. So I lost my job.

When you first met black people in South Africa, did you discuss this issue of colour?

No, I didn't. I completely felt at ease with them, with Johnny Gomes, with [E. J.] Brown, with James La Guma.[9] So I got involved with those people and I was introduced to the discussion on the 'Native Republic', the Black Republic. Now that is something of great honour to the Communist Party of South Africa, because it was the first and only organization that put forward majority rule — the first organization on the African continent that had put forward the idea of one vote for every person, irrespective of race and colour. And there was raging the debate about it — whites in the Communist Party who hadn't approved of it left the party.

Well, I was completely in agreement with this slogan of Black Republic, because that was to me a sensible thing, democracy. I couldn't visualize anything else. One of the comrades had said that I should give them the reasons why I am supporting the Black Republic, so I put down the reason as democratic rights: Africa is black, South Africa is a black man's country, and therefore it should be a black republic. I said to them, 'But this is ordinary democracy, one man, one vote — we can't tolerate this white autocracy here.' So they accepted me like this.

What about the rank-and-file union membership, did they accept you? And the white workers, how did they feel?

In all the Cape Town factories you had a mixed group of workers, whites and coloured, working together. There wasn't this nonsense that came afterwards. Now the first time that I succeeded to organize a union was the Commercial Employees Union. I worked in the shop and I organized the shop assistants. You know that we used to work Christmas — before Christmas Day and before New Year's Day and before Easter Day, till eleven o'clock at night, Fridays till nine p.m. — and we succeeded in reducing the working hours.

Now at this stage, when I got so many benefits for them, I walked in the street with Comrade Shuba,[10] and two of the shop stewards, two Afrikaans girls, they went and lodged a complaint with the Cape Federation of Labour Unions that I was walking with a 'kaffir'[11] and insulted them by greeting them. So they organized a big campaign that I must be removed as the secretary of the Commercial Employees Union — that was all done by the reactionary leaders of the Cape Federation of Labour Unions. So I'm summoned to a meeting and they expect that I would resign.

But I didn't resign. I made my speech and I said that I'll help any worker, irrespective of their colour or race or religion, to improve their wages and conditions of work. I said, 'What you have, the benefits you have obtained as a result of my work, is due to the fact that Comrade Shuba had trained me.' And elections took place, and although one of the trade union federation leaders went round and told people not to vote for me, I got re-elected with flying colours. And then this matter is discussed by our comrades and it's all agreed that I'm in a way wasting my time on these white girls — that I should devote all my energies in organizing the coloured and African workers.

Why was that decided?

Because the base for our work is the black people — that is as it was and as it is still today, you see.

As it happened, that lesson learned — that the impetus for changing South Africa would come from the most exploited group — was not so straightforward. Some trade unionists felt that while they endorsed non-racialism in theory, in practice a form of racial differentiation within the unions offered tactical advantages in building a powerful workers' movement. For others, this represented a betrayal of principles and undermined the position of black workers.

Food and Canning Workers Union officials (left to right): Betty du Toit, Oscar Mpetha, Ray Alexander, Maria Williams and David Jantjies.

James Phillips, a cutter in the garment industry and chairman of the Garment Workers Union Number Two Branch for 'non-Europeans' from 1940 until his banning in 1953:

In fact, the early beginnings of the clothing industry in the Transvaal came mainly from the Afrikaner community, so that my first job was working for a firm which had a Jewish employer and mainly Afrikaner girls. There was always a strict line barring you from any close relationship with the whites. You worked in the factory and you saw to their needs as far as work was concerned — out in the street you were nobody.

Were these Afrikaner women members of the union?

Yes, well, it's a peculiar thing about the way things go in South Africa. Solly Sachs had established the Garment Workers Union, and initially it was based on membership who came from the Afrikaner community, you see, mostly women. At some stage, when I suppose they could not get enough white labour for the industry, there was then an influx of coloureds and Indians, you see. Their numbers were growing and so around 1939, '40 they felt that they'd have to do something about providing some sort of union membership for these coloureds and Indians, and so they called a meeting and established the Number Two Branch.

Now Solly's attitude was that because the Afrikaners were essentially very racist in their outlook, you couldn't get them to sit at the same table with blacks to discuss their problems which were mutual to themselves, and so the Number One Branch would meet and discuss the same problems as the

Number Two Branch — but separately, you see. We then reached a stage where we felt that since they professed that trade unions looked after the interests of all workers, irrespective of race, why did Solly and his colleagues call themselves socialist or whatever, when in fact, they are carrying out a policy which means that we are apart? So that we found ourselves in the Number Two Branch actually waging a campaign to bring the union together. But they wouldn't have it, because the feeling expressed by Solly Sachs was that if we did so the Afrikaners would resent it and it would split the union.

It's a strange thing, there were lots of contradictions. There was a dispute in 1943 when we were all locked out by the employers — some 400 factories throughout Johannesburg were just closed. I'd been working for this firm for a number of years, and though working with these Afrikaner girls meant that we kept our distance from each other, in the factory there was a kind of link. I was busy running in between the factory and the union office and so forth, and they wanted to select a shop steward. They found that the one they had was useless, and an Afrikaner girl said, 'Well, there's Phillips, let's make him our shop steward.' And so a message was sent across to our union office: 'They say they want Phillips to act for those girls in South African Shirt and Underwear Manufacturers.' And the union officials, Solly Sachs and his colleagues, turned it down. They said, 'No, you must appoint a white person.'

Another time it was decided that there should be a cutters' association, and most of the cutters in the industry then were Afrikaners, with a sprinkling of coloureds and Indians. And this meeting was called and we discussed the question of forming this association, and it was all agreed and they said we need a chairman. So an Afrikaner got up and he says, 'I nominate that man.' And they said, 'Who?' And he said, 'Phillips.' So I was appointed unanimously at this meeting.

Solly was away and returned a few days later and saw the minutes of the meeting, called me to the office and he said, 'You shouldn't have become the chairman, you should have let an Afrikaner become the chairman.' I said, 'But they elected me and it was unanimous.' Well, he wouldn't have it. But this is something on which I was in dispute with Solly over a long, long period. I thought, here was an opportunity where we might be able to break those barriers by these little links.

This was the thing about the Garment Workers Union: it never politicized the workers. They made them just think in terms of bread and butter — unlike us, who felt that we didn't fight for bread and butter issues, but wider issues, that politics comes into it. I think when I was elected as chairman, and where these workers wanted me to be their shop steward, an attempt should have been made to try it out and not to just reject it outright, and to see what would happen. But Solly adopted a very special position: he felt that the time would come when the Afrikaners would open their minds, you know, and that they would actually lead to change things in South Africa.

And what did you feel, having worked with these whites on the shop floor?

I felt that in order to advance ourselves as workers we would have to group ourselves together, and by the force of our numbers and our strength and our politics and our links with the movement in general, this is how we would come to be respected. But then it had gone too far, and this is why the position is what it is today, that the minds of the whites have been so completely warped.[12]

An Appeal to all *Garment Workers and to all other Workers and Citizens.*

Keep the Workers' Ranks United and Free from Racial Hatred.

Do Not Make Your Hard Life More Difficult.

FELLOW WORKERS,

The recent events in Johannesburg and in other parts of the country which have served to inflame racial hatred in the hearts of hundreds of thousands of people impel us to direct this appeal to you.

Violent inter-racial hatred is sweeping the whole country. Afrikaners hate non-Afrikaners and even some of their own fellow Afrikaners.

Britishers hate Afrikaners. Citizen against citizen. Worker against worker, all common sense is thrown to the devil. Young and old, men and women, all join in this orgy of racial hate. Hardly a day passes without some incident which inflames this hatred. When some bearded men attack a soldier, or some soldiers attack a bearded man, the trouble is not confined to the actual combatants, but tens of thousands of hearts all over the country on both sides flare up with deep and passionate hatred.

This is a national tragedy. Our national life is being poisoned for many years — even generations — to come. This poison has also entered our own ranks, and quarrels amongst workers are taking place in factories with increasing frequency.

Workers of South Africa! Have you stopped to think where all this will lead? Your life is full of hardships and is becoming increasingly difficult.

Are you going to make it completely unbearable?

Afrikaner worker! How will your life become better and happier by hating every Britisher?

British worker! What pleasure will you derive from hating the Afrikaner?

For your own sake, for the sake of your children, for the sake of the generations to come; you must do all in your power to stop the racial poison which pervades every phase of your life, every heart and every home. Racial hatred is the very negation of all that is decent in life, of true Christianity and of human conduct.

Have we sunk to the level of beasts? Or have we still left in us a spark of reason, sense and human decency?

By all means seek freedom and independence, strive for happiness, spread your culture, treasure and preserve your traditions, but drop racial hatred which has nothing in common with freedom, independence, happiness, culture or national traditions. Concentrate your hatred not on fellow human beings, but rather on the poverty, starvation, insecurity and the other evils from which the masses of workers and poor people suffer.

We make this urgent appeal to our members and to all others.

(1) Think with your head and not with your heart.

(2) Do not offend those who hold views which differ from your own. You may both be wrong.

(3) Do not take part in any brawls or any other acts of hooliganism.

(4) Keep calm yourself and calm those who are inclined to get excited in case of an incident.

(5) Teach those who share your views to keep calm and not to start squabbles.

(6) Seek and strive for true happiness for the masses of people; for decent homes instead of hovels; for clothes instead of rags; for good food instead of mieliepap; for real security instead of the uncertainty of the tomorrow.

Racial hatred will bring endless sorrow and suffering to all.

Racial peace and working class unity will bring us real happiness and a better life.

Away with racial hatred! Away with poverty and insecurity. Up with working class unity!

Let us fight for real social, economic and political freedom for all mankind.

For the Garment Workers' Union,
ANNA SCHEEPERS, President.
E. S. SACHS, General Secretary.
JOHANNA CORNELIUS, National Organiser.

Above are three women workers: One English, one Afrikaans, one Jewish. Why should they hate each other?

A Garment Workers Union pamphlet addressed the issue of ethnic prejudice among workers, but focussed only on the whites.

Notes

1. One hundred years later, the National Union of Mineworkers responded to 'the pomp and advertising hype of the Chamber's centenary celebrations' with a full-page advertisement in several South African newspapers labelling the Chamber 'the exploiter of our nation', citing a pay differential between whites and blacks of ten to one, and charging that 'racial segregation and the denial of basic human and trade union rights are the cornerstones of the industry'.
2. Apart from the Garment Workers Union in the 1930s and 1940s, there was little serious disruptive action on the part of white labour until the 1970s.
3. The first category included ISL and CPSA founder member Bill Andrews, the only South African ever elected to the executive of the Comintern; the second included Solly Sachs, a Lithuanian immigrant who led the Garment Workers Union for more than twenty years; the third, S.P. Bunting, an early CPSA chairman who advocated the recruitment of Africans. For a more detailed analysis of early white radicalism in South Africa, see John Daniel, 'Radical Resistance to Minority Rule in South Africa: 1906—1975', unpublished Ph.D thesis, State University of New York at Buffalo, 1975.
4. The white railway union participated in separate but supportive action with the ICU and IWA until the government responded with a concession that prompted the white workers to scab.
5. The gravity of this concern is evidenced by extensive government probes into the 'poor white problem' in the first three decades of the twentieth century.
6. One of the first South African-born white communists.
7. The Negro Commission, a sub-committee of the Colonial Commission of the Sixth Congress of the Comintern, which analyzed race and nationalism in South Africa and the US.
8. Sheltered employment for unskilled whites, extended by Prime Minister Barry Hertzog's Pact government (Nationalist-Labour) in 1924.
9. Gomes, Brown and La Guma (father of ANC leader and author Alex La Guma) were CPSA members from Cape Town's coloured community.
10. James Shuba was secretary of the Cape Laundry Workers Union, elected to the first national council of the South African Trades and Labour Council and a member of the CPSA.
11. A derisive South African term for blacks, stemming from an Arabic word meaning 'infidel'.
12. For more on the vision of non-racialism peculiar to Solly Sachs's trade union experience, see Leslie Witz, 'A Case of Schizophrenia: The Rise and Fall of the Independent Labour Party', in Belinda Bozzoli, ed., Class, Community and Conflict, Ravan, 1987.

3 The Battle of the Bantu

The incipient non-racialism of the working-class socialist movement was rivalled by a joint venture of white liberals and black elites. European missionaries who came to South Africa in the late eighteenth century built a base for a liberal alternative to crude white domination of black. The assimilation of a faithful black middle class was seen as the best means of ensuring the stability of the society defined by race.

A group of mission-educated black professionals and traditional chiefs founded the South African Native National Congress in 1912 'to so avoid the exploitation of Native fears and grievances by irresponsible agitators'.[1] The SANNC's liberal allies were heartened by its focus on racial discrimination as an affront to the dignity and aspirations of the elite, and by its keen hostility to a class analysis of black oppression.

The early nationalists spent much of their time and energy petitioning governments for reforms. Dr Walter Rubusana, Thomas Mapikela, Revd John Dube, Saul Msane and Sol Plaatje (left to right) led a delegation to Britain in 1914.

Letter from Sol Plaatje, first SANNC secretary-general, writing to De Beers Consolidated Mines Ltd in Kimberley about the company's donation of an old shed for use as an 'Assembly Hall for Natives', 3 August 1918: [2]

I beg to explain the cause of my delay in answering your letter. I had to attend the Native Congress in Bloemfontein to prevent the spread among our people of the Johannesburg Socialist propaganda. I think you are aware of our difficulties in that connection. The ten Transvaal delegates came to Congress with a concord and determination that was perfectly astounding, and foreign to our customary native demeanour at conferences. They spoke almost in unison, in short sentences, nearly every one of which ended with the word 'strike'.

It was only late on the second day that we succeeded in satisfying the delegates to report, on getting to their homes, that the Socialists' method of pitting up black and white will land our people in serious disaster, while the worst that could happen to the whitemen would be but a temporary inconvenience.

When they took the train for Johannesburg at Bloemfontein station, I am told that one of them remarked that they would have 'converted Congress had not De Beers given Plaatje a Hall'. This seems intensely reassuring as indicating that Kimberley will be about the last place that these black Bolsheviks of Johannesburg will pay attention to, thus leaving us free to combat their activities in other parts of the Union. Only those who saw the tension at this Congress can realize that this discussion hall of ours came at just the right time for South Africa.

The alliance of white philanthropists and black nationalists paralleled that of white workers and the ruling class, in that the black partners were also accomplices in the continuing exploitation of the majority. The elites were concerned about securing a niche within the colonial system, not about changing the system itself.

No restructuring of the economy was envisaged, nor was there even a challenge to racial differentiation, for this approach was not non-racial but 'multi-racial'. White and black reformists recognized the value of 'constructive segregation'.[3] This philosophy in the 1920s and 1930s, combined with the renunciation of militant trade union and Communist Party activists, coincided with an all-time low in the popular support of the African National Congress, as the SANNC was renamed in 1923.[4]

An important international influence on this evolving multi-racialism came from the United States. Philanthropic initiatives like the Phelps-Stokes Fund promoted African education and training along the lines of a model developed in the American South. South African intellectuals — whites and some blacks — were encouraged to travel to the US to witness the multi-racial society firsthand.

(Opposite) Educated on a German mission station in the Cape Colony, Plaatje was the foremost campaigner against racial segregation of his generation, as author, journalist, linguist and politician. This poster advertised his 1921 visit to New York.

COME AND HEAR

Mr. SOL
PLAATJE
Of Kimberley, South Africa

Gives thrilling account of the
condition of the Colored Folk
in British South Africa.

A Touching Message well and kindly told

*The story has gripped nearly a thousand
audiences in England, Scotland, Canada & U.S.A.*

IT WILL THRILL YOU

Bethel A. M. E. Church
West 132nd Street, bet. Lenox and 5th Aves.

Sunday, March 13, 11 a. m.
THE BLACK MAN'S BURDEN IN SOUTH AFRICA

Friday, March 18th, 8 p. m.
THE BLACK WOMAN'S BURDEN IN SO. AFRICA
Interspersed with Quaint African Music sung in his own native tongue

Free Will Offering for Brotherhood Work among the South African Tribes

ADMISSION FREE
COME EARLY AND AVOID THE CRUSH ! !

Dr. MONTROSE W. THORNTON, Pastor

A one-time apologist for segregation, academic Edgar Brookes returned from his Phelps-Stokes-sponsored trip to America a zealous convert to the cause of incorporating a black middle class into the white-dominated system. In 1929, with the additional aid of another New York-based funding agency, Carnegie, Brookes founded the South African Institute of Race Relations (SAIRR). According to the 'race relations' concept South Africa was not a unitary society, but rather one of distinct races with inherently different interests stemming from their diverse cultures. Resolution of conflict between the races thus demanded a reconciliation of the immutable elements of this multi-racial society.[5]

Edgar Brookes, delivering the Phelps-Stokes lecture at the University of Cape Town, 1933:[6]

Bantu[7] nationalism must reach out towards Bolshevism. How could it be otherwise? If there is a clearly defined proletariat anywhere in the world, it is in South Africa. Happier or wiser countries postpone or altogether avoid a Marxian 'class war' by the creation of common interests, by opening doors of opportunity enabling the ambitious member of the proletariat to escape into the governing class, at the very least by ostentatious professions of a single national unity transcending class distinctions.

In South Africa we follow a different course. We try to prevent the multi-plication of common interests, we close almost every door of opportunity, and we loudly proclaim the impossibility of union in a single nation. Class becomes associated with something definite and tangible such as colour. The stage is inevitably set for the 'class war'. As a member of the bourgeoisie myself, I hope it is not set for the 'dictatorship of the proletariat'. As a liberal, I believe that only swift and far-reaching reforms and many more opportunities for self-realization on the part of the Bantu can create the impossibility of such a dictatorship. I insist that those who are fighting the Battle of the Bantu are the real friends of the white man and the whole South African community.

Multi-racialism must be seen in its historical context. While Brookes eventually joined the Liberal Party, others branched off the multi-racial path, ultimately arriving at an endorsement of the non-racialism of the popular movements. One such case was that of Bram Fischer, the dis-tinguished Afrikaner advocate, grandson of the Prime Minister of the Orange Free State, and son of the judge-president of the province's Supreme Court, who died serving a life sentence for attempting to over-throw the South African government.

Bram Fischer, speaking about his political experiences in the 1920s, in a speech from the dock during his trial for sabotage and membership of the underground South African Communist Party (SACP), 28 March 1966:

Though nearly forty years have passed, I can remember vividly the experience which brought home to me exactly what this 'white' attitude is, and also how artificial and unreal it is. Like many young Afrikaners, I grew up on a farm. Between the ages of eight and twelve, my daily companions were two young Africans of my own age. I can still remember their names. We roamed the farm together, we hunted and played together, we modelled clay oxen and swam. And never can I remember that the colour of our skins affected our fun or our quarrels or our close friendship in any way.

Then my family moved to town and I moved back to the normal white South African mode of life, where the only relationship with Africans was that of master to servant. I finished my schooling and went to university. There one of my first interests became a study of the theory of segregation, then beginning to blossom. This seemed to me to provide the solution to South Africa's problems and I became an earnest believer in it.

A year later, to help in a small way to put this theory into practice — because I do not believe that theory and practice can or should be separated — I joined the Bloemfontein Joint Council of Europeans and Africans,[8] a body devoted largely to trying to induce various authorities to provide proper, and separate, amenities for Africans. I found myself being introduced to leading members of the African community. I found I had to shake hands with them. This, I found, required an enormous effort of will on my part. Could I really, as a white adult, touch the hand of a black man in friendship?

That night I spent many hours in thought, trying to account for my strange revulsion when I remembered I had never had any such feelings towards my boyhood friends. What became abundantly clear was that it was I and not the black man who had changed, that despite my growing interest in him, I had developed an antagonism for which I could find no rational basis whatsoever.

One night, when I was driving an old ANC leader to his house far out to the west of Johannesburg, I propounded to him the well-worn theory that if you separate races you diminish the points at which friction between them may occur and hence ensure good relations. His answer was the essence of simplicity. If you place the races of one country in two camps, said he, and cut off contact between them, those in each camp begin to forget that those in the other are ordinary human beings, that each lives and laughs in the same way, that each experiences joy or sorrow, pride or humiliation for the same reasons. Thereby each becomes suspicious of the other and each eventually fears the other, which is the basis of all racialism.

I believe no one could more effectively sum up the South African position today. Only contact between the races can eliminate suspicion and fear; only contact and cooperation can breed tolerance and understanding. Segregation or apartheid, however genuinely believed in, can produce only those things it is supposed to avoid: interracial tension and estrangement, intolerance and race hatreds.

Bram Fischer was an exceptional person and his response to his Joint Council experience was also exceptional. Most whites were little moved by interracial contact, and most blacks saw the Joint Council movement as at best ambiguous, and at worst, a scheme to co-opt and depoliticize African nationalists. As a result, the Joint Councils never gained political support beyond a small section of the black middle class, and were rejected even by the conservatives who then led the ANC.

Perhaps the most significant effect of this period of collaboration between white and black elites came in the form of a building black backlash against what African nationalists perceived as white control. By the late 1930s, the ANC's leadership was under pressure to adopt a more militant political stance.

Notes

1. Principal SANNC founding member Pixley ka I. Seme, in describing the purpose of the body. Note also that a female counterpart to the SANNC was formed in 1913: the Bantu Women's League, which grew out of the 1913 women's anti-pass campaign in the Orange Free State (OFS). Led by the OFS Native and Coloured Women's Association, the protest included both African and coloured women, and thus marked the first non-racial unity in struggle among South African women.
2. Cited in Brian Willan, *Sol Plaatje: South African Nationalist 1876—1932*, Heinemann Educational Books and Ravan Press, 1984, a work that succeeds in illuminating Plaatje's literary and political contributions, as well as the role he (and other early nationalist leaders) played in buffering the ruling class from more militant challenges.
3. Jan Hofmeyr, a liberal cabinet minister in the Smuts government, in 1930, rejecting the two 'extreme' policies of repression and equality; quoted in William Minter, *King Solomon's Mines Revisited: Western Interests and the Burdened History of Southern Africa*, Basic Books, 1986.
4. For further exploration of this theme, see Paul B. Rich, *White Power and the Liberal Conscience: Racial Segregation and South African Liberalism*, Ravan, 1984.
5. Other factors were also relevant, e.g., the rise — albeit short-lived — of the ICU, the CPSA's own serious decline in membership, and the ousting of ANC President Josiah Gumede after his visit to the Soviet Union.
6. Quoted in Robert Davies, *Capital, State and White Labour in South Africa: 1900—1960: An Historical Materialist Analysis of Class Formation and Class Relations*, Harvester Press, 1979.
7. An Nguni word, meaning 'people', the term describes southern African ethnic groups, but was co-opted by the apartheid regime to refer to Africans, e.g., Bantu Education.
8. The Joint Council movement, with councils in the major South African cities, was launched in 1921, following the African miners' strike and a tour of South Africa by Phelps-Stokes Fund Director Thomas Jesse Jones and its African member, Dr J. E. K. Aggrey of the Gold Coast (now Ghana), who proselytized about 'interracial cooperation' and the model of American 'negro' industrial training offered by Booker T. Washington's Tuskegee Institute.

4 The Class of '44

The Second World War — a period of accelerated industrialization and urbanization in South Africa — gave rise to a new generation of militant political leaders. These impatient young Africans were distanced from their rural roots, for they had grown up in the new urban ghettos or, at least, gone to school in town. Though most were not workers themselves, the popular struggles of the emergent industrialized working class had made them respect that motor force for change. The young militants sought the unity of all Africans — not only across ethnic lines, but across class lines, too. This generation was known as 'The Class of '44', for the year that they founded the ANC Youth League. The first assertion of this broad African nationalism also repudiated the liberalism of their predecessors — or, as it was known then, 'Trusteeship'.

'ANC Youth League Manifesto', 1944:

To mislead the world and make it believe that the Whiteman[1] in South Africa is helping the African on the road to civilized life, the Whiteman has arrogated to himself the title and role of Trustee for the African people. The effects of Trusteeship alone have made the African realize that Trusteeship has meant, as it still means, the consolidation by the Whiteman of his position at the expense of the African people, so that by the time national awakening opens the eyes of the African people to the bluff they live under, White domination should be secure and unassailable.

These conditions have made the African lose all faith in all talk of Trusteeship. He now elects to determine his future by his own efforts. He has realized that to trust to the mere good grace of the Whiteman will not free him, as no nation can free an oppressed group other than that group itself. Self-determination is the philosophy of life which will save him from the disaster he clearly sees on his way, disasters to which Discrimination, Segregation, Pass Laws and Trusteeship are all ruthlessly and inevitably driving him.

The formation of the African National Congress Youth League is an answer and assurance to the critics of the national movement that African Youth will not allow the struggles and sacrifices of their fathers to have been in vain. The Congress Youth League must be the brains-trust and power-station of the spirit of African nationalism, the spirit of African self-determination, the spirit that is so discernible in the thinking of our Youth.

Dan Tloome, a trade unionist and ANC and CPSA member since the late 1930s, who served on the ANC national executive from 1945:

I found that at the time I first joined, the ANC was an organization of teachers, intellectuals, clergymen — all the elite of African society. Young people were not very much interested in the ANC. They felt it was an organization of elderly people. As a result, the ANC never became progressive until it was joined by younger people: the Tambos, Mandelas and so on. Those were members of the Youth League of the ANC. It was when those young people came into the ANC that there was transformation in so far as the ideology was concerned, because in the past the elderly people believed in demonstrations, reconciliation with the powers that be and so on. They weren't very much interested in action against the government.

Yet it seems that while you supported the Youth League's militancy, you were also critical of their definition of the enemy.

Their outlook was that our fight is against the white people. 'We are nationalist here, and these white people took away our land' — that was the type of approach. Then I would get up and say, 'You can't take the white man and throw him into the sea. He was born in South Africa and we will have to stay with them here.' There was too much focus on the white people: 'White people are oppressing us, they have taken our land,' and so on and so forth.

I felt that it was not really the question of white people that was the point. The point was exploitation of people, irrespective of whether they are white or black. I came to understand that what we are fighting against is not a white man — we are fighting against exploitation of the working people.

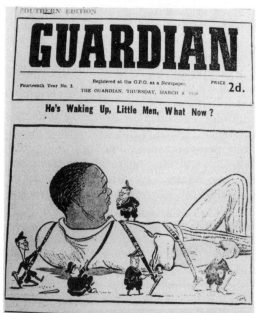

Front page of the Guardian, *9 March 1950, a progressive weekly newspaper founded in 1936 which played an important role in mobilizing anti-fascist opinion and support for the ANC. Banned in 1952, it reappeared as the* Clarion, *then* Advance, New Age *and* Spark, *before the banning of its staff led to its demise in 1963.*

Oliver Tambo and Nelson Mandela were both founder members and leaders of the ANC Youth League. Tambo went on to become ANC secretary-general, then ANC president after he left South Africa in 1960, while Mandela's leadership of the ANC culminated in his imprisonment under a life sentence in 1964. They are shown here together at a conference in Addis Ababa in 1962.

My concept of non-racialism is quite different from what many people think about it being an issue between white and black. My approach is that this whole thing means a question of profits. It is the economic motive of it which one should take into account. People talk about racism, but I'm not so much bothered about it — I'm bothered about the motive of it.

Look, these were not my enemies — they were my friends. We used to sit together, have a drink and discuss these things, you know. They were very, very hostile against the CP. Their cardinal point was that communism is a foreign ideology and that we shouldn't follow it because it's not applicable to South Africa. It's the question of colour bar in South Africa, therefore we should just restrict ourselves to the question of segregation and apartheid and things of that kind in our struggle.

African militancy was further spurred by the raising and dashing of expectations for progressive change in South Africa during and after the Second World War.

Graham Morodi, who was among some 120,000 South African blacks who joined the South African army in the Second World War:

In 1941 I joined the army. We handled a gun, but never to shoot. We were only carrying *assegais* [spears]. We didn't like it. We were demobilized in 1945. I was given a khaki suit, a blanket and a lot of certificates and some medals and nothing else but five pounds pocket money,[2] and promised that we'll get something when we're at home: we won't carry passes, and we'll be given houses which we are not going to rent for so much. But all those things never happened.

Then I started to say, 'Now I'm going to join the ANC and fight against this government which has robbed me and told me a lot of lies.' At that time, too, the ANC was very small, it was an organization of rich people and intellectuals – although in 1944 it changed. That's when they formed the ANC Youth League and it went militant, but that time I was in the army myself. Then I had army friends who were ANC members, but I was not much interested because I was interested in sports. But I usually went to public meetings.

In Sophiatown[3] the youth was very strong during that time of '45, '46, and then I started to see what the ANC is because of the mine strike and other strikes that were going on, public meetings and so on. So in 1950, when the shooting went on in the strike of May Day, then I joined the ANC. I got fed up and I said, 'But how can they just shoot a person who's unarmed? I'm going to join the ANC and we are going to beat the whites.' I was committed from that time.

So were you anti-white then?

When I was in the ANC, then I started to see whites, then I definitely accepted them. They were addressing meetings and so on. I saw them myself, personally, and other people explained to me our struggle, that we are not a racialist group, we are fighting apartheid, we can't have another apartheid – although at first I said no, because I thought that we are fighting the white people, you see. But now I accept it.

When I saw all these whites now in the struggle, then I started to see that it's a correct thing, we must unite ourselves. Because even the government is using the blacks to come and arrest us, to come and get information from us, so why should we say the whites should not be with us? So that's how I accepted the whites, although there were groups, like what we call 'Africanist', which were advocating that we should have nothing to do with other racial groups.

Why didn't you support the Africanists?

Because I felt their line was wrong – it supports apartheid. It's not a matter of removing a white person and replacing him with a black. I thought a non-racial society, where everybody lives together and enjoys the wealth of the country, is better because it ends hatred among people.

The Africanists within the ANC were rejecting any non-African racial group to be associated with the ANC. They were very much anti-communist. I'm not a communist but I don't hate communists. I think that at present we are fighting the same enemy against racialism and fascism, and I think we can be allies with the communists because they are prepared to fight. The idea is to push the fascists out with all forces that are interested.

I worked with J. B. Marks,[4] I worked with Moses Kotane, I've worked with many, many other communist leaders. But Kotane always said, when he addressed the ANC cadres, 'Those who think they are communist here in the ANC, they should not discuss their communist politics with the ANC — they must discuss ANC politics, or else they must get out from the ANC.'

With its adoption of the militant 'Programme of Action' in 1949 and the election of Youth Leaguers to the national executive, the bold new ANC gained confidence. Resistance to cooperation with non-Africans lessened, as did its anti-communism.

Stanley Mabizela, who joined the ANC's 'Masupatsela' (Young Pioneers) as a child in the 1940s, then entered the ANC Youth League, and became a fully-fledged member of the Eastern Cape regional ANC in 1952:

We did query the policy of non-racialism. We were young and we said, 'Why can't we fight and drive the whites away?' But our elders in the organization were very patient people. They told us the history of the ANC and took pains to explain why the ANC must be non-racial. It was something which was not very easy to accept at the beginning, because of immaturity, because of youthfulness.

We would tell our seniors that we don't agree with the policy, but this was a topic which was handled so many times that gradually you got to understand the reasoning behind it: that first and foremost, whites in South Africa came over three hundred years ago and they now have nowhere to go. Secondly — and this is the stressed point in the ANC — whites are human beings like ourselves, except that they have got the wrong ideology in their heads. And with time they will change and we will stay with them as brothers and sisters, as our fellow human beings.

As a practising Catholic, how do you regard the ANC's working relationship with the Communist Party?

I have worked with communists and I have never had any problems with them. I've worked under Govan Mbeki[5] and I admire him. He never tried to interfere with the fact that I'm a religious man. He always respected that between such and such an hour I would be in church. Communists are in the ANC as members of the ANC, not as members of the South African Communist Party.

No one is allowed to criticize or to be vindictive to me simply because I'm a Christian, no one's allowed to be vindictive to another simply because he has discovered that the other one is a member of the Communist Party. We are all members of the ANC. Just as you will not be allowed to be vindictive to another person simply on tribal grounds, so that has been the position between me and the communists in the ANC. Together we've been in the thick of things. They've never reneged, they've never sold us out.

Notes

1. 'Whiteman' as a single word, the capitalization of 'Trustee' and 'Segregation', etc. are in keeping with the usage of that time. In later eras, 'Black' and 'White' were capitalized with less consistency, thus in subsequent chapters such words are not capitalized, in keeping with the most common usage in South Africa today.
2. The South African monetary system was based on pounds, shillings and pence until 1961, when the decimal system of rands and cents was adopted.
3. A black freehold area of Johannesburg where the mingling of races and classes inspired a vibrant non-racial culture. The government began demolishing it in 1955 and by 1960, despite resistance organized by the ANC, Sophiatown's residents had been forcibly removed to racially segregated areas. Most Africans were dumped in the South Western Townships, known as 'Soweto' (where they were further segregated according to specific ethnic background, e.g. Zulus to the Meadowlands section, Sothos to Diepkloof), while coloureds, Indians, whites and even Chinese were each relocated in separate living areas.
4. A trade unionist who led the 1946 mine strike, and an ANC and CP member, Marks was classified coloured but chose to align himself with the black workers.
5. An ANC and CP leader sentenced to life imprisonment in 1964 for his activities in the ANC's armed wing, Mbeki was released by the government in response to domestic and international pressure in late 1987.

5 Natural Allies

While the new militancy in the ANC emanated from the growing cooperation between young African intellectuals and workers, Indians, coloureds and whites of all social backgrounds were also part of the political rejuvenation of the war years. The evolving forms of resistance in each of these communities were similar in the non-racial and cross-class associations they forged to counter the state's divide-and-rule tactics. Still, South Africa's race-specific oppression inevitably shaped distinct histories.

Initially imported from India in 1860 as indentured farm labour under the 'Natal Coolie Law',[1] South Africa's Indians were the first oppressed group to mount an effective non-military challenge to the government. Mahatma Gandhi inspired *Satyagraha* — passive resistance to discriminatory legislation — during the 21 years he spent in South Africa (from 1893). This tradition was then overtaken by the accommodationist policies of the Indian business class, until the Second World War period spurred the radicalization of Indian resistance politics.

Dr Goonam,[2] *one of the young militants involved in challenging the old guard of the Natal Indian Congress (NIC) in the early 1940s:*

Hitherto we had only a group of capitalists, mostly people who could afford, really, to follow the leaders of that particular group — men who talked to the government and compromised and got a few concessions at the mercy, really, of the Indian people's name, because they sold us every time they went to see [Prime Ministers] Smuts and Hertzog those days. It did not suit us at all because we followed their antics and their manoeuvring and we felt that something must be done. So we challenged the old guard.

Each indentured worker arriving in South Africa by ship from India was identified by number.

We said that we have to challenge them, this is the only hope we have to form a new congress, a congress that is built on the principles of Mahatma Gandhi.

We had a very big meeting at Curries Fountain [Durban]. We got all our workers — workers we had because they had faith in us, that we were going to have a voice that is going to represent all sections of the community. We said if we do that now, then later we can get our Africans and the coloured people — but first let us put our house in order. We said, 'Are you going on the same path these people have led you, which has spelt ruin for all of us? Or are you going to now consider changing? The Group Areas³ means a complete destruction of everything that we have — not only for us, but for the Africans and for the coloured people — because we're all going to be shoved into some hell-and-gone place. So this is how we came into being in the Natal Indian Congress, representing all shades and all sections of the people. That was a first sign of awakening of the women. Women who had never ever been to a public meeting came to our meeting, because we told them what it meant for themselves and the future of their children. I talked to them in their own language, Tamil,⁴ and appealed to them that this is the movement that Gandhi has laid down for us. So they came in droves, left their children and they came — which was surprising, because these were women who never left their home before.

It was my duty to go along and canvass for the women because it could not be just a male-dominated organization. For a few years they wouldn't have me at all. I did not think like them and I did not behave like them. Perhaps I was little difficult, you know. I smoked a cigarette and wore short dresses and wore lipstick and drove a car, night or day, alone. And all that was not in keeping with the tradition of the Indian people. They were still in the Victorian Age of thinking, you see.

Gandhi founded the Natal Indian Congress to fight anti-Indian laws in 1894. He is pictured here with the staff of his law firm.

Were you aware that Nelson Mandela, Walter Sisulu and Oliver Tambo were involved in the same kind of exercise of deposing the old guard in the ANC Youth League?

They were eliminating the old ones there and we were eliminating the old ones here. It was quite a nerve-racking job because wherever you went they said, 'You will probably want us to join forces with all sorts of people' — meaning Africans. And we had to sit and talk to them, explain to them. It meant hours of explaining to very old people whose views cannot be changed overnight. Talking to them in their own language helped a lot. Quite a lot of Indians said, 'Now you want us to marry the Africans, isn't that what it is?' I said, 'No, I don't think they want to marry you. We are living in one country — is this your country? Do you want to live here?' And I said, 'How are you going to live? In a little pocket, or are you wanting to live nicely, in a friendly way with Africans?' Then they said, 'Yes, but how? Because they won't trust us.'

I said, 'You can look at the papers every day, you can see how the whites hate us — they want us to leave. But the Africans do not say that at all. This is our country. If we are going to live here at all, we also have to play our part. A lot of those Africans are also exploited by those Indian people: they don't pay them decent wages, they don't give them decent homes. The Africans are also human. I work with them and I know what they go through. So it is for you people, for every one of you, to try to foster this friendship amongst them.'

The style of these young, new leaders differed radically from those they ousted: the era of meek petitions to authority was over.

M. D. Naidoo, elected secretary of the NIC after the radicals won elections for a new executive in 1945:

After we were elected, one of the first things we did was to ask the government to receive a deputation of the Indian Congress. Field Marshal Smuts was then prime minister and he agreed, and a very big delegation went up in November 1945.[5]

The interview lasted barely half an hour. Smuts heard our representations and the memorandum we presented to him, and he said, 'Gentlemen, there is nothing for us to discuss. You have brought a political manifesto to me and you can't expect me to talk to you about it.' That convinced me that we were living in two different worlds, and I, personally, was at that time convinced that there didn't seem to be any possibility of peaceful evolution in our country.

We warned Smuts that if he was not prepared to talk to us we would have no choice but to go back and mobilize our people into mass action, and we did precisely that. We now met similar left elements in the Cape Province and in the Transvaal, and we then developed a strategy for passive resistance, and in 1946 we embarked on the campaign.

That campaign went on from '46 to '47. We extended it and led a series of groups of people from Natal into the Transvaal, refusing to take permits to cross from the one province to the other. Some 2,000 of us spent a substantial period in prison in 1947 and '48. Then the Nationalist Party came to power and that involved a rethinking and a realignment of strategy altogether. This brought us now into very much closer contact with the African National Congress.

The mobilizing success of the passive resistance campaign ensured the dominance of the young radicals in Indian politics, and allowed them to pursue cooperation with the ANC in the late 1940s.

Passive Resistance Council report, 13 June 1946 – 13 May 1947, from the NIC Agenda Book:

The bold Congress policy of resistance has had effects far wider than among the Indians. A profound impression has been made among the other non-European sections, particularly the Africans. They have seen a community with a population vastly inferior in numbers to theirs and with much less justification for struggle than themselves refuse to accept the government terms. They have seen this small community humiliate the seemingly invincible power of the South African rulers. And they have drawn the necessary conclusions.

It is noteworthy how much more militant the African people have become during the year, as evidenced by the anti-pass conference at Johannesburg last year, the African miners' strike involving over 100,000 workers, the 'passive resistance' of the Natives Representative Council which adjourned after the miners' strike and to date has refused to meet, the Bloemfontein emergency conference,[6] the burning of the passes in Cape Town, and the militancy displayed by the shanty-town movement in Johannesburg and Durban.[7]

The Indian people have now learnt the fallacy of sectional and iso-lationist principles. By their experience in the resistance struggle they have learnt the necessity of allies, and that their natural allies are the other oppressed non-European groups, together with the progressive Europeans.

The Africans, too, have learnt from the passive resistance struggle that the Indian people are their friends, and despite their smallness as a community can be very valuable allies. For years the Africans have regarded the Indians with suspicion. Their doubts were bred from the government's divide-and-rule policy, and by the sectional attitude of the old Indian leadership. But when the passive resistance campaign began, they quickly realized that a success for the campaign would benefit them immensely in their own fight, and from the beginning it had their full sympathy.

H. I. E. Dhlomo, African poet and ANC Youth League regional convener, speaking at a mass meeting held before a march through the streets of Durban to protest the restriction of Indian property rights, 1946:

Justice is not Indian and neither is freedom Indian. We want all people to be free. The young people in the ANC support the struggle of the Indians.

A Passive Resistance Campaign meeting at Durban's Red Square in 1946.

The transformation of South African Indian politics from isolationist to activist cannot only be attributed to the policies of the leadership. This trend paralleled the maturation of the Indian working class from rural labourers to urban wage-earners, which in turn led to the growth of trade unions. Thus workers, intellectuals, merchants and professionals all helped to shape the new policies of the Indian Congress.

Kay Moonsamy, a trade unionist who joined the militant new NIC:

I left the factory to join the Passive Resistance. Like thousands in those days, we left work and went to defy and to court imprisonment. Prior to 1944, the Indian Congresses in South Africa were led by leaders who did not want to have any cooperation between Indians and Africans or coloureds. The new leadership called upon all the democratic forces to work together, that is, for the closest cooperation with the African people, because we feel that the majority in our country are the Africans − if they're not liberated, then I don't think the others will be liberated. So we believe that the main content of our revolution is the liberation of the African people, and the Indian Congress worked for that.

And what was the motivation for you to get involved in passive resistance? Was it Indian-oriented in any way, or was it purely political?

The overwhelming majority of the Indians are part and parcel of South African society and the majority of us do not look towards India. Of course, there is the special affinity because our forefathers hailed from India. And then, of course, India, as you know, was one of the first countries to take up the whole question of racial discrimination at the United Nations way back in 1946, and in fact it was during the passive resistance campaign that this question was raised at the UN, to highlight not only the plight of Indians, but the whole question of oppression.

Cooperation between Indians and Africans was symbolized by the 'Doctors' Pact' signed in 1947 between ANC President Dr A. B. Xuma and the leaders of the Transvaal and Natal Indian Congresses, Dr Yusuf Dadoo and Dr G. M. Naicker. Less than two years later the pact faced its most serious test, when fighting between Indians and Africans broke out in Durban.

R. D. Naidoo, trade unionist and NIC and CPSA activist who witnessed first-hand the clashes of 1949:

It was on a Friday afternoon, I remember, in the Victoria Street area, in one of the Indian cafes: a little African boy stole a cake, you know — just took a cake — and the man actually hit him with a bottle on his head! And the rumour went around that the boy's neck was cut off and they placed it in a mosque, and as a result of this the riot broke out. I was in Durban with Congress then and I was in the Riots Relief Committee. I lived in Mayville, the area that was affected most.

How do you assess the origins and background of those clashes?

Well, in those days we used to call it the 'colour bar' system, and it was very, very heavy against the Indian businessman and the Indian working class. At one stage I remember the ruling class even said that we should pack up the Indians and send them back to India. They had an immigration scheme which provided for the state to finance you to go to India.

I attribute the 1949 riots to the policy of the government. The anti-Indian agitation that was going on, year in and year out, had been soaked into the black man, pointing out to him that these are the people that are taking your jobs, these are the people opening businesses and shops and depriving you. The word 'coolie' was a very common utterance. It wasn't a black people's vendetta against the Indian people — I blame it on Nationalist policy. State propaganda was largely responsible for giving birth to this riot.

Pamphlet issued in 1950 by the Supreme Council of the Federation of Bantu Organizations, an obscure group formed to oppose the joint political action of Africans, coloureds, whites and Indians, with a particular anti-'Asiatic' focus:[8]

The Bantus consider the presence of Asiatics amongst them as a menace to their interests and advocate for complete segregation. The Bantus strongly resent and deplore: commercial domination by Asiatics in areas proclaimed Bantu by law; financial destitution as a result of blackmarket, unfair transactions, together with gambling snares and dens; evils arising from Asiatics' liquor sales; resentment-stirring exhibition of sophisticated supremacy and seduction of Bantu women by Asiatics. Consequently the Supreme Council earnestly appeals to Asiatics for an abrupt halt to the above practices in order to avoid their attendant repercussions.

What is the Salvation of the Black Man? We leave it to presumptuous fools in their asylum of dreams to dream of our liberation being gained through Asiatic or Communistic leadership. Let us rather assiduously organize for the National Advancement and the local self-government of the Bantu Race, in which we will have the assistance of all right-thinking men, even those in high positions. Let us become our own shopkeepers in areas locally administered by our chosen representatives and so build up the Bantu Race by positive action.

Indian-African cooperation weathered the racist storm: the solidarity forged in the 1940s provided a platform for continued non-racial unity between the two communities throughout the 1950s.

Some Indian indentured labourers rose from farm worker to street vendor and then to shopkeeper. The trading store was a point of contact between the white-controlled industrial economy and black consumers; as a result, the Indian shopkeeper was often the focus of popular resentment.

Notes

1. A British Crown Colony from 1843, the province of Natal suffered from a critical labour shortage because the Zulus resisted work on European farms, hence the move to import 'coolie' labour.
2. Although Gail M. Gerhart and Thomas Karis, *From Protest to Challenge: Political Profiles,* Volume 4, Hoover Press, 1977, identify Goonam as having the first name of Kasavello, she maintained that it is 'my father's name, not mine'. She remained steadfastly cagey about her full name, claiming that she was always known simply as 'Dr Goonam', refusing to disclose any first or middle name, and denying the widely held view that her real name is Goonam Naidoo. When pressed as to how she was known before she became a medical doctor, when she was a small girl, she answered, 'Small Girl, that's what they called me!' She was equally circumspect about her age; it is estimated that she was born in 1905.
3. The Asiatic Land Tenure and Indian Representation Act of 1946 — known as the Ghetto Act — prohibited Indians from buying land and occupying property except in certain 'exempted areas'. It was this legislation that gave rise to the passive resistance campaign. The Group Areas Act of 1950 designated separate urban residential areas for each race group, and also gave rise to great resistance.
4. The largest single language group among Indians in South Africa originated in the Tamil-speaking provinces of India; the second-largest group is Hindi-speaking, and most others speak Gujerati, Telegu and Urdu. In terms of religious background, the large majority are Hindu and most of the rest Moslem, with a small minority of Christians, plus Buddhists and Parsees.
5. This was to be the last meeting between members of the Congress movement and a leader of the South African regime until the 1989 meeting over tea between Nelson Mandela and then-President P. W. Botha.
6. An 'Emergency Conference of All Africans' was convened to debate the question of continued ANC participation in the Natives' Representative Council; Africans were exhorted to boycott future elections to this council.
7. The mass evictions of black people from white farms and the overcrowding in the reserves led to severe housing shortages in the 1940s, as people converged on the towns in search of a means of livelihood. They formed organized communities of squatters, often led by popular messianic figures, who resisted all attempts by the state to move them by simply picking up their shacks and setting them up in other empty fields.
8. A probe into the group by the SAIRR in 1950 uncovered allegations that the Council was sponsored by members of the right-wing Afrikaner Broederbond, with the express aims of counteracting ANC influence and promoting anti-Indian feelings among Africans. The SAIRR also found out that the Council had schemed with *tsotsi* (thug) elements to 'bring the leaders of Congress into conflict with the authorities by committing atrocities during any strikes and boycotts which the former may organize'; and had also 'incited *tsotsis* to force Indian businessmen from African areas by burning their shops during strikes'. Suspicions that this pro-separate development body was state-supported were compounded by its use of apartheid terminology such as 'Bantu' and 'Asiatic'. On one specific occasion, before a Congress call for a strike in June 1950, the Council was reported to have received assistance from the government's Railway Police in distributing leaflets.

6 Tomorrow It's Going to Be You

Those classified 'coloured' by the South African government shared a community of interests only because they were defined as a separate community – not because of any innate characteristics uniting them. The descendants of indigenous Khoikhoi, San, and Bantu peoples, imported Asian and African slaves, and European settlers developed an identity that existed solely in contrast with the other race groups: less privileged than the whites, but better off than the Africans. Government 'coloured preference' policies[1] aimed at ensuring that the coloureds remained in this buffer, precluding any sense of either solidarity with other blacks or equality with whites. Non-racialism in the coloured community evolved out of a rejection of this arbitrary ethnic category based on the notion of 'miscegenation' of supposedly pure races.[2]

The most influential political trends among coloureds have traditionally emanated from the Western Cape, where the population is centred, outnumbering Africans as well as whites. The most active and militant regional structure of the ANC in the late 1920s was its Western Province branch. It organized Africans and coloureds from all classes on a non-racial basis at a time when the elite African leadership of the ANC was attracted to Marcus Garvey's 'Africa for the Africans' movement.[3] In the 1930s, the breakaway Independent ANC of the Southern Cape publicly attacked the 'Natives only' policy of the then-conservative national ANC,[4] complaining that contact between African and coloured was confined to leadership level.

The coloured community was further politicized along non-racial lines by the government's creation of a Coloured Affairs Department (CAD) in 1943. Widespread opposition to the segregated administrative body gave rise to the Anti-CAD, and then the more radical Non-European Unity Movement.[5] While most coloured militants were ardent advocates of non-racialism in theory, in practice they mobilized around issues that affected their narrow community base.

Dennis Brutus, active in the Unity Movement-oriented Teachers League of South Africa (TLSA) in the Eastern Cape in the 1940s and 1950s:

The history of the coloureds was totally different from the Africans and the Asians. They had the franchise, they only lost the franchise in 1956.[6] Too, you must remember that the Cape was always seen as a kind of liberal place — it was certainly where a lot of the inter-marriages took place, with sailors who came into the port and so on — so you had an enormously mixed population, racially, culturally. You'd had a history of liberal city councils that were much slower to enforce apartheid than elsewhere, like in the Transvaal or the Free State.

Do you think the coloured community has suffered from the insecurity of a minority?

I think that's important, but there is something more important: there was always the promise of the white dominant group that the coloureds would be treated as an appendage: 'They are our step-children, you know, our half-children, our bastard children.' In a sense, they were given the kind of crumbs from the white man's table, which gave them more hope — especially with the retention of the franchise, when it was being lost all over the country. They came into the Union of South Africa with something which the Asians didn't have and the Africans didn't have, and this gave them some privileged status, however illusory. So out of that comes a certain reluctance to take on the system. There's the hope that there are crumbs for you in the system.

Cape Town's District Six, one of the best-known coloured areas in the 1940s and 1950s, was declared white and demolished by the 1960s.

But there is also a very strong insistence by other coloureds that the race categories are irrelevant and that one ought to transcend them — which is my position. On the other hand, the fact that for many years coloureds could own property, could become petty-bourgeois to some degree, was clearly a barrier against fusing both with the Africans in Nyanga and Langa [Cape townships], and also with the coloured working class. They were contemptuous of the coloureds who were hawking fish or vegetables in the street. So this stratification is very strong and there's no point in disputing it.

Why was it that the the Unity Movement and the Teachers League had such appeal in the coloured community?

That's self-evident: a most powerful formative influence in the coloured community was the teacher. So you really have to ask, how did the teachers get to be Trotskyist? That was through contact with the people at Cape Town University, who were Marxists but had formed the breakaway organization called the Spartacus Club, which consisted mainly of people who took a pro-Trotsky[7] position. If they were to define themselves, they would've said that they belong to the intelligentsia, out of whom a vanguard party would come. But it is quite true that the TLSA and the Anti-CAD and the Unity Movement tended to draw their support from educated coloureds and professionals, the teachers.

The sense of alienation from the mainstream of African-dominated resistance was a further impetus to separate coloured organization. The most significant of these groups, the Unity Movement, was led by an African, yet in terms of his background, he felt he had more in common with the coloured intellectuals who made up the majority of his constituency.

I. B. Tabata, President of the Unity Movement since its founding:

I happen to be a person born in a particular place in a particular way which is not typical of a black man's life in South Africa. First of all, my father came from people who could be called, not farmers, but landowners. You see, if you can imagine that milieu, I had no cause to be anti-anything, anti any white man. For me, there was nobody higher than my father.

You know, the Afrikaner in those days was not like the Afrikaner of today. Those days they knew only two things: you are either a man or a *skepsel* [creature]. If you possess the same things as they've got, then you are a man. My father was a farmer and was entitled to all the privileges of farmers.

So when you went to school at Lovedale mission, was that the first time you mixed with coloureds and Indians?

That's right. The other fellows came from the reserves, and some came from places where they were under chiefs and they believed in certain things — that kind of life which I did not know because I grew up on a farm. So I didn't know so much about the customs and that kind of thing — I had to come across this later, when I was older. Consequently, when I now met the coloured boys and the Indian boys, I took to them quite naturally because they lacked the same things that I lacked: you know, the tribal customs. My approach to the whole thing was intellectual.

Your left-wing friends who attended the Cape Town political clubs, they were not Africans, generally?

Of course not, ja.

That didn't bother you, that there weren't many African people involved?

Given my background, it didn't.

Would you agree that Unity Movement supporters have tended to come from middle-class backgrounds?

That was the very essence of it. You see, we said you cannot fight for socialism in the same way as England and Germany and so on — you have to have a national organization. That national organization was founded under the leadership of the petty bourgeoisie. It couldn't be otherwise, it had to be. The workers can't form an organization that's going to liberate itself of themselves — it has never happened anywhere in the world and it can't. Ideas come from the bourgeois class — even the ideas of socialism came from outside the workers, from the sense of the bourgeoisie. And it can't be otherwise.

In contrast to this view, a non-racial trade union movement had developed in the Western Cape in the 1940s. While many unions allowed their legal, separate, race-based branches to perpetuate coloured labour preference policy, some Cape unions — notably the Food and Canning Workers and the Stevedores and Dock Workers — managed to organize both coloured and African workers.

Zola Zembe, a migrant worker from the Eastern Cape who became a full-time trade unionist in Cape Town:

Well, coloureds were prejudiced against Africans, particularly those who were not urbanized but rural. First of all, we had no language with them: we speak Xhosa. More or less, they were people who were between whites and Africans, and some of them were extreme, very bad indeed, because they've got to shout more to compensate. But also ourselves, we never accepted them at first, until you know them.

You see, the trade union is very important. It's more important than political organization because there is the organization in the factory where you are equal, you are all workers. Somebody is being ill-treated by a foreman there in the presence of another one, and you're affected by this thing because tomorrow it's going to be you. It doesn't matter whether it's a white or a coloured or an African — you feel very bad. Because you are with this chap for eight hours and you talk to him — even though you don't know English sometimes, or Afrikaans — you develop a language of communication.

Whereas politics is completely different, particularly that time, because the ANC had not gone down to the masses of our people. We just followed because, well, we were oppressed. In other words, at first you regard some of the coloureds as similar to the whites, the way they're behaving and so on, but as you go along with them you learn how they are and you see that these are not whites, and as you go along they make friends with you.

African and coloured workers at the 1945 Food and Canning Workers Union conference in Cape Town's Trades Hall.

Can you tell me about your experience of organizing coloureds and Africans together in one union?

The story that sticks in my mind is when we organized about 200 coloured women in a zip factory. At the time we had applied for conciliation board, so the union could be registered and they could apply for bargaining position. We went to these coloured women and said, 'Listen, now, it's more than a month the government has not answered your letter of applying for a conciliation board and therefore you've got the right to strike.' That thing was different to me: there were coloureds and I was the only African leading them. I was there at lunch-time and the plan was that even if the bell goes at two o'clock, we continue the meeting. And we continued our meeting as if nothing's happening. Of course, the police were called, and then of course they rush to me when they see an African, saying, 'You are arrested!'

They took me to Maitland Police Station, but after an hour I was rushed back to where I was because those coloured women were there demanding me: 'If that person is not back, that's the end of it, you might as well close this factory.' So you see what I mean: if workers are organized effectively, colour just disappears completely. Here I'm an African — and not even an articulate African at that time — but I was a symbol of unity to them and so they said, 'That chap must come back here.' I was brought back to them and then they went back to the factory and we won our strike — an African leading coloureds. You know, to me, it was a great thing indeed, because South Africa is organized in a segmented form and people find it difficult to follow people of other racial groups, but in the trade union movement these coloured women were prepared to follow an African person.

The trade union helps a great deal with this. For instance, people have been arrested — you see amongst the arrested people are whites. You know, once you organize for the people you will be arrested, whether you're white, pink or green. You understand that, you see it doesn't need a book, it's clear as A, B, C: when people in South Africa go on strike, the first thing they get is the police — they bash you. The government, it's just an organization created by those who have got money to protect themselves, and nothing else.

So you found that was the kind of argument that made workers understand non-racialism?

That's right, they learn. Politics are very understandable to people when there's a struggle. Even the question of racism itself, it's easy to understand. You don't have to be educated for that. And they know that Ray Alexander slept in the bloody rural fishing compounds in Saldanha Bay and other places with them, for organizing them — that is not lost.

That's why I'm always coming back to the trade unions, because trade unions bring you nearer all the time with the hot line. It's not a theoretical thing. You come closer to somebody's factory and your honesty is proved — whereas in politics you're not always challenging employers. The trade union, it's a school of politics, no doubt about it — it's wonderful.

Notes

1. The decades-old preference for coloured over African labour in the Western Cape was institutionalized by the 1955 Coloured Labour Preference Policy, which aimed to create a distinct 'coloured nation', according to Prime Minister Hendrik Verwoerd's Secretary of Native Affairs, W. W. Eiselen.
2. For a thorough treatment of this theme, see Ian Goldin, *Making Race: The Politics and Economics of Coloured Identity in South Africa*, Longman, 1987.
3. See Willie Hofmeyr, 'Agricultural Crisis and Rural Organization in the Cape, 1929—1933', MA thesis dissertation, University of Cape Town (UCT), 1985 for a discussion of the minimal impact on Cape politics of the Jamaican leader who advocated the emigration of African-Americans to Africa in the early twentieth century. Hofmeyr concludes that lack of enthusiasm for African separatism was due to the longstanding integration of coloureds into ANC structures in the Cape.
4. The Independent ANC (IANC) was founded in Cape Town in late 1930 by militants opposed to the ANC's conservative leadership and was crushed by state repression in 1932. Hofmeyr (see previous note) characterizes the IANC's programme of action as 'the most militant to emerge out of the national movement until the late 1940s', and argues that 'the ease with which the Food and Canning Workers Union was later able to organize in the Western Cape rural areas suggests that at least some awareness of the value of organization had been developed' as a legacy of the militant elements of the ANC (Western Province) and the IANC.
5. Most often simply called the Unity Movement.
6. When the Nationalist government succeeded in removing coloured voters from the Cape common roll.
7. According to Brutus, the Spartacus Club tried to get Leon Trotsky himself to adjudicate a debate on 'the relative importance in the revolutionary struggle of the peasantry versus the proletariat — whether the revolution would take its energy from the urban workers in Cape Town or the peasantry in Transkei'. Trotsky replied ('Remarks on the Draft Theses of the Workers Party of S.A.', 24 April 1935), vindicating the view that the peasantry was crucial, but adopting a far less dismissive approach towards the Black Republic policy of the CPSA and the ANC than his South African disciples. However, it was then alleged that the courier had doctored the document in transmission, so the debate raged on.

7 Against the Common Enemy

Although the Second World War was fought against fascism, few whites made the link between Nazi persecution of Jews in Europe and the oppression of blacks in their own country. The Army Education Service aimed to 'inculcate a liberal, tolerant attitude of mind'[1] to counter the considerable Nazi support in South Africa,[2] but the only effort to organize soldiers in a way that related their war experience to the situation back home came from a group called the Springbok Legion.

Fred Carneson, who was amongst the first South African soldiers to see active service in 1939, serving in the North African and Italian campaigns:

We started what we called a Union of Soldiers. Then we heard about the Springbok Legion that had started almost simultaneously, from servicemen who for one reason or another found themselves back in South Africa, and from then onwards we were busy recruiting for the Springbok Legion. It became a vehicle in the South African Army for a lot of progressive thinking, on the race issue as well, amongst white South African soldiers.

You see, when you look at the problem of bringing the whites across, as an abstract theoretical thing you can see all sorts of bloody problems. But given the right climate, as existed, for instance, amongst soldiers during the war, we were able to do an enormous amount of work in a progressive direction amongst them. We took up all sorts of issues there − not only the question of increasing family allowances and things that were hitting their pockets and their families, but on political issues calling for sterner measures against the Broederbond[3] and against the Ossewa Brandwag.[4] We were able to do that sort of work.

Don't forget, the bulk of the South African Army were Afrikaners, not English-speaking, and they were also bloody fed up with this lot. Some of them were being beaten up when they went to their home towns and their *dorps* [villages] by these anti-war elements. The Springbok Legion organized a huge demonstration in Johannesburg which smashed up a Nationalist Party conference, again with whites turning out in force, and a hell of a lot of Afrikaners and ex-servicemen. I remember one huge Afrikaner coming along there carrying a rope, and he says, 'If I put my hands on Malan[5] I'm going to hang the bastard!' I mean, that was the strength of feeling that arose then against those they regarded as traitors, who tried to stab them in the back when they were fighting.

And one could see how, given the right circumstances, you can win political support from whites behind particular progressive demands. For instance, when the government was scared to arm the Africans and the

coloureds and the Indians in the face of the opposition from the right-wing
and the anti-war elements, amongst the soldiers you could get across the
line that, look, why shouldn't they be armed? The question of making a
maximum contribution to the war, let's get this bloody thing over. So you'd
be bringing in the colour issue around concrete things.

Also, you know, soldiers being soldiers, going through Africa, Abyssinia
[Ethiopia], and so forth and so on, a hell of a lot of white soldiers made
contact with black women for the first time in their lives. The Immorality
Act[6] didn't apply as far as the soldiers were concerned, I can assure you —
that's the last thing they thought about.

It's funny, you seldom heard any anti-black sentiment amongst the white
soldiers. If you're in an army and a man's on your side, you respect him, you
see. They saw people of different races fighting together on the same side
against the common enemy. This couldn't but have an effect on their
general thinking. How long it lasted after the war, I don't know, but I'm sure
a hell of a lot of it stuck. I doubt if it would have been possible for any South
African government, at that stage, to use the South African Army against
the black people as they've been doing.

Only a minority of Springbok Legion members returned home from the
war radically politicized, but of those who did, many developed a life-
long commitment to political change.[7]

*Wolfie Kodesh, who joined the South African army after finishing high school,
and was recruited to the Springbok Legion soon after its formation in 1941,
while training in North Africa for the Allied offensive in Italy:*

I wasn't really that interested before the war, but once I got into the
Springbok Legion, I felt I'm really doing some good here. Because after all,
why should we go and fight and then come back and be treated like we were
told the First World War soldiers were treated: the big heroes when the war
was on, and then they came back to nothing?

That, in theory, together with what I actually saw with my own eyes, I
thought, no, this can't be right, there's something wrong, you know — when I
saw these people coming out of the hills, ragged, obviously poor people, and
the richer ones were thriving and living in good houses that hadn't been
touched. What I saw there in Italy I think probably politicized me even
more than anything else. Because when we advanced on towns and cities,
you couldn't help noticing that the places that were destroyed by air and so
on were not the big, nice houses — it was always sort of the poor hovels.

There's no doubt about it, I'm absolutely certain that there was a policy of
doing that type of thing — bombing the poor peasants rather than the
wealthy. That had a terrific impact on me, because I equated these poor
people with the coloured people that I knew lived in hovels and the
Africans who lived in tin shanties that I knew and had seen in South Africa.

We had Afrikaners in the army and they made the connection — though not sympathetically. The way they treated those poor people in southern Italy, the working class types who were eating dogs and cats and everything, the Afrikaners said, '*Hulle is net soos ons kaffirs.*' [They are just like our *kaffirs.*] And I thought, now these people are not black, and yet the Boers are saying they are like kaffirs. Then I started thinking and then I started reading.

The Springbok Legion were getting newsletters to us, and I had some books that I managed to get hold of — some were Marxist and some were on the subject of race. Wherever I went I'd be looking round for books and discussing with people who were in advance of me politically, and finding out what this was all about, you see. Finally I decided that now I was going to get involved in the movement, and if possible, full-time, to overcome this racialism, which was like poison.

After all, Hitler had been a racist against the Jews — he said he was going to do the same thing to the blacks. Here were the South African whites doing the same thing as Hitler said he would do — they were already doing it. And you know, it all came together and I thought, no, this is wrong, man, and I have to do my bit towards getting rid of it. I'd gone to meetings and it all fitted in with what was going on in my mind, and I knew that's where I belong — never mind about luxury and business and, you know, being rich.

The entry of the Soviet Union into the war in 1941 opened up further opportunities for politicizing South Africans along non-racial lines, for the 'Red threat' was now 'our glorious ally'. Soon after the Soviet consulate opened in Pretoria in 1942, the Friends of the Soviet Union (FSU), a small anti-fascist group, was reinvigorated, receiving popular support from even government ministers.

'Meeting of Spirit of East with Spirit of West: Soviet Friendship Congress Opened in City', Star, *7 July 1944:*

The spirit of the East and the spirit of the West would soon meet across the stricken body of Nazi Germany, said the Minister of Finance, Mr. Hofmeyr, when he opened the Southern Africa-Soviet Friendship Congress before a large audience in the Great Hall of the University of the Witwatersrand last night. On the platform were members of the Diplomatic Corps and representatives of the Church, the Army, education, the trade unions and other aspects of public life. A message was read from the Prime Minister, General Smuts, in which he said the influence of the Soviet Union for peace would be immense, and much good could come from the continuous exchange of information among the United Nations in building up a more enlightened civilization.

The Soviet Union's popularity also helped swell the ranks of the Communist Party in South Africa, its membership rising from hundreds to thousands during the war years. The CPSA's call for white members to join the army was instrumental to the founding of the Springbok Legion, and by 1942 the party was sponsoring 'Defend South Africa' rallies around the country. The government noted these displays of patriotism: after veteran white labour leader Bill Andrews was elected CPSA chairman in 1943, he was asked to broadcast a pro-war May Day message to workers on the government-run radio service.

For the first time since the 1920s, there was more than a token focus on recruiting whites to the CPSA. Communist candidates contested various elections in 1943, winning two seats on the Cape Town City Council and one on East London's, and the next year securing one on the Johannesburg council and two more in Cape Town.[8] This outreach even extended to the launch by CPSA members of an Afrikaans-language newspaper.[9]

Esther Barsel, a CPSA member active in the FSU in the 1940s and 1950s:

I would say up till the war years we didn't really get to the whites of the country. But from the time that the Soviet Union entered the war in 1941, there was this feeling of solidarity with the Soviet Union, so it really was an opportunity for the FSU to get to the whites, to put our point of view about the Soviet Union. Because there was so much literature coming in, for the first time the whites who knew nothing about the Soviet Union were able to find out more about what was happening there.

In telling people about the Soviet Union, you were popularizing the socialist system — which most whites knew nothing about. In fact, up till the time that the Soviet Union entered the war, Russia was something you fought against. Certainly during the war years, that accent changed. From becoming violently anti-communist, people became sympathetic to the Soviet Union and the Soviet system. We hoped that this would be an ongoing process, but after the war came the Cold War, and it was not so easy. After the end of the war, it was blacks that came into the FSU.

But a lot of whites remained, like the Jewish Workers' Club,[10] for instance. A lot of their members came from Eastern Europe and some came from the Soviet Union, and that organization certainly flourished during and after the war and did a lot to popularize the Soviet Union. And when they had meetings, if they could have blacks as well, they did have. And in that way there was again a mixing of black and white.

Virtually all the considerable war-time political gains of the FSU and the CPSA were reversed by the Suppression of Communism Act of 1950. That law not only banned the Communist Party, but it unleashed a ruinous offensive against non-racial organizations. The militancy stoked by the Springbok Legion fizzled out, despite a spurt of activity in the early '50s led by an ex-servicemen's association called the Torch Commando.[11] The Soviet Consulate in Pretoria was closed in 1956, although the South African Society for Peace and Friendship with the Soviet Union, as the FSU was renamed, staggered on until its banning in 1963.

Communists regrouped underground, later to resurface as the South African Communist Party (SACP). The abortive effort to woo whites had once again vindicated the view that the SACP's most viable base was among the black workers.

ASTORIA THEATRE

(AFRICAN CONSOLIDATED THEATRES LTD.)

WOODSTOCK   WOODSTOCK

MONDAY & TUESDAY, DEC. 29 & 30.

The first official Soviet Film to be shown in South Africa

AT LAST!   THE VEIL IS LIFTED.

SEE HOW 200,000,000 SOVIET CITIZENS LIVE, WORK AND PLAY!

"A Day in Soviet Russia"

Soviet naval units assembling in the Uritski Square, Leningrad. "A Day in Soviet Russia" provides thrilling views of the Soviet naval strength.

A Film So Gigantic it Took 97 Cameramen to make it. Life in the Soviet revealed for the first time.

★ *Read what the Trade Union Secretaries have to say about* "A DAY IN SOVIET RUSSIA".

Russia is a country that will never be beaten, not only because of her vast distances and great population, but because Russia is a land where the people of many races, religions, colour, languages and cultures are free, equal and united.

Russia is a Socialist state: this means that the common people, the working man and woman, are the owners of factories, fields, mines and railways; they are the rulers of their country, that is why Russia is unconquerable.

Come and see the new life. Come, see the country about which more has been argued and written in the past twenty years than about any other country.

Fellow-worker, Trade Unionist, this is a chance you must not miss!

I. BABOO (Sweet Workers' Union).
    (Wine and Brandy Industrial Workers' Union).
ROY DU PREEZ (Textile Workers' Union.
    (Leather Workers' Union).
RAY ALEXANDER (Chemical Workers' Union).
    (Tin Workers' Union).
    (Food and Canning Workers' Union).
B. J. JANUARY (Laundry, Cleaners' and Dyers' Workers' Union).
JOEY FOURIE (National Union of Distributive Workers).
J. CORNELIUS (Tobacco Workers' Union).
JACK FLIOR (Garage Workers' Union).
L. H. MSILA (Dairy Workers' Union).
    (Timber Workers' Union).
    (Printing Labourers' Union).

                                        ☆ STEWART

The FSU showed films like this one, with the message that, 'Russia is a land where the people of many races, religions, colour, languages and culture are free, equal and united... a socialist state where the common people are the rulers of their country.'

Notes

1. In her interview for this book, Helen Joseph quotes this as a goal of the Education Service, in which she served as an Information Officer, along with Brian Bunting, Miriam Hepner and others.
2. There was considerable support among Nationalist Party ranks for the pro-German fascist movement, the Ossewa Brandwag (OB), 'Oxwagon Sentinel'. (The oxwagon used by nineteenth-century Boers to 'trek' from the Cape was a symbol of Afrikaner independence and resistance to British imperialism.) Nationalist leaders tried to distance themselves from the OB, but several OB activists, including John Vorster, who became South Africa's prime minister in 1967, were interned during the war for their Nazi sympathies.
3. This Afrikaner nationalist body grew out of a group formed in 1918 called Jong Suid-Afrika (Young South Africa). The Broederbond ('Brotherhood') established its key public front, the Federasie van Afrikaanse Kultuurverenigings (Federation of Afrikaans Cultural Associations) in 1929, and then concentrated on building the right-wing cross-class alliance that won political power in 1948.
4. See note 2, above.
5. D. F. Malan, a member of the pro-Nazi Ossewa Brandwag who successfully campaigned in the 1948 elections on a pro-apartheid ticket and became prime minister.
6. The Immorality Amendment Act of 1950 forbade extramarital sexual intercourse between whites and blacks, extending a 1927 law to include coloureds and Indians. The Mixed Marriages Act of 1949 prohibited marriages between whites and members of other races. Both laws were scrapped as a reformist concession in 1985.
7. Among those ex-Springbok Legion members who went on to play important roles in South African political organizations were Carneson, Kodesh, Joe Slovo, Jack Hodgson, Brian Bunting, Rusty Bernstein, Ivan Schermbrucker and Cecil Williams. Bram Fischer, Vernon Berrange and others joined the Legion's Home Front League.
8. The best-known CPSA election victory was that of Hilda Watts (now Bernstein) in the Johannesburg municipal poll. For more on the popularity of the CPSA in this period, see *South African Communists Speak: 1915—1980*, Inkululeko Publications, 1981. For a critique of the CPSA's war-time strategies, see 'Class Conflict, Communal Struggle and Patriotic Duty: the CPSA during the Second World War', Tom Lodge, African Studies Seminar Paper, University of the Witwatersrand, 1985.
9. *Die Ware Republikein* (The True Republican) was aimed at Afrikaner workers.
10. Formed in the late 1920s, its support had waned by the time its Johannesburg office burned down in 1948.
11. Formed in 1951 by a small group of English-speaking white war veterans opposed to the government's unconstitutional plans for removing the coloureds from the voters' roll, the Torch Commando joined with the United Party and the Labour Party to form the 'United Democratic Front' in 1953, but faded from the scene after the Nationalist Party's re-election.

PART TWO
1950—1968

The Nationalist Party's 1948 election victory brought the introduction of apartheid policies reflecting the white obsession with 'swamping' (oorstrooming) by blacks.

8 The Shape of Things to Come

Afrikaner nationalists consolidated their unity in the post-war period with a campaign that manipulated white anxieties over growing black labour militancy. The ruling United Party crushed a massive black miners' strike in 1946, but its subsequent attempts at reform prompted panic among white farmers worried about their labour supply drifting toward the cities and white workers who feared competition from lesser-paid blacks. A new policy of 'apartheid' — a newly coined Afrikaans word for separateness — promised to solve these problems for whites through stricter pass laws, job reservation, forced removals of blacks out of 'white areas' into the overpopulated rural labour reserves, tighter restrictions on black political activity, and state support for Afrikaner farms and businesses. Behind the promise lay the reality of 'volkskapitalisme' (people's capitalism): the economic empowerment of the Afrikaner middle classes at the expense not only of blacks, but of their poorer white partners in the cross-class alliance as well.

The Reunited Nationalist Party[1] won political power in the 1948 elections. The apartheid legislation that followed met with some opposition from liberal whites, notably around the Nationalists' anti-constitutional efforts to remove the coloureds from the common voters' roll. However, the most serious challenge came from the rejuvenated African National Congress (ANC), now including Youth Leaguers in its leadership and a fiery new spirit of cultural nationalism in its rhetoric.

Statement on a National Day of Protest against the Unlawful Organizations Bill (later the Suppression of Communism Act) by the Central Executive Committee of the Transvaal ANC Youth League, 31 May 1950:

The protest is to us a manifestation of all those divine stirrings of discontent of the African people since 6th April, 1652, onward — through the period of the so-called Kaffir Wars, through the days of Dingana, through the days of Moshoeshoe, through the days of Sekhukhune against the Grondwet [constitution], through the days of the Treaty of Vereeniging, through the days of the White Union Pact of 1910.[2]

What is more significant to us is that for the first time since 1652, African National Leaders are going to stage simultaneously a forceful opposition to our oppressors. If Makana, Dingana, Khama and Sekhukhune had defended their country jointly, Africa would have been saved for posterity.[3] The African people have pledged themselves to liberate South Africa — black, white and yellow — and to that end the impending national crisis presages the shape of things to come.

Our cause is just, our aspirations noble; Victory cannot but be ours. *Vuka Afrika!* Up You Mighty Race! *Tsoga Afrika!*

Resistance ideology was in transition. This formative stage in the development from nationalism to non-racialism pointed up the need for unity and joint action in an African-led opposition.

M. B. Yengwa, a Natal ANC Youth League member who was elected to the ANC National Executive Committee in 1952:

I had become very much politically aware during the Passive Resistance campaign of the Indian Congress. I was very, very, very much impressed by the determination of the Indians in fighting against the segregation of the Ghetto Act, to the point that they were prepared to go to jail. I felt that one must fight for his rights.

When I got married in 1945, I wanted to get a house in the housing scheme. You can't get a house without a pass, and up to that time I avoided taking out a pass. Now I will tell you my traumatic experience. When I went into the Native Administration Department I queued up in a very long line, and when we went into the hall it was shattering: we were ordered to expose our male organs! This was a very rude order, which is not mentionable in Zulu, literally: '*Vul' umthondo*', expose your penis. We were in a line, no respect for privacy, and the white man examined our private parts, just casually, and then said, 'Go away, you must go and wash yourself.' Such humiliation I'd never seen, and I felt that the white man was such a horrible oppressor. And I went back so disgusted that I felt I would have to fight against passes because I was so humiliated, and I didn't like to face the experience again.

So I went up to apply for membership of the ANC: it represented the blacks fighting against white oppression. At that particular point I didn't have any idea of alliances with the coloureds and the Indians, but as the struggle grew, we became aware of the need for a united front.

How did you become aware of that?

First we became aware through the tragedy of the Indian riots during 1949. It was the incitement to racial animosity which was responsible for the riots. We felt that we had to confront the question of our deprivation of rights together, and fight as a united organization. We had joint sessions with the South African Indian Congress.

We were then in the Youth League, and the ANC in Natal was still led by Mr A. W. G. Champion. Mr Champion was not prepared to cooperate with the Indians, but from our experience we felt that the Indians were to be trusted to go along with us because they were in the Passive Resistance campaign. We argued that we have no alternative but to work with the Indians, that we are fighting the same enemy. We won, Champion was deposed, and Chief Albert Lutuli replaced him as leader of the African people.

When I first joined in 1945, I regarded the ANC as not very militant at all. I felt that this was a body which was doing absolutely nothing. It was based on the support of the chiefs, and the chiefs were dependent on the government's goodwill. The methods of passing resolutions and deputations had been proved to be of no effect. The Youth League had been formed in 1944, proposing very, very, very drastic reforms through the Programme of Action, and it had stated that Africans must be united through African nationalism and we must devote our energies on strikes and civil disobedience.

When you said you wanted to make the ANC more militant, did you feel it should be more pro-African, more anti-white?

It was not an anti-white thing. We became more and more aware that our struggle is not against the white man — our struggle is against apartheid. Of course, generally, our whole thrust was African nationalism. African nationalism was, as we saw it, a uniting force and a driving force towards overthrowing white oppression. As we developed our own philosophy of African nationalism, we discovered that we had common goals — it didn't matter whether you are black or white. In other words, we evolved towards non-racialism. I think you can't fight against racism and then substitute racism. Racism is a philosophy which is very destructive — it's very soul-destroying.

How did you actually make that change away from African nationalism?

Well, from the actual struggle. The National Party made laws against the Communist Party, it made laws against the coloureds, the Group Areas Act, and so forth. We felt that, no, we are all lumped up together and we must all fight together. This was a natural process of learning about our common struggle against apartheid, and we were able to discover in actual practice that our fight was against the common enemy. The whole concept of non-racialism developed imperceptibly, slowly, but I've become a convinced non-racialist. I am repeating this point over and over and over again: the struggle made me a non-racialist.

In 1952, the ANC launched a campaign that was to swell its membership to an all-time high of 100,000. The Campaign for the Defiance of Unjust Laws was the first major action to draw support from all race groups.

Dorothy Nyembe, in the leadership of the Natal ANC, the ANC Women's League, and the Federation of South African Women (FedSAW) in the 1950s:

When I first heard about the ANC, I was walking in town [Durban]. I was returning from school and I heard people shouting, '*Mayibuye! Mayibuye i'Afrika!*' [Let Africa return!]. We saw a large group of Africans and Indians singing, and we sat down and listened to what they were saying. They were talking about land which was taken from us by the Afrikaners. One of my friends told me that they were talking about the history that we were taught at school.

It was in 1952. From that very first day, I decided to join the ANC. People at the meeting did not advocate for whites to be driven out of the country.

They wanted to be free, to live wherever they pleased, to have the right education, to have a say in the making of laws in this country. I started to be a card-carrying member shortly after the Defiance Campaign. I was a full-time member and not just a tea-maker. Our mentor was Chief Albert Lutuli. He taught us that men and women were equal, and that it all depends on one's dedication.

Dorothy Nyembe and Lilian Ngoyi leading a 1952 Durban march.

There were Indians we lived with. We were close to them and went to school together, but I got to know them well at Cato Manor, in the struggles we waged together. I was fascinated by the contact we had with them, because we respected one another and lived together happily.

We were locked up for a month during the Defiance Campaign. It was my first jail experience. We did hard manual labour. It was a bad experience. We crushed large rocks with hammers, but our determination was not crushed. We were determined to get liberation, no matter how demanding it may be.

Other groups which emerged argued that we should not mix with whites. But Chief Lutuli taught us that every person born in this country had a right to stay and be free, whether he is Indian, African or white. We fought side by side. There were other white people who did not believe in racism and oppression. They were known as 'democrats'.

Such democrats had been active for years, in the trade unions and political organizations, but it was the participation of whites in the Defiance Campaign that publicly highlighted their involvement.[4]

Albie Sachs, an ANC-supporting activist in the Cape in the 1950s and 1960s:

I met a crowd off campus called the Modern Youth Society. And that was my great moment of transformation. Because these were young people — mainly, but not exclusively, whites — who were struggling for a free, liberated, non-racial South Africa. They had all the values that were lying latent inside me. But they were my pals, my generation, my crowd. I wasn't doing things for my parents.[5] I developed a definite reaction against that. Immediately, this is where I wanted to be, I knew. At that stage — this was '52, onwards — the Modern Youth Society was the only non-racial organization in the whole of the Union of South Africa. Apart from the CP, deep underground, there wasn't a single non-racial organization — social, cultural, political — in the whole country. Even the churches were racially divided.

We had a lot of activities. We organized a youth festival, we also used to have what we called non-racial dances. It was a most straightforward social activity, having fun but defying the laws — in the sense that the serving of liquor was always controlled, in terms of race. But the real defiance was in terms of the fact of black, white, brown just dancing together.

We were white-dominated, there is no doubt about that. We were always eager to have blacks in positions of leadership, and somebody would roll up at a meeting and three weeks later might be the chairman. It was a bit artificial. And almost invariably these people turned out to be police spies. It was because we accepted the importance, in principle, of black leadership of a people's movement.

How did this political involvement relate to your own personal background?

My parents were Jewish in a kind of cultural sense. There are certain characteristics of style and humour, sometimes little things that one eats and so on, that one can say is part of a Jewish tradition. But they were involved in the struggle for liberation of everybody, not just for the Jews. I know when I went to Czechoslovakia, and in Prague saw the two synagogues that had survived the holocaust — the guide told me that these synagogues had been preserved by the Nazis to be a museum, a museum for an extinct race — I wept, it just came pouring out, because I know that a lot of my family had been annihilated and this was something that had touched me. But the result of that was not to make me want to identify with Israel or the Jewish cause — it was all a part and parcel of the struggle against oppression everywhere.

It wasn't just millions of Jews who had died in the holocaust: it was millions of Poles and Russians and half-a-million gypsies. So there was no need to distinguish gradations of horror. It was a ghastly episode, and fascism and Nazism had to be combatted wherever it was. So in that sense, the world I grew up in wasn't a world of identification with Jewry — it was a world of identification with struggle against oppression.

How would you explain the disproportionate representation of Jews in South African resistance politics?

I think that there are sociological and cultural reasons for that. They came from poor families, immigrants. The way the South African economic structure was established, Jews could enter the professions, the liberal professions in particular, through education. But even though they could be very successful in professional terms, they were excluded largely from government, they were excluded from the multi-national part of industry, and also there was a lot of very strong anti-semitism which was promoted by the internal racists.

Did the whites in your circles have a political relationship with the ANC?
We worked with the ANC Youth League and every Saturday afternoon we would go out to the locations to show the non-racial quality of the ANC.

Nineteen fifty-two was a very important year for me, the year of the Defiance of Unjust Laws Campaign. We were told to go to some hall in Salt River, a sort of working class coloured area. The hall was packed, and suddenly there was this commotion and in walks Johnson Ngwevela, one of the ANC leaders. He was one of the first to receive a banning order and he was now attending a meeting in defiance of the banning order. And everybody stood up and sang, and then the police came in and took him away and we carried on singing, and then we sat down and someone said, 'Comrades, you have seen Comrade Ngwevela defying the unjust laws – we now call for volunteers.'

People were rushing forward, saying, 'Take my name, take my name!' and everybody was given great cheers, and I was saying to the comrade next to me, 'You say it is a freedom struggle – why can't whites participate? It is for everybody. We believe in a non-racial South Africa, why can't I join?' They responded with, 'Wait, wait, it is not time yet – we are just starting.' So I said, 'At least the question has got to be taken up.' So he said, 'Okay, we will take up the question.'

By about August or September the word comes through: the leadership in Jo'burg say it is okay for whites to join. So we went and sat down on a 'Blacks Only' post office bench in a huge post office in Cape Town – and nobody would arrest us. Now any black who took part in the Defiance Campaign was whipped off in no time, but people actually went out to get us a cup of tea, we were waiting so long to be arrested. And by then I would say a thousand people, black people, had gathered around, and two colonels came to arrest us. So we weren't even arrested by any old sergeant. And I turned to the crowd and shouted, '*Mayibuye!*' and the blacks shouted back, '*i'Afrika!*' three times. Later the court was packed; they were happy that there were young whites willing to participate in their campaigns.

In a sense, we operated at two levels. There were the Modern Youth Society activities that were overtly non-racial in character but white-dominated. And then there was organizing work that was all semi-secret, and that was black-dominated – where we would be doing the driving, we would be called in for study classes. The ANC would tell us where they wanted support from us – it could be anything from politics to the history of South Africa.

I had book knowledge, a lot of it. The people wanted that. I'd been recruited for that, but for me, this was my real university: going into a tin shanty. The workers would be there, it had a very intense emotional quality, the interaction between us, for them and for me. It had even an intense visual quality, because it was all by candlelight. So it was very, very much a two-way thing. You had to learn not to have a complex about the advantages of growing up in a privileged white society. Complexes help nobody. You had to learn to take everything that you'd got from that privilege and put it at the service of the people's struggle. And that is what the people wanted.

They didn't want us to voluntarily impose upon ourselves all the limitations that apartheid society imposes upon people. That is a kind of a self-sacrificial idea that was totally out of keeping with the concept of liberation.

Years later, I met Moses Kotane. I think he always had this special feeling for me because he had known me as a kid. He now sees I am in the Defiance Campaign, so I think he is feeling quite pleased. But he gives me a little lecture. He says, 'You whites, you all love running to the location [black township]. You get big cheers from the people.' He says, 'Water always follows the path of least resistance. We don't have access to the whites, we can't organize amongst them. That is really where you people have to be, but you always run away from that. Because it is more difficult.'

It was to this difficult task of organizing in their own community that progressive whites were asked to address themselves when the ANC appealed for their support. While many whites would have preferred to join an organization open to all races, the ANC argued that the time for one united non-racial body had not yet come, and that the goal of non-racialism could best be achieved through building organizational bases in the existing segregated communities. Even the ANC Youth League, regarded as anti-white only a decade before, exhorted whites to work with the ANC through its own wing of the Congress Alliance.

Afrika, *journal of the ANC Youth League, November 1953:*

Last month a very important conference was held in Johannesburg, consisting largely of progressive Europeans [whites]. The aim of this conference was to establish an organization in South Africa of all those Europeans who believe in and are committed to struggle for the achievement in this country of the principles of the African National Congress. This is a most significant step in the political history of this country.

This is a national movement of Europeans pledged to a policy of working with and under the leadership of the Congress. We would like to pause here to draw attention to a fact that is often lost sight of. The expression, 'liberation', from the point of view of a European democrat, cannot bear the same meaning as when it is used by the African. Thus liberation, from the point of view of a democratic European, would concretely mean freedom from class oppression. In other words, every time a European in this country speaks of liberation, his mind must jump to the concept of freedom from economic exploitation under capitalism.

As for the African, the tendency is for him to think in terms of the removal of caste or national oppression whenever the expression, liberation, is employed. The fact that national oppression and class oppression are twin problems, interlinked and interlocked, is what occurs to him when he thinks again. This, crudely put, is the contradiction that has always existed between the European and African democrats in this country. The formation of the Congress of Democrats (COD) is an important step in the resolution of the internal contradiction within the democratic camp.

Helen Joseph, a COD founder member:

How did you feel about the job of working among whites?

I tried, but it was very hard. I am the world's worst canvasser, I can't sell anything to anybody. I was the secretary of our Hillbrow branch and one of our tasks was to get literature out, COD pamphlets and *Fighting Talk* and *Liberation*,[6] going flat by flat to sell it. I was hopeless.

I respected COD tremendously for what it was trying to do, but I don't know what impact we made on the white people in Jo'burg. We certainly did not get around to the ordinary people in the street. I never see the Congress of Democrats as a failure, though. I tell you where I think we did make an impact: not in the personal contact, not in wooing people in, but we certainly were an important 'ginger group'. We made people think, through our literature, letters to the paper. There wasn't a topic that we didn't bring out a pamphlet or document on. Anything, apartheid at the zoo, anything that came up that was a topical issue, COD was out with a pamphlet or an article or booklet. We were the most indefatigable writers of letters to the papers.

And we certainly had, I think, a great effect upon the Liberal Party, because we were always one or two or three steps ahead. We were the people who were recognized, who were part of the Congress Alliance – equal partners in it. The Liberal Party was still trying to buffet its way in, but handicapped by its concern for its membership. You know, the Liberal Party started on a qualified vote, and it took them eight years to get rid of that one. Whereas we were in immediately. That was their mistake: the Liberal Party didn't move far enough.

You see, there was a split among the people that attended the meeting called by the ANC and the SAIC to discuss the formation of a white organization. The people that later made the Congress of Democrats stood on universal franchise and the liberals stood on a qualified franchise. And I suppose I acquired a form of contempt for the liberals because of that. I was so enthusiastic about this new world of mine that I tended to be very critical of people who wouldn't accept universal franchise. That was what we fought for, that was what I had been in the army for: for democracy, and democracy means universal vote.[7] That's what the United Nations Declaration of Human Rights says, so why can't these people accept it? I really was intolerant of them. I knew some lovely individuals, but as a group, we in COD had contempt for them – yes, we did. We have always been ahead of them, you see.

But I have canvassed for the liberals. We would always work with them and we would have been very happy if we had got closer to the liberals. But the liberals were very suspicious. Don't forget, in the 1950s there was tremendous anti-communist suspicion, and the liberals were very suspicious of COD – which some of them still see as a communist front.

Misgivings among liberal whites about the African-led mass movement were highlighted by the exaggerated response to a wave of riots in the

Eastern Cape during the Defiance Campaign. Despite the ANC's claim that the unrest had been fomented by government agents aiming to discredit the well-disciplined campaign, a group of distinguished liberals issued a statement counselling patience for the defiant 'non-Europeans'.

'Equal Rights for All Civilized People', statement issued by 23 signatories from Johannesburg, Cape Town and Durban, including Edgar Brookes, Alan Paton, Leo Marquard and Donald Molteno,[8] 14 October 1952:

We have watched with dismay the situation that has developed from the growth of the non-European movement of passive resistance against unjust laws. We believe that it is imperative that South Africa should now adopt a policy that will attract the support of educated, politically conscious non-Europeans by offering them a reasonable status in our common society. This can be done by a revival of the liberal tradition which prevailed for so many years with such successful results in the Cape Colony. That tradition, an integral part of South African history, was based on a firm principle: namely, equal rights for all civilized people, and equal opportunities for all men and women to become civilized. On their side, we ask the African and Indian leaders to recognize that it will take time and patience substantially to improve the present position.

The Congress Wheel,
symbol of the Congress Alliance.

The logo of the Congress was a wheel, with four spokes representing the ANC, the Indian Congress, COD and the South African Coloured People's Organization (later renamed the Coloured People's Congress). Of all the spokes of the Congress wheel, it was this last one that encountered most difficulty in establishing a base in its community. As with whites and Indians, there was some suspicion among coloureds about the position of a small minority in the African-dominated Congress Alliance.

George Peake, national chairman of the Coloured People's Congress (CPC), speaking at a joint rally with the ANC at Cape Town's Parade, October 1954:

With the object of achieving freedom in our lifetime, we have joined forces with the African National Congress, the Congress of Democrats and the South African Indian Congress. Almost too late, we coloureds have come to realize that the few privileges we enjoy are won at the expense of our African and Indian comrades. Too long have we accepted the policy of divide-and-rule of the South African government, always believing and hoping that the attacks made on the liberty of other sections would not affect us.

And friends, most tragic of all, too many of the coloured people believed for too long that because at a certain stage in the history of South Africa, Dutchmen, Englishmen, Frenchmen, Germans — in fact, men of most of the races of Europe — have embarked on married life with, or violated, Hottentots and Bushmen, yes, we believed we were their descendants. But when we realize facts, we see that we are not an appendage of the European people. We must be oppressed, humiliated and deprived of rights which in democratic countries are the liberty of all people. My advice, friends, is not to delay one moment longer. The government is not wasting time in oppressing you, so don't waste time in fighting back. Don't be lulled into a sense of false security and believe that it is not for you, that it is for Africans only.

Join in the struggle through your national organizations. Throw in your lot with the Congress movement, and show the world at large that although oppressed, we are not browbeaten, and have the courage of our convictions to fight and strive for a place in the land of our birth. Forward to Freedom!

Reg September, CPC founder member:

You know, questions of suspicion of the African community, in my experience, have come mostly from the more privileged section of the coloured community, not from the poor section — which in my opinion have proved to be the most involved in struggle. A big percentage of the coloured community is very poor, and to me, this is the section which is most amenable to organization, because they've got more to fight for. They are closer to the African because they are poorer, and more likely to respond to appeals for supporting the struggle than the average artisan.

It's not necessarily a homogeneous community that you're dealing with. You're dealing with a community which has a class structure within it, very much so, and we've got to take this into account throughout in organizing the community. We have a need to pay particular attention to the poorer section of the community in order to draw them into struggle. The rest of the community will be drawn in as the movement gathers momentum. This is my belief.

From your experience in trying to mobilize coloured people, were there any particular leaders or heroes whose names could be invoked to win a greater response?

Perhaps it's one of the things that we've lacked in the community. We've never had a Lutuli or a Mandela or a Xuma — this is one of the problems. In its heyday, the community did have a Dr Abdullah Abdurahman. At a later stage, it did have a Cissie Gool, who was the leader of the National Liberation League (NLL), but since then, I would not claim that there was anybody in particular who stood out as a leader of the coloured community.[9]

As a result, did the coloured community accept the African leaders?

I think that, more and more, as they gained experience, they understood that it was inevitable that the African people would lead South Africa — but a lot of these things come about as a result of practical experience, don't they, not just talking about them.

Notes

1. The party that made an election pact with the Afrikaner Party in 1947 in order to campaign as a united Afrikaner nationalist front. Once in power, it presided over the rapid centralization of Afrikaner capital and the emergence of monopoly corporations controlled by a small minority of the volk. This led to increasing differentiation between the various class forces that had initially united behind Afrikaner nationalism, laying the ground for the ruptures in its ranks in the 1980s.
2. The 'Kaffir Wars', frontier clashes between settlers (usually supported by British troops) and Xhosa from 1779 to 1879, are now known as the Wars of Dispossession. Dingana succeeded Shaka as Zulu king and is remembered for his attack on Boer leader Piet Retief and his followers, and the subsequent defeat of the Zulu army at the Battle of Blood River on 16 December 1838. Basotho chief Moshoeshoe succeeded for a good part of the nineteenth century in playing off Boer against Briton to salvage independence for what is now Lesotho. Pedi chief Sekhukhune, the last independent African chief in the Transvaal, was defeated by a combined force of English, Boers and Swazis in 1878.
   The Boers conceded defeat to the British with the treaty of Vereeniging in 1902. The four South African colonies — Transvaal, Cape, Natal and Orange Free State — united in 1910, embracing white supremacy.
3. Makana was a Xhosa leader during the war of 1818−19 who was sentenced to life imprisonment on Robben Island and then drowned while attempting to escape. Khama was chief of the Bamangwato, the largest Tswana polity.
4. The white participant in the Defiance Campaign who received the most publicity at the time was Patrick Duncan, son of a former Governor-General of the Union of South Africa. Duncan went on to edit the Liberal Party-supporting newspaper, *Contact*, opposed the ANC's alleged communist domination, and became the first white member of the PAC.
5. Albie Sachs's mother, Ray Edwards, was secretary to Communist Party leader Moses Kotane; his father was the Garment Workers Union leader, Solly Sachs; and his parents named him after Albert Nzula, the first African to hold the post of CPSA general-secretary, in 1929.
6. COD publications.
7. Joseph served as an Army Information Officer during the Second World War, giving weekly lectures on current affairs and South African government to Air Force women — an experience she regards as her initial politicization.
8. Paton wrote *Cry the Beloved Country* and, along with Marquard and Molteno, was in the national leadership of the Liberal Party from its founding in mid-1953; Brookes became chairman of the Party in 1964.
9. Abdurahman was president of the Cape Coloured-dominated African People's Organization from 1905 until his death in 1940. The NLL, founded in 1935 by radical coloureds, inspired the formation in 1938 of the non-racial Non-European United Front, led by Dadoo.

9 The Freedom Front

The practical experience that taught Congress Alliance members most about building non-racial unity was the organizing of the Congress of the People in June 1955, by a newly-created National Action Council (NAC) consisting of eight members from each of the four sponsoring bodies.

'Call to the Congress of the People', leaflet issued by the NAC, 1954:

We call the people of South Africa, black and white — Let us speak together of freedom!

We call the farmers of the reserves and trust lands. Let us speak of the wide land, and the narrow strips on which we toil. Let us speak of brothers without land, and of children without schooling. Let us speak of taxes and of cattle, and of famine. Let us speak of freedom.

We call the miners of coal, gold and diamonds. Let us speak of the dark shafts, and the cold compounds far from our families. Let us speak of heavy labour and long hours, and of men sent home to die. Let us speak of rich masters and poor wages. Let us speak of freedom.

We call the workers of farms and forests. Let us speak of the rich foods we grow, and the laws that keep us poor. Let us speak of harsh treatment, and of children and women forced to work. Let us speak of private prisons, and beatings and of passes. Let us speak of freedom.

We call the workers of factories and shops. Let us speak of the good things we make, and the bad conditions of our work. Let us speak of the many passes and the few jobs. Let us speak of foremen and of transport and of trade unions; of holidays and of houses. Let us speak of freedom.

We call the teachers, students and the preachers. Let us speak of the light that comes with learning, and the ways we are kept in darkness. Let us speak of great services we can render, and of the narrow ways that are open to us. Let us speak of laws, and government, and rights. Let us speak of freedom.

We call the housewives and the mothers. Let us speak of the fine children that we bear, and of their stunted lives. Let us speak of the many illnesses and deaths, and of the few clinics and schools. Let us speak of high prices and of shanty towns. Let us speak of freedom.

Let us speak together. All of us together — Africans and Europeans, Indian and Coloured. Voter and voteless. Privileged and rightless. The happy and the homeless. All the people of South Africa; of the towns and of the countryside. Let us speak together of freedom. And of the happiness that can come to men and women if they live in a land that is free. Let us speak together of freedom. And of how to get it for ourselves, and for our children. Let the voice of all the people be heard. And let the demands of all the people for the things that will make us free be recorded.

Freedom Volunteers wearing posters depicting the Congress wheel, canvassing support for the Congress of the People.

We call all the people of South Africa to prepare for the Congress of the People — where representatives of the people, everywhere in the land, will meet together in a great assembly, to discuss and adopt the Charter of Freedom.

This Call to the Congress of the People is addressed to all South Africans, European and Non-European. It is made by four bodies, speaking for the four sections of the people of South Africa: by the African National Congress, the South African Indian Congress, the Congress of Democrats, and the South African Coloured People's Organization.[1]

When South Africa's first non-racial trade union coordinating body was formed, the South African Congress of Trade Unions became part of the Congress Alliance. SACTU's members joined with the thousands of other Congress Volunteers in canvassing demands for the Freedom Charter. The active involvement of SACTU in this and many other Congress campaigns derived from its belief that organizing workers is inextricably linked to engagement in the wider political struggle, and that both workplace and community issues are the concern of a committed trade union.

Declaration of Principles adopted at the foundation conference of SACTU, 5 March 1955:

We firmly declare that the interests of all workers are alike, whether they be European, African, Coloured, Indian, English, Afrikaans or Jewish. We resolve that this coordinating body of trade unions shall strive to unite all workers in its ranks, without discrimination and without prejudice. We resolve that this body shall determinedly seek to further and protect the interests of all workers, and that its guiding motto shall be the universal slogan of working class solidarity: 'An injury to one is an injury to all!'

The NAC drafted the Freedom Charter from the demands for a non-racial South Africa collected from all over the country. It was adopted at the Congress of the People, held in Kliptown, outside Johannesburg, on 26 June 1955. The delegates included 2,222 Africans, 320 Indians, 230 coloureds and 112 whites: non-racialism in overt, self-conscious and affirmative form, projecting a vision of the future South Africa after the defeat of apartheid. Delegates and volunteers then reported back to their constituencies and began popularizing the Freedom Charter.

Delegates to the Congress of the People in Kliptown.

The Freedom Charter:

WE, THE PEOPLE OF SOUTH AFRICA, DECLARE FOR ALL OUR COUNTRY AND THE WORLD TO KNOW:

That South Africa belongs to all who live in it, black and white, and that no government can justly claim authority unless it is based on the will of the people;

That our people have been robbed of their birthright to land, liberty and peace by a form of government founded on injustice and inequality;

That our country will never be prosperous or free until all our people live in brotherhood, enjoying equal rights and opportunities;

That only a democratic state, based on the will of the people, can secure to all their birthright without distinction of colour, race, sex or belief;

And therefore, we the people of South Africa, black and white, together equals, countrymen and brothers, adopt this Freedom Charter. And we pledge ourselves to strive together, sparing nothing of our strength and courage, until the democratic changes here set out have been won.

THE PEOPLE SHALL GOVERN!

Every man and woman shall have the right to vote for and stand as a candidate for all bodies which make laws;

All the people shall be entitled to take part in the administration of the country;

The rights of the people shall be the same, regardless of race, colour or sex;

All bodies of minority rule, advisory boards, councils and authorities shall be replaced by democratic organs of self-government.

ALL NATIONAL GROUPS SHALL HAVE EQUAL RIGHTS!

There shall be equal status in the bodies of state, in the courts, and in the schools for all national groups and races;

All national groups shall be protected by law against insults to their race and national pride;

All people shall have equal rights to use their own language and to develop their own folk culture and customs;

The preaching and practice of national, race or colour discrimination and contempt shall be a punishable crime;

All apartheid laws and practices shall be set aside.

THE PEOPLE SHALL SHARE IN THE COUNTRY'S WEALTH!

The national wealth of our country, the heritage of all South Africans, shall be restored to the people;

The mineral wealth beneath the soil, the banks and monopoly industry shall be transferred to the ownership of the people as a whole;

All other industries and trades shall be controlled to assist the well-being of the people;

All people shall have equal rights to trade where they choose, to manufacture and to enter all trades, crafts and professions.

THE LAND SHALL BE SHARED AMONG THOSE WHO WORK IT!

Restriction of land ownership on a racial basis shall end, and all the land be redivided amongst those who work it, to banish famine and land hunger;

The state shall help the peasants with implements, seed, tractors and dams to save the soil and assist the tillers;

Freedom of movement shall be guaranteed to all who work on the land;

All shall have the right to occupy land wherever they choose;

People shall not be robbed of their cattle, and forced labour and farm prisons shall be abolished.

ALL SHALL BE EQUAL BEFORE THE LAW!

No one shall be imprisoned, deported or restricted without fair trial;

No one shall be condemned by the order of any government official;

The courts shall be representative of all the people;

Imprisonment shall be only for serious crimes against the people, and shall aim at re-education, not only vengeance;

The police force and army shall be open to all on an equal basis and shall be the helpers and protectors of the people;

All laws which discriminate on the grounds of race, colour or belief shall be repealed.

ALL SHALL ENJOY HUMAN RIGHTS!

The law shall guarantee to all their right to speak, to organize, to meet together, to publish, to preach, to worship and to educate their children;

The privacy of the house from police raids shall be protected by law;

All shall be free to travel without restriction from countryside to town, from province to province, and from South Africa abroad;

Pass laws, permits and all other laws restricting these freedoms shall be abolished.

THERE SHALL BE WORK AND SECURITY!

All who work shall be free to form trade unions, to elect their officers and to make wage agreements with their employers;

The state shall recognize the right and duty of all to work, and to draw full unemployment benefits;

Men and women of all races shall receive equal pay for equal work;

There shall be a forty-hour working week, a national minimum wage, paid annual leave, and sick leave for all workers, and maternity leave on full pay for all working mothers;

Miners, domestic workers, farm workers and civil servants shall have the same rights as all others who work;

Child labour, compound labour, the tot system[2] and contract labour shall be abolished.

THE DOORS OF LEARNING AND CULTURE SHALL BE OPENED!

The government shall discover, develop and encourage national talent for the enhancement of our cultural life;

All the cultural treasures of mankind shall be open to all, by free exchange of books, ideas and contact with other lands;

The aim of education shall be to teach the youth to love their people and their culture, to honour human brotherhood, liberty and peace;

Education shall be free, compulsory, universal and equal for all children;

Higher education and technical training shall be opened to all by means of state allowances and scholarships awarded on the basis of merit;

Adult illiteracy shall be ended by a mass state education plan;

Teachers shall have all the rights of other citizens;

The colour bar in cultural life, in sport and in education shall be abolished.

THERE SHALL BE HOUSES, SECURITY AND COMFORT!

All people shall have the right to live where they choose, to be decently housed, and to bring up their families in comfort and security;

Unused housing space to be made available to the people;

Rent and prices shall be lowered, food plentiful and no one shall go hungry;

A preventive health scheme shall be run by the state;

Free medical care and hospitalization shall be provided for all, with special care for mothers and young children;

Slums shall be demolished and new suburbs built where all shall have transport, roads, lighting, playing fields, creches and social centres;

The aged, the orphans, the disabled and the sick shall be cared for by the state;

Rest, leisure and recreation shall be the right of all;

Fenced locations and ghettos shall be abolished and laws which break up families shall be repealed.

THERE SHALL BE PEACE AND FRIENDSHIP!

South Africa shall be a fully independent state, which respects the rights and sovereignty of all nations;

South Africa shall strive to maintain world peace and the settlement of all international disputes by negotiation, not war;

Peace and friendship amongst all our people shall be secured by upholding the equal rights, opportunities and status of all;

The people of the protectorates, Basutoland, Bechuanaland and Swaziland, shall be recognized, and shall be free to decide for themselves their own future;

The right of all the peoples of Africa to independence and self-

Graffiti supporting a clause from the Freedom Charter, downtown Johannesburg, 1956.

government shall be recognized, and shall be the basis of close cooperation;

LET ALL WHO LOVE THEIR PEOPLE AND THEIR COUNTRY NOW SAY, AS WE SAY HERE:

'These freedoms we will fight for, side by side, throughout our lives, until we have won our liberty.'

ANC photographer Eli Weinberg had originally planned to stage this group picture of all the Treason Trial defendants in Johannesburg's Joubert Park, but permission was withdrawn when a government official learned that blacks and whites were to be seated together. The defendants were then photographed in smaller groups and Weinberg prepared a montage.

The rest of the 1950s saw countless campaigns: among the best remembered are demonstrations against the demolition of racially mixed freehold areas like Johannesburg's Sophiatown, boycotts of buses to protest fare increases, and of potatoes to highlight the conditions of farm labourers. The demands of the Freedom Charter for a non-racial South Africa provided a focus for unity in all these struggles, and the front was widened to include organizations not affiliated to the Congress Alliance.

Sechaba: Bulletin of the Transvaal ANC, *September 1956:*

Let us face it! The Nationalists have driven the African people to the point where many who were formerly not involved in political movements — who are today still outside the African National Congress — are up in arms against apartheid and for their rights. This is inevitable and must be welcomed. We believe that all vanguard fighters for freedom are led in the final analysis by the militant programme and actions of the ANC, but this does not mean that the ANC should expect or try to claim a monopoly of all anti-apartheid fights of the people. Many actions may originate outside the ANC, some locally, some initiated by other leaders and groups. But if they are for the right policies, the ANC must welcome such actions and campaigns, and fight with them in the overall freedom fight.

The Women's Federation[3] represents a great working unity between the different women's organizations representing the different sections of South African women. To suggest that it is unnecessary or that the ANC Women's League 'could have done the job' is in the same breath to attack the very basis of the Congress movement itself. Why then do we not say to the Indian and Coloured Congresses and to COD, 'Why a National Action Committee? Why not come in with us?'

On the women's fighting front, the Women's Federation is the counterpart of the alliance built by the Congress movement. It is composed of the bodies that campaign together, that stand for the same programme, yet it is something mightier than all its independent parts, built by their cooperation on the basis of unity in action. Coloured, Indian and democratic European women, though not affected by passes today, have opposed these evils inflicted on African women because they know this is apartheid at work and no women's rights in future are safe under apartheid.

So the Women's Federation is part of the freedom front. It augments and strengthens it. It is a full-blooded member of the freedom movement and must not be regarded — or treated — as a step-child. Part of the Congress front, the Federation must nevertheless have freedom of action within it.

The South African government had been closely monitoring the ground-swell of support for the Freedom Charter. Police barred busloads of delegates from attending the Congress of the People, and Special Branch agents backed up by hundreds of armed police on horseback searched the crowd at Kliptown. The state collected Congress documents in raids over the next year, and then in December 1956, some 156[4] people — two-thirds African and the rest Indian, coloured and white — were arrested and charged with High Treason. In a trial that lasted four years, the state tried to prove that the Freedom Charter was a communist document, part of a conspiracy aimed at instigating a violent overthrow of the state. The attempt failed: the trial ended with the acquittal of all defendants.

While the Congress movement suffered from this deactivation of its leadership, it also benefited from the lengthy and intensive contact between activists from all over the country afforded by the marathon trial. The wide spectrum of political views among the treason trialists has been summed up as 'ranging in outlook from Moses Kotane to Chief Lutuli'.[5] In fact, since the defendants were seated in alphabetical order, the Communist Party leader and the Christian nationalist forged an intimate relationship, personally and politically, during the months they spent sitting next to each other in court. Similarly, blacks who had never experienced firsthand the non-racialism they had endorsed through the Freedom Charter interacted as equals with whites. Thus the developing unity, despite diversity, of the Congress movement owed a big debt to the Treason Trial.

Notes

1. It was the call for the Congress of the People that prompted the South African Coloured People's Organization (SACPO) to formally change its name to the Coloured People's Congress (CPC).
2. Practice whereby coloured farmworkers were rewarded with periodic shots of wine or brandy throughout the working day, ostensibly to ensure productivity.
3. The Federation of South African Women (FedSAW), formed in April 1954, is best remembered for organizing an anti-pass demonstration on 9 August 1956, when 20,000 women from all over South Africa marched to the Union Buildings in Pretoria to present a petition to Prime Minister J. G. Strijdom.

10 A Dynamic and Irresistible Force

The non-racialism of the Congress Alliance was not without opposition. By the late 1950s, the tensions that arose a decade before in the ANC Youth League began to coalesce, and two different camps emerged: the non-racialists and the Africanists.

A. B. Ngcobo, a Natal ANC Youth League member who was part of the Africanist breakaway from the ANC:

My father was the chairman of the local ANC branch in Melmoth in Zululand. He had been an ANC member from 1913. At the time there was definitely no other movement — it was run by black people for black people. There wasn't a family that wasn't an ANC family — if you came from an African background, there was no other movement at the time. You might not have held office, you might not have paid subscription, but you said that if you are part of the nation, you are ANC.

What debates were going on in the ANC Youth League when you first got involved?

What we discussed was the whole question of national self-determination of the African people, and ways and means of improving their economic output. And unfortunately, all people in the bandwagon came into this — we think with ulterior motives. They didn't want to carry out the programme of the Youth League, which the ANC had accepted. The white members of the Communist Party came into the mainstream of our activity and they put a stop onto the Programme of Action that we had. They came in as the Congress of Democrats and they pressurized to have that alliance. Of course, the alliance came in because they had the money and we didn't have — we have the numbers. We felt that the whites, now if they're on the right, they want to control you through overt apartheid — if they are on the left, they still want to have you in control. And in fact, this is what ultimately happened. [Gerard] Ludi, who was regarded as the most important member of the Congress of Democrats, gave the most damning evidence against Mandela himself.[1]

But couldn't you name just as many black people who testified against their comrades?

Ah, but they don't do it because it is in their interest — black collaborators are manipulated by the system itself. I'm saying people join the police force, not because they like to be controlled by the police and so forth, but because it's a question of livelihood. [Transkei Chief] Matanzima's different from [South African Prime Minister] Vorster. You are talking to an Africanist here, and to me, an African collaborator is a different species from a white oppressor.

Can you tell me how you came to be increasingly critical of the ANC?

What we were following on was the traditional view that the Africans are going to be their own liberators, and the Youth League underlined that. And then it was the Freedom Charter that in fact spelt out the break in the ANC, because the Freedom Charter spelt out that, 'South Africa belongs to all who live in it, black and white.' In fact, the 'Charterists' moved away from the mainstream of African thought, which was that the Africans are going to strive for national self-determination. This Charter thing was never drawn by us. And this alliance, with equal members from each of the four organizations — equal members from the blacks, from the whites, from the Asians, and then from the coloureds — we also opposed that.[2]

What did you see as the place of coloureds and Indians and whites?

The coloureds are as indigenous as anybody else because they are born of miscegenation between the whites and our sisters or our daughters. We say the bulk of the coloureds come from the loins of the Africans, they are part of the African nation. But what I'm saying is that the whites and the Asians, those are the people that were manipulating. The Africans, that is their struggle in the first place, and they've got to lead that struggle. The Indians should not lead the struggle — they've got to support. For instance, they didn't carry passes and the whites didn't carry passes, and therefore they couldn't understand anything about passes. With the whites, we say that it's not for them to say the struggle must go this way or that way, as in fact, has happened. Within the ANC there has been a wave of dissatisfaction with the whites in the movement.

By 1958, we decided we can't take any more the policies that the ANC was carrying on. African emancipation could only be realized by the return of the land that had been taken away. The ANC had been established in 1912 in order to espouse that, with the question of the land being paramount. As [Anton] Lembede[3] said, there's a mystic connection between the soil and the soul. The economic system we inherited from our fathers, where there was no starvation, where there was no exploitation — we wanted an economic system based on those principles.

Would you call it a socialist or a capitalist system?

The trouble with you is that you think either socialist or capitalist. You think in terms of a white person's viewpoint, because capitalism comes from Europe and so does Marxism. We want to create a new social order, original in concept, out of Christian orientation, democratic in form, socialist in content, and that is our view.

I am an Africanist. The communist doctrine, subsequently we have found that it is an irrelevance to our struggle. We can pursue our struggle pursuing Africanist ideals, and therefore the question of being anti-communist or pro-communist doesn't arise. We want to determine an Africanist state in South Africa which will be democratic, and we will admit people to South Africa who come with their acceptance of and their allegiance to African nationhood. We are saying that ours is an African country.

John Nkadimeng, who was recruited to the ANC when he arrived in Johannesburg from Sekhukhuneland to seek work, but never joined the Youth League, out of opposition to its Africanist leanings:

You see, at the time when I came in, apparently the Defiance Campaign crushed that tendency. When I really got involved in active politics that thing was dying out. It was a certain comrade called Flag Boshielo[4] who, more than anybody else, told me that in this movement we have got white people who are very close to us, who agree with us completely. One of the reasons why he wanted to read this paper, the *Guardian*, with me was to try to sort of indicate that particular concept to me. That's how I was con-scientized, politically.

You know, later on during my work with Flag, he personally used to take me to Nelson Mandela. We used to go to Mandela fortnightly at his house in Orlando. They used to argue — I used to like listening to them. Sometimes I thought Mandela was going to chase us from his house.

Mandela didn't think whites should be involved?

Well, he was of the view, at the time, that they should not be given so much influence inside the movement, while Comrade Flag was saying that it must be in terms of the amount of work they are doing. Comrade Flag brought me in contact with people like Ruth Slovo, and later on I worked with her husband, and he also brought me in contact with people like the late Mike Harmel and Rusty Bernstein — those people.[5] I was in a position to learn a lot of things from these people. They seemed to be very clear about anything they were discussing — that is what struck me, you see, because on any question I raised, they would not discourage me. They would do everything to help me to become effective.

In fact, I found that Ruth used to encourage me a lot. She would say, 'Look, I'm going to talk to you about such-and-such, and I need you to point out some of the problems which you see out of what I'm saying. I will try to be as simple as possible so that you must understand, and if you disagree with me, don't be shy — speak.' She was one of the white people who really made me to feel that she wants me to know as much as she does, you see. But Potlako Leballo,[6] people like Andrew Setlhane, who was the editor of the Youth League paper, the *Lodestar* — they used to dislike these white people I used to come to the ANC office with.

Do you have any insight as to what motivated those who were anti-white, anti-Indian and anti-communist?

I will again come to Comrade Flag, because he was the person who was saying to me, 'You must not be surprised if some of the people, especially Africans, are suspicious of the white people — it must be your job to convince them. You must show them that in our struggle, if there could be Africans who are on the other side, why can't there be whites on our side?'

What were your views on the communist issue, the Africanist claim that it's a foreign ideology?

I thought it was nonsense, because I always thought even the Bible is a foreign ideology — it's not ours. If they accept the Bible, why can't they accept communism? That's always been my argument — and the fact that we accepted even speaking in English in our meetings.

Lesoana Makhanda, who joined the Africanists as a secondary school student:

There was this potato boycott and it was carried in *Drum* magazine, the situation in the farms there, what they do with prisoners. And it just stuck in my mind, the galling picture of the African convicts who were arrested and thrown to the farms and dying and then being used as manure. I used to go out and, you know, talk. I would never go to school and see a student eat potatoes — I would hit them off, you know. So the potato boycott became a rallying point of our actions.

At that time I was about ready to carry a pass, so I could identify much more easier that one time I could also myself be arrested for a pass and sent to these prisons. So when the potato boycott was called off, I was somehow left very empty inside, because I didn't see any changes. So I got totally disillusioned.

I then lost interest in politics, until one friend of mine came one day and said to me, 'Look, there's another group within the Youth League now that has the same thinking that you have.' I came to later know that those were the Africanists within the ANC. That's when I started learning about the 1949 Programme of Action of the ANC, and why it was very important in the development of the political positions. Then I stuck with the Africanists. Of course, at that time I did not know that they were having this internal fight within the ANC.

How would you describe your own political views at that stage?

I understood then that there were two classes in South Africa, the white class and the black, that there was a demarcation of white people and black people, and that in order that there be equality, the black people will have to strive to better their position so that they can also be on the same level with the white people — that is what I understood.

Would you reject a class analysis?

I would reject a class analysis of South Africa because with apartheid you cannot talk of classes — the Boers are the ones that use race.

The Africanist dissidents tried to seize power at a Transvaal ANC conference in late 1958, and, when they failed, quit the ANC. They then regrouped in early 1959 and, with support mainly in the southern Transvaal and the Cape, formed a rival party, the Pan-Africanist Congress (PAC).

PAC President Robert Sobukwe, delivering the opening address of the PAC inaugural convention, 4 April 1959:

The Africanists take the view that there is only one race to which we all belong, and that is the human race. In our vocabulary, therefore, the word 'race' as applied to man has no plural form. We do, however, admit the existence of observable physical differences between various groups of people, but these differences are the result of a number of factors, chief among which has been geographical isolation. In South Africa we recognize the existence of national groups which are the result of geographical origin within a certain area, as well as a shared historical experience of these groups. The Europeans are a foreign minority group which has exclusive control of political, economic, social and military power.

Then there is the Indian foreign minority group. In the South African set-up of today, this group is an oppressed minority, but there are some members of this group − the merchant class in particular − who have become tainted with the virus of cultural supremacy and national arrogance. This class identifies itself by and large with the oppressor, but significantly, this is the group which provides the political leadership of the Indian people of South Africa. And all that the politics of this class have meant up to now is preservation and defence of the sectional interests of the Indian merchant class. The downtrodden, poor 'stinking coolies' of Natal who alone, as a result of the pressure of material conditions, can identify themselves with the indigenous African majority in the struggle to overthrow white supremacy have not yet produced their leadership. We hope they will do so soon.[7]

The Africans constitute the indigenous group and form the majority of the population. They are the most ruthlessly exploited and are subjected to humiliation, degradation and insult. Now it is our contention that true democracy can be established in South Africa and on the continent as a whole only when white supremacy has been destroyed. And the illiterate

Robert Sobukwe and supporters give the PAC open-palmed salute.

and semi-literate African masses constitute the key and centre and content of any struggle for true democracy in South Africa. The African people can be organized only under the banner of African nationalism in an All-African organization, where they will by themselves formulate policies and pro- grammes and decide on the methods of struggle, without interference from either so-called left-wing or right-wing groups of the minorities who arrogantly appropriate to themselves the right to plan and think for the Africans.

In conclusion, I wish to state that the Africanists do not at all subscribe to the fashionable doctrine of South African exceptionalism.[8] Our contention is that South Africa is an integral part of the indivisible whole that is Afrika.[9] She cannot solve her problems in isolation from and with utter disregard of the rest of the continent.

It is precisely for that reason that we reject both apartheid and so-called multi-racialism[10] as solutions of our socio-economic problems. Against multi-racialism we have this objection: that the history of South Africa has fostered group prejudices and antagonisms, and if we have to maintain the same group exclusiveness, parading under the term of multi-racialism, we shall be transporting to the new Afrika these very antagonisms and conflicts. Further, multi-racialism is in fact a pandering to European bigotry and arrogance. It is a method of safeguarding white interests, implying as it does proportional representation, irrespective of population figures. In that sense it is a complete negation of democracy.

We aim politically at government of the Africans, by the Africans, for the Africans, with everybody who owes his only loyalty to Afrika and who is prepared to accept the democratic rule of an African majority being regarded as an African. We guarantee no minority rights because we think in terms of individuals, not groups. To sum it up, we stand for an Africanist Socialist Democracy.

Joe Seremane, an ANC Youth League member in the West Rand who joined the PAC soon after its inception:

We knew that there was a new party, like a football club breaking from another football club, but as months went on we got to understand now this was an organization that was prepared to fight, that was openly talking of armed struggle.

Whereas the ANC wasn't?

At the time it wasn't. It had a history all along, but in my area that sound was not heard — it was this other group, the PAC, and that was how I got involved and became a member. It was just you feel aggrieved and there's no other body articulating your frustrations except the body which we respectfully regarded as our mouthpiece and with all the history. The ANC had that aura, that respectability — up to now it is the people's organization — but now here was a group that seemed to be addressing what the angry young people wanted to do or see done, the fight part of it. So the answer was this new one,

The PAC attacked the ANC's joint action with Indians in the campaigns of the Congress Alliance. In this photo the ANC's Mandela and Transvaal Indian Congress leader Dr Yusef Dadoo are shown together, breaking their banning orders and addressing a prohibited meeting.

which consists of younger people, who have been in the ANC, you see. The PAC was appealing to the anger that was existing in the young people. So that is how one got involved.

It is a burning issue: who is oppressed? It is the African first and foremost, and it is the Africans' problem, and they, themselves, alone, will have to solve that problem. The ANC, they took that into consideration but they said, 'We can also allow those in our midst who are not African, if they feel strong about the point, to do it with us.' Our understanding was that, no, they can't do it with us — if they want to help us, they can mobilize, correct the attitudes of their people there, and we'll have a converging point when we have tackled the business of an oppressive government and removed that one. We will have a common point if we owe that same loyalty, we are common citizens, and the colour is irrelevant.

Flyer issued by the PAC, 1959:[11]

The Pan-Africanist Congress (*Amafrika Poqo*)[12] has a message for the down-trodden black masses of Afrika. We of the PAC say:
(a) Africa must be free by 1960, from Cape to Cairo, Madagascar to Morocco;
(b) Africa for the Africans, Africans for Humanity, Humanity for God;

(c) Under the banner of African Nationalism, we say that once we launch (it does not matter what campaign) there is no bail, there is no defence, there is no fine;[13]

(d) We are one with Dr K. Banda, the great Jomo Kenyatta, Tom Mboya and Dr Kwame Nkrumah, 'the architect of the United States of Afrika';

(e) Down with imperialism, colonialism and domination! Forward then to independence! To independence now! Tomorrow the United States of Afrika!

The Pan-Africanist Congress is on the verge of launching a union-wide positive decisive campaign against the pass laws. You are seriously affected by the administration of these fascist laws of a white foreign minority pseudo-government in our fatherland. These laws must be brought to a complete standstill. They must be blown to oblivion this year, now and forever. Are you with the downtrodden black masses or are you with the enemy? You must make up your mind now. Tomorrow may be too late. *Izwe Lethu, i-Afrika!!* [Africa is ours!]

Max Sisulu, an ANC Youth League member who opposed the PAC break-away:

When you grow up in Soweto, you identify colour with the system: it's a white policeman who sends a black policeman to arrest you, and it's the blacks who work for the whites. So you grow up hating the system, you grow up wanting to do something to put an end to this oppression — but it's only when you grow up that you see that the best way of going about it is not by individual acts of bravery, but by working within an organizational structure and mobilizing people to fight.

When we were students, when the PAC broke off from the ANC, we said, 'All right, fine, but how do you go about removing the regime?' We said, 'You need also to work amongst the white population, you need to work among the Indian population, you need to work amongst the coloured population.' So it started through that, in understanding that although they're not as oppressed as the Africans, they are also oppressed by the system, and therefore they have a lot to benefit from removing the system.

The peculiarity of the South African situation is that people live in segregated areas, and in order to mobilize we've got to go where the people are. It is a lot easier, for example, for an Indian to go and mobilize the Indians in his area, or a white amongst the whites. You can't, as an African, go and mobilize the whites — it's impossible. Part of the process of struggle is that you recognize obstacles and you find ways of bypassing them. How do you do it? You don't do it by sitting back and saying, 'We don't recognize these boundaries, we don't recognize race.' You actively fight against racism: that is the essence of non-racialism.

In the discussions with the youth in the PAC I think we managed to broaden the debate, so it was not just a question of white and black, but a question of what kind of society do you want after apartheid goes, in a liberated South Africa? And this is the work that was done mainly by the young people in the Congress Alliance.

Francis Meli, an ANC Youth League member in the Eastern Cape, stronghold of the non-racial camp:

Actually we never regarded non-racialism as the opposite of black nationalism. Black nationalism was part of our thinking and non-racialism was also part of our thinking. One would say, perhaps, that black nationalism is a step towards non-racialism, especially during our time. I mean, in those early days we were involved in the movement because we were against apartheid. And we were against apartheid because the dignity of the black man was threatened and trampled underfoot.

If you look at the leaders of the ANC, they all started with African nationalism. The first consciousness is anti-white and then they develop, through practical political involvement in the struggle, to this broad non-racial outlook of the ANC. The PAC was actually not a militant or revolutionary strand.[14] It was more of a right-wing deviation from the ANC position, because the ANC was getting involved with the Indians and the coloureds and the democratic whites. The Freedom Charter was the embodiment of the aspirations of the people and the PAC was refusing to move with the times, and in that sense it became a retrogressive step.

What about the ideological question of the PAC being closer to the West, criticizing the ANC for its alliance with the communists — was that something that was discussed?

The PAC was accusing the ANC of all sorts of things: that the ANC are lackeys of communism, the Freedom Charter being a document adopted in the Kremlin. That was discussed quite openly, but of course, at that stage, I must admit that we didn't know much about communism. All we were saying was, 'Look here, if somebody is tramping on your foot, you remove the one who is tramping on your foot first — then you'll see to that one who's still coming.' You don't start complaining about the one who is still coming — you complain about the one who is actually hurting you. That is how we argued those days.

You see, the Communist Party was banned in 1950 and dissolved itself. It reconstituted itself in 1953, and then in 1961 it came out publicly. We would get some books and pamphlets and things like that about Marxism and whatnot, but we didn't understand all these things. 'Proletarian', what is that? Now we know the workers, but what does this mean, 'working class leadership'? Those were all complicated concepts for us.

'Congress and the Africanists', in Africa South, *the ANC journal, July – September, 1959, by Walter Sisulu, then-banned Secretary-General of the ANC:*

In recent months much has been published in the South African press about the 'Africanists' and their attempt to capture the leadership of the African National Congress. It would be wrong for any student of politics in this country to ignore the significance of this development. Even though the Africanists have not evolved any definite programme and policy, the general trend of their ideas is manifest: it lies in a crude appeal to African racialism as a reply to white arrogance and oppression.

The principal target of their attacks is the broad humanism of the African National Congress, which claims equality but not domination for the African people, and regards South Africa as being big enough and rich enough to sustain all its people, of whatever origin, in friendship and peace. This broad outlook of Congress finds its clearest expression in the opening sentence of the Freedom Charter, which boldly declares that, 'South Africa belongs to all who live in it, black and white.' It is precisely this formulation which is most strongly attacked by the Africanists. The intention is clear: it is a denial that any section of the population, other than the descendants of indigenous Africans, have any rights in the country whatsoever.

In the first place, it should be stated as emphatically as possible that the Africanists' principal charge — that Congress has departed from its traditional purpose and policy — is untrue and unfounded. It has never advocated the replacement of exclusive rights for whites with exclusive rights for Africans, as now proposed by the Africanists. In putting forward this conception, it is they who are departing from the original objectives and purposes of the founders of Congress.

The Freedom Charter is in a direct line of succession to the many statements of Congress policy and principle down the years: that the rights of all people shall be the same, regardless of race, colour or sex. Its ten famous chapters are identical in spirit and closely parallel in content to the eleven points of the 'Bill of Rights' as published in 'Africans' Claims',[15] and specifically endorsed in the 1949 'Programme of Action'.

Congress has repudiated the idea of 'driving the white man into the sea' as futile and reactionary, and accepted the fact that the various racial groups in South Africa have come to stay. Congress has at all times welcomed and taken the initiative in achieving cooperation with other organizations representing different population groups, provided always that such co-operation was on a basis of equality and disinterested adherence to mutual aims.

Thus the so-called 'African nationalism' of the Africanists turns out to be a mere inverted racialism, foreign to the spirit and traditions of the African people, and more in line with the Afrikaner Nationalist Party than with the progressive liberationist nationalism of Congress. This type of racial exclusiveness has been condemned the world over, and not least by the progressive African national movements of this continent.

Yet these truths should not blind us to the fact that there are men and women amongst them who genuinely believe that the salvation of our people lies in a fanatical African racialism and denunciation of everything that is not African. In a country like South Africa, where the whites dominate everything and where ruthless laws are ruthlessly enforced, the natural tendency is one of growing hostility towards Europeans. In fact, most Africans come into political activity because of their indignation against whites, and it is only through their education in Congress, and their experience of the genuine comradeship in the struggle of such organizations as the Congress of Democrats, that they rise to the broad, non-racial humanism of our Congress movement.

The Africanists have thus far failed, but their mere appearance is an urgent warning to all democratic South Africans. In certain circumstances, an emotional mass-appeal to destructive and exclusive nationalism can be a dynamic and irresistible force in history. We have seen in our own country how, decade after decade, the Afrikaner people have followed yet more extreme and reactionary leaders. It would be foolish to imagine that a wave of black chauvinism, provoked by the savagery of the Nationalist Party (and perhaps secretly encouraged and financed by it too), may not some day sweep through our country. And if it does, the agony will know no colour-bar at all.

Africanists on the march in 1960, with placards featuring their slogan, 'Africa for Africans'.

Notes

1. Gerard Ludi was a Security Police spy recruited while a University of the Witwatersrand student by the then head of the Security Police underground division, Colonel Hendrik van den Bergh. Ludi infiltrated COD and the underground SACP, but was by no means regarded as COD's 'most important member'. While he testified against Bram Fischer, by far the 'most damning evidence' of the 173 witnesses for the prosecution against Mandela came from an African ex-Umkhonto we Sizwe cadre, Bruno Mtolo.
2. The disproportionate weight given to the SAIC, CPC and COD on the joint executive, despite the huge numerical majority of the Africans in the ANC, is the point of Africanist criticism that is given most credence by defenders of the non-racial approach to political cooperation across ethnic lines. The ANC's 'Strategy and Tactics', adopted in 1969, specifically argues against such 'mechanical parity between the various national groups' (see Chapter 12).
3. The first president of the ANC Youth League and chief ideologue of the Africanist faction of the ANC, Anton Lembede, died in 1947, at the age of 33.
4. An ANC and Communist Party activist who was later killed while serving in Umkhonto we Sizwe.
5. The Johannesburg editor of the *Guardian*, Ruth First was married to Joe Slovo, and both were active in the CPSA and COD. Michael Harmel was a member of the CPSA central committee until its banning, edited the *African Communist* after he left South Africa, and published *Fifty Fighting Years: The Communist Party of South Africa* under the pseudonym of A. Lerumo in 1971. Rusty Bernstein, a Communist

Party leader arrested in the Rivonia raid, was acquitted of membership of Um-khonto we Sizwe in the 1964 trial.

6. Editor of *The Africanist* and chairman of the Orlando Youth League, Leballo was elected National Secretary at the founding of the PAC, then named Acting President from 1962 until he was deposed in 1979.

7. On the contrary, a significant number of working-class Indian leaders had emerged by then, e.g. Billy Nair, George Ponen, M. P. Naicker, H. A. Naidoo.

8. Here, Sobukwe understands the term 'South African exceptionalism' as differentiating the South African struggle from anti-colonial struggles in the rest of Africa (for reasons such as its much larger white population). In a critique of Sobukwe that appeared in *Liberation*, July 1959, 'Africanism under the Microscope', the ANC's Joe Matthews called the Africanists' rejection of the concept of class struggle in South Africa 'the worst example of South African exceptionalism'.

9. A peculiarly Africanist spelling.

10. By the end of the 1950s, most ANC supporters had adopted the term 'non-racialism' as opposed to 'multi-racialism' to denote democracy without reference to race. However, there was still some confusion over terminology, with some ANC supporters using multi-racialism when they clearly meant non-racialism; likewise, the PAC often used the term non-racialism to describe its notion of accepting only 'the human race'.

11. No date is cited for this pamphlet (reproduced in *From Protest to Challenge*, Karis and Carter, cited previously) but it seems apparent that it was issued in mid- to late-1959.

12. 'Poqo', a Xhosa word meaning 'standing alone', was a peasant-initiated PAC offshoot in the Western Cape and Transkei, noted for uncoordinated attacks on whites and seemingly arbitrary targets.

13. A reference to the slogans of the PAC's anti-pass campaign — hastily called for 21 March 1960 to pre-empt the ANC's plans for a protest on 30 March — which resulted in the massacre at Sharpeville, outside Vereeniging in the Transvaal. Many of those charged did subsequently accept a legal defence and pay bail and fines.

14. The fact that Africanist leader Potlako Leballo was working for the United States Information Service and that the PAC was formed at the USIS library raised some suspicions about the PAC's links with the West, especially in light of its anti-communist views. Another commonly held misgiving about the PAC was voiced by Dennis Brutus in the interview conducted for this book. Noting that the newspaper that supported the PAC, the *Bantu World*, was owned by Anglo American, he concluded: 'The mining bosses saw the PAC as a black movement which they could espouse because it was challenging apartheid on capitalist terms — in terms of a more rational economy, better wages, abolition of migrant labour and so on. What they did not want was any whisper of socialism, communism, so they would inflate the importance of the PAC in order to use it as a battering ram to attack the ANC.'

15. A key achievement of the ANC under Xuma, 'Africans' Claims in South Africa' (1943) articulated the ANC's response to the Atlantic Charter and its vision of post-war political restructuring, and included a Bill of Rights but no timetable. The 'Programme of Action' followed in 1949, prodded by militant youth leaders.

11 Against White Domination and Black Domination

Both the ANC and the PAC were banned by the government in April 1960, following the massacre by police of 69 unarmed pass law protesters in Sharpeville. In the period that followed, it was the response to the challenge of underground conditions, more than the debate over non-racialism, that determined the level of mass support of the two organizations.

When the ANC called an 'All-in Conference' in May 1961 to draft a 'non-racial democratic constitution for South Africa', the PAC opted out. When the ANC organized a national stay-at-home, the PAC distributed leaflets aimed at sabotaging the campaign. These actions did little to build mass support for the fledgling PAC. The ANC, on the other hand, was able to rely on its historical reputation to such an extent that the launch of the first organized military response to apartheid — identified only as being under the guidance of 'the national liberation movement' — was immediately embraced as a Congress initiative.

Flyer issued by 'command of Umkhonto we Sizwe' (Spear of the Nation), 16 December 1961:

Units of Umkhonto we Sizwe today carried out planned attacks against government installations, particularly those connected with the policy

Police shot into a crowd demonstrating against the pass laws on 21 March 1960 in the black township of Sharpeville, outside the Transvaal town of Vereeniging, killing 69 people.

of apartheid and race discrimination. Umkhonto we Sizwe is a new, independent body, formed by Africans. It includes in its ranks South Africans of all races.

Umkhonto we Sizwe fully supports the national liberation movement and our members, jointly and individually, place themselves under the overall political guidance of that movement. It is, however, well known that the main national liberation organizations in this country have consistently followed a policy of non-violence. But the people's patience is not endless. The time comes in the life of any nation when there remain only two choices: submit or fight. That time has now come to South Africa. We shall not submit, and we have no choice but to hit back by all means within our power in defence of our people, our future and our freedom.

We hope — even at this late hour — that our first actions will awaken everyone to a realization of the disastrous situation to which the Nationalist policy is leading. In these actions, we are working in the best interests of all the people of this country — black, brown and white — whose future happiness and well-being cannot be attained without the overthrow of the Nationalist government, the abolition of white supremacy, and the winning of liberty, democracy and full national rights and equality for all the people of this country.

Indres Naidoo, among the first Umkhonto we Sizwe recruits:

I was one of those they recruited to the armed struggle. Maybe it was because people heard that I was one of those who said, 'To hell with non-violent struggle!' and maybe openly talked of taking up arms. My immediate reaction was, 'Fantastic, Umkhonto has come up.' But we had become quite respectable leaders of the Indian community — what would the reaction in the Indian community be?

We debated the question of moving from the Gandhian philosophy — how would we justify our movement away from non-violence? But if one looks at the struggle from the turn of the century, you would find there's been a move all the way, there'd been a difference from Gandhi to my grandfather, and from my grandfather to my father, who was talking of more radical action.

We operated as an MK [Umkhonto] unit from 1961 right up to 1963. The reaction of our people during the sabotage campaign was that the debate became even more hotter. People were now looking to join MK. At the Rand Youth Club one Saturday evening, an activist raised the question and openly said, 'You know, it's time we all joined MK. You fellows still believe in your Gandhian philosophy and it's about time you abandoned it. You'll get nowhere.'

The units at that time were racially comprised, because it's easy to move around that way. I mean, two o'clock in the morning, if you find one African in the heart of Johannesburg riding around with three whites you already become suspicious, but when you find four Indians, there's less suspicion. We, as an Indian unit, had a much broader scope to work in.

We were amongst the very first MK cadres to be arrested. In April '63 we were the first MK guys to appear in court, and this had a tremendous influence amongst the Indian youth. People of all races filled the court, it was just impossible to move. I would say we had firmly established (1) the non-racial aspect of the struggle, and (2) the need to take up arms.

Denis Goldberg, tasked by the Umkhonto we Sizwe High Command to develop weaponry for sabotage:

For me, it was a relief when Umkhonto we Sizwe was formed, because I'd been arguing for it amongst some groups of people I knew. Eventually when I was asked to join Umkhonto we Sizwe at the time of its formation, I said yes, and the person who asked me said, 'Go away and think about it.' And I said, 'But I've been arguing for it for over a year — what's there to think about?'

Were there any specific implications of you being one of the few whites in a largely black organization?

I think there were possibilities that developed because of my skills. That's where my training as an engineer was important, you see, because technical skills were in short supply — it's one of the effects of racism in South Africa. I was known amongst some of my comrades as 'Mr Technico' — I didn't mind getting my hands dirty, covered in ink and things like that, you see. When it came to buying duplicators, it was much easier for a white to go into a shop and buy a duplicator, or to buy hacksaws to cut iron tubes, or to buy a rope or whatever — it was just easier. And then there was always the question of access to cars, and time. Whites didn't have to work such long hours or travel so far, so you could do things. So in the facilitation sense, it helped.

I felt that that was what I could contribute, and I felt morally bound to contribute. Because we lived in white South Africa I got a university degree, and that was part of the privilege of being white. Once I understood that, it was necessary to give back that privilege. If you support the movement only, then you give it back in another way — you get rich quick and you pay conscience money. If you're in it you use your skills that you've got, as a result of your privileges, for that movement, in that movement. That was my approach to it, so I never resented it at all, never.

One of the bitternesses of prison was that we were deliberately kept away from our comrades. I was sentenced with seven other comrades — I could not see them from the day we were sentenced, because they are black and I am white. The officials said to me, 'We maintain a policy of apartheid even though we know you don't — we will never put you with them.' It's a very bitter thing. We lived together, we cooked for each other, but we couldn't be in prison together.[1]

I remember a prison officer on more than one occasion saying, 'Nelson Mandela, we can dislike, but we can respect him for fighting for his people — after all, Afrikaners have stood up and fought for Afrikaners. But you, with everything in front of you that white society could give you, you're a traitor — we hate you.' And by God, they hated me.

But I didn't regret those days in prison. I'll tell you why. When we were taken to prison, the armed struggle was new. We were amateurs, we did what we could. I think we changed the course of South African history, and it was important to do that at that time. And when the armed struggle was started, we knew that one day that regime could be toppled. We didn't know when – they looked so solidly in power, so self-confident. Well, they're now ripe to be toppled, it's going to happen. That's why it was worth it: it was necessary to do it, and we did it because it had to be done.

The inevitable turn to illegality and violence in response to the banning of the legal organizations prompted further repressive legislation. The state was obsessed by a white-led conspiracy, premised on the racist conviction that blacks cannot organize without white leadership. It was mainly whites who were hit by the first house arrests and banning orders, the Congress of Democrats and the white-edited *New Age* that were banned. Whites were also over-represented in the first detentions under a new law that allowed people to be held without trial, in solitary confinement, for periods of up to ninety days.

Sondagblad *(Afrikaans Sunday newspaper), 22 October 1961:*

John Vorster, the new Minister of Justice, has promised drastic action. Accordingly, the cabinet is discussing legislation to limit the freedom of speech and movement of 'agitators'. As has happened in the past, it can be done by confining a person to a certain area, or town, or even to his house. The form of house arrest which was used during the war was that a person was allowed only to go to his work, but in the evenings and at weekends he had to stay at home. Although the legislation is aimed at all 'agitators', it is intended primarily for whites. They are the most dangerous and the state knows who they are.

While the ANC was waging guerilla warfare through underground Um-khonto cells, the PAC and its militant wing, Poqo, attempted a kind of spontaneous mass uprising. Although the government worried about the non-racial ANC because 'it has many more white brains at its disposal',[2] the anti-white Poqo alarmed the white public more, especially after crowds of Poqo supporters killed several whites in incidents in Paarl and Transkei in late 1962 and early 1963.

Poqo's efforts – seemingly unaffected by the lessons of failed armed revolts throughout the history of African resistance[3] – were easily crushed. The knockout blow to the PAC came when the boasts of its acting leader, Potlako Leballo, from neighbouring Basutoland (now Lesotho) led to raids that netted extensive membership lists, resulting in massive arrests of PAC supporters inside South Africa and the continued detention of its president, Robert Sobukwe.[4]

The Sabotage Act of 1962, which gave the government even greater powers to act against 'security threats', sparked protest from ANC supporters and liberals, blacks and whites.

'The ANC Spearheads Revolution — Leballo? No!', ANC leaflet, May 1963:

The ANC tells the people straight: the struggle that will free us is a long, hard job. Do not be deceived by men who talk big with no thought for tomorrow. Freedom is not just a matter of strong words. It is no good to think in terms of *impis* [Zulu military units] and not of modern guerilla war. PAC leaders like Leballo talk of revolution but do not work out how to make revolution. War needs careful plans. War is not a gesture of defiance. For a sum total of nine whites killed — only one of them a policeman, and he killed by accident — hundreds of Poqos are in jail serving thousands of years imprisonment.

Don't mistake the real target. Poqo is said to have killed five white road-builders in the Transkei recently. There are more effective ways of busting the white supremacy state. Instead, smashed railway lines, damaged pylons carrying electricity across the country, bombed-out petrol dumps cut Prime Minister Verwoerd off from his power and leave him helpless. And these acts are only the beginning.

Why make enemies of our allies? The Leballos spurn men of other races. We say that just as Africans bear the brunt of oppression under the white state, so will the white state be broken by the main force of African people.

But this is no reason, we say, to reject comrades of other races whom we know are ready to fight with us, suffer, and if need be, die.

Find a way — but not the Leballo way. Umkhonto we Sizwe, army of the liberation movement, is for activists. We have struck against the white state more than 70 times (boldly, yet methodically). We are trained and practised. We shall be more so. We attack PAC-Leballo policy not out of petty rivalry but because it takes us back, not forward along the freedom road. Genuine freedom-fighters must find a way to fight together, in unity, in unbreakable strength. There is room in the freedom struggle for all brave men — and women. With your support we will win.

The ANC's military campaign was far more effective than the PAC's but soon it, too, was smashed. In mid-1963, police raided the secret headquarters of the Umkhonto we Sizwe High Command in a wealthy white suburb of Johannesburg called Rivonia. For Nelson Mandela, the first accused in the 'Rivonia Trial', it was an unrivalled opportunity to explain the historical development of his movement's ideology and practice. Mandela laid special emphasis on two much-misunderstood issues: non-racialism and alleged communist influence.

Statement from the dock by Nelson Mandela, 20 April 1964:

The ideological creed of the ANC is, and always has been, the creed of African nationalism. It is not the concept of African nationalism expressed in the cry, 'Drive the white man into the sea!' The African nationalism for which the ANC stands is the concept of freedom and fulfilment for the African people in their own land.

The most important political document ever adopted by the ANC is the Freedom Charter. It is by no means a blueprint for a socialist state. It calls for redistribution, but not nationalization, of land; it provides for nationalization of mines, banks and monopoly industry, because big monopolies are owned by one race only, and without such nationalization, racial domination would be perpetuated, despite the spread of political power. The ANC has never at any period of its history advocated a revolutionary change in the economic structure of the country, nor has it, to the best of my recollection, ever condemned capitalist society.

The ANC, unlike the Communist Party, admitted Africans only as members. Its chief goal was and is for the African people to win unity and full political rights. The Communist Party's main aim, on the other hand, was to remove the capitalists and to replace them with a working class government. The Communist Party sought to emphasize class distinctions, whilst the ANC seeks to harmonize them. This is a vital distinction.

It is true that there has often been close cooperation between the ANC and the Communist Party. But cooperation is merely proof of a common goal — in this case, the removal of white supremacy — and is not proof of a complete community of interests. I joined the ANC in 1944, and in my younger days I held the view that the policy of admitting communists to the ANC, and the close cooperation which existed at times on specific issues between the ANC and the Communist Party, would lead to a watering down of the concept of African nationalism. At that stage I was a member of the African National Congress Youth League, and was one of a group which moved for the expulsion of communists from the ANC.

This proposal was heavily defeated. Amongst those who voted against the proposal were some of the most conservative sections of African political opinion. They defended the policy on the ground that from its inception the ANC was formed and built up, not as a political party with one school of political thought, but as a parliament of the African people, accommodating people of various political convictions, all united by the common goal of national liberation. I was eventually won over to this point of view and have upheld it ever since.

It is perhaps difficult for white South Africans, with an ingrained prejudice against communism, to understand why experienced African politicians so readily accepted communists as their friends. But to us the reason is obvious. Theoretical differences amongst those fighting against oppression is a luxury we cannot afford at this stage. What is more, for many decades communists were the only political group in South Africa who were prepared to treat Africans as human beings and their equals, who were prepared to eat with us, talk with us, live with us and work with us. They were the only political group which was prepared to work with the Africans for the attainment of political rights and a stake in society.

Because of this there are many Africans who today tend to equate freedom with communism. They are supported in this belief by a legislature which brands all exponents of democratic government and African freedom as communists, and bans many of them (who are not communists) under the Suppression of Communism Act. Although I have never been a member of the Communist Party, I myself have been banned and imprisoned under that Act.

It is not only in internal politics that we count communists as amongst those who support our cause. In the international field, communist countries have always come to our aid. Although there is a universal condemnation of apartheid, the communist bloc speaks out against it with a louder voice than most of the white world. In these circumstances, it would take a brash young politician, such as I was in 1949, to proclaim that the communists are our enemies.

I now turn to my own position. I have always regarded myself, in the first place, as an African patriot. Today I am attracted to the idea of a classless society, an attraction which springs in part from Marxist reading and in part from my admiration of the structure and organization of early African societies in this country. The land, then the main means of production, belonged to the tribe. There were no rich or poor and there was no exploitation.

It is true that I have been influenced by Marxist thought, but this is also true of many of the leaders of the new independent states. Such widely different persons as Gandhi, Nehru, Nkrumah and Nasser all acknowledge this fact. We all accept the need for some form of socialism to enable our people to catch up with the advanced countries of this world and to overcome their legacy of extreme poverty. But this does not mean we are Marxists. I have been influenced in my thinking by both West and East.

Basically, we fight against two features which are the hallmarks of African life in South Africa and which are entrenched by legislation which we seek to have repealed. These features are poverty and lack of human dignity, and we do not need communists or so-called 'agitators' to teach us about these things. Above all, we want political rights, because without them our disabilities will be permanent. I know this sounds revolutionary to the whites in this country, because the majority of voters will be Africans. This makes the white man fear democracy.

But this fear cannot be allowed to stand in the way of the only solution which will guarantee racial harmony and freedom for all. It is not true that the enfranchisement of all will result in racial domination. Political division based on colour is entirely artificial, and when it disappears so will the domination of one colour group by another. The ANC has spent half a century fighting against racialism. When it triumphs it will not change that policy.

During my lifetime I have dedicated myself to this struggle of the African people. I have fought against white domination and I have fought against black domination. I have cherished the ideal of a democratic and free society in which all persons live together in harmony and with equal opportunities. It is an ideal which I hope to live for and to achieve. But if needs be, it is an ideal for which I am prepared to die.

ANC publications recalled the Rivonia trialists and kept alive the ideals that led to their imprisonment.

After making that statement Mandela was sentenced to life imprisonment, along with Walter Sisulu, Govan Mbeki, Ahmed Kathrada, Raymond Mhlaba, Andrew Mlangeni, Elias Motsoaledi and Denis Goldberg. With most of the rest of the ANC's leadership also imprisoned, banned or exiled, anti-apartheid resistance waned, and thus began a period that has come to be known as 'the lull'.

Notes

1. Black political prisoners were sent to Robben Island, the maximum security prison off the Cape coast, while whites went to Pretoria Central Prison. Racial segregation in South Africa's prisons has been repeatedly criticized, most recently by warders at Pollsmoor Prison (where most of the key ANC leaders were moved from the Island) who formed the Police and Prisons Civil Rights Union (Popcru). 'There is no white crime or black crime,' said a Popcru member, 'Why aren't all offenders treated the same?' Upon his release from Pretoria Central in 1989, a white ANC member, Roland Hunter, made a public call for black and white prisoners to be jailed together.
2. Prime Minister Vorster, quoted in Hansard, House of Assembly, 12 June 1963.
3. The last desperate armed uprising against white domination before the 1960 Pondoland unrest was Zulu Chief Bambata's battle against government troops in 1906, in which the chief and more than 500 of his warriors were killed.
4. Under the 90-day act legislation of 1963, Sobukwe's three-year prison term then due to expire was extended (though with special privileges); many observers concluded that the continued sidelining of Sobukwe was at least a partial goal of Leballo's bravado. Sobukwe was not released until May 1969, when he was restricted to Kimberley, where he remained until his death in 1978.

12 The Lull

The white government was never more smug about its power than in the late 1960s. The resistance movements had been smashed. Profits soared with the inflow of foreign investment and the white standard of living reached record heights. A new divide-and-rule strategy ensured the continued supply of cheap labour.

Work had begun in earnest on the grand social engineering schemes envisaged by the apartheid theorists: Africans not needed in town and families living on white farms were forced out into remote rural dumping grounds, destitute 'ethnic' communities teeming with the unemployed, women, children and the elderly. Under the 1959 Promotion of Bantu Self-Government Act, eight 'bantustans' (later ten 'homelands') were eventually to be granted 'independence', with their 'citizens' stripped of all rights as South Africans. To the white minority, everything looked possible.

Prime Minister Hendrik Verwoerd, known as the 'architect of apartheid', after his return from the 1961 Commonwealth Conference. Verwoerd pre-empted anti-apartheid campaigners by withdrawing from the Commonwealth, which accelerated the post-Sharpeville outflow of capital. But South Africa defiantly declared itself a republic, and by the end of the decade the economy was booming.

Various opposition groups attempted to fill the political void in this bleak period: one was the Liberal Party. Formed in 1953 by whites who stayed out of the Congress Alliance, the liberals had largely survived the repression that devastated the ranks of Congress-allied whites. (The Congress of Democrats was not banned until 1962, but scores of its members had already been restricted from political activity through individual banning orders and house arrests.) The Liberal Party had attracted few blacks in the past, but now the lack of any other legal option induced others to join.

'Where the Liberal Party Stands', Liberal Party pamphlet, 1966:

The Liberal Party stands for a combination of private enterprise with state ownership, broadly similar to the present system in Great Britain. We believe that public services such as transport, power supplies, etc. are best managed by the state. We stand for non-racial trade unions and no job reservation. Under the Liberal Party all races will be taxed equally and from these monies funds will be made available for heavily subsidized housing schemes. The Party stands for universal adult suffrage — one man, one vote.

The Liberal Party deplores the present position, where 20 per cent of the population own 87 per cent of the land. The Party would abolish the Group Areas Act, and aims to have the state buy large areas of farmland with a view to making farms available, in particular to non-whites, for purchase free-hold on easy terms.

The Liberal Party would respect the wish of any group to maintain its identity, provided always that there is no infringement of the rights of others. The Party rejects the extreme Black Nationalism which would place the interests of Africans before the interests of the other inhabitants of our country. The Party holds no truck with Communism, which it regards as a totalitarian system with no concern for individual human rights.

Ian Mkhize, a one-time member of the Pietermaritzburg ANC branch:

When the screws really did turn on the ANC, people were just nowhere to be found. I must say, it seemed for a while that the ANC had a demise — it seemed like it was virtually dead. And its place was seen to be taken at that time by the Liberal Party. I saw it as the forefront organization at that moment. It was in 1963 that I joined the Liberal Party. It certainly was, in my own view, going the same way as ANC at that moment. I mean, as far back as 1960 it had abolished the qualified franchise thing — it was then an open organization. They were the only alternative that was available. I would have taken a stand against them being anti-communist, but we had no option. Somehow we had to get a political platform.

Why were you opposed to the Liberal Party's anti-communism?

I had an inclination towards socialism. We had always looked forward to a society, albeit in a utopian manner, of equality, of equal opportunity and so on, and in a completely free enterprise situation you don't get that. I mean, if you look at America, it has been free for a number of years, but because of free enterprise you still have very poor people and very rich people.

In 1963 and '64, the Liberal Party had every promise to be a powerful party. It was attracting quite a number of Africans, they were coming in their numbers – particularly people who were facing removals in the northern areas of Natal. I think they just sought a political home, like I had, a form of protest. But in about 1965 the screws were turned on the party like anything: people were banned. So again, the Liberal Party seemed to be going the ANC way, in that now people just seemed to fear it.

And yourself, did you stick with the Liberal Party?

To its dissolution, in 1968. It was a terrible thing, looking at our party dissolve when this Prohibition of Improper Interference Act[1] was passed.

On balance, how do you feel about the work of the Liberal Party?

History has it that white liberals have wasted people's time, that liberals have done a lot to lead blacks up the garden path, but I think it really depended on the individuals involved. It was such an amorphous thing, there were so many personalities. In some areas it was very much like a 'tea party' party, as it were, but then there were times when principles had to be stood for, and that is where you would admire such characters as [Liberal Party chairman] Peter Brown and Alan Paton. Paton, of course, changed dramatically since then.[2] At the same time, one really understood they were from a completely different background, and the struggle was really our struggle. In the final analysis, this is an African working-class struggle, and the Liberal Party recruited its members from the middle class and upper class of whites.

The same disheartening lack of political options spurred a small group of whites to form the African Resistance Movement (ARM).

'Political Intelligence Unit – Confidential', document found by police in ARM leader Adrian Leftwich's flat, 4 July 1964:

The unit will act for the furthering of the broad aims of non-racial social democracy in South Africa; the concepts as understood by the non-communistic sections of the ANC, the official leadership of the PAC, the left wing of the Liberal Party, and possibly more progressive Progressives.[3] The members of the group will have no particular party loyalty but to the broad belief in basic social and democratic principles and a concern for the future of South Africa.

Stephanie Kemp, recruited to ARM while studying at the University of Cape Town:

In Cape Town, certainly at that period, in 1962, '63, there was no contact between ordinary whites and any blacks. So that the whole ARM thing, really, was what was possible for an ill-informed white who was radical and who didn't come from a political background. I think they were a group of liberals — I mean a handful, really, in the Cape, mainstream Liberal Party people — who I believe now were almost entirely motivated by an anti-communism and a lack of confidence in the mainstream of the movement, a feeling of their own historical importance, a kind of white arrogance.

I think what the ARM didn't recognize was the importance of African nationalism — as a concept, as a real thing in this process — so that they recognized a sort of non-racialism that obliterated all that. You know, people were just people, and the fact that they were African or white was unimportant. Yet it was important for them to establish their credentials by ensuring that they had some black support — and they had very, very little.[4]

I stayed with them till I was arrested, simply because it happened so quickly that I didn't have a chance to really consider anything else, and in a way, nothing else presented itself. Basically, there was no overt political activity, really, except the Liberal Party, and that was no longer really something towards which one looked, because I think it was so obvious that South Africa wasn't something for which whites had to find a solution, but something for which the solution would come from the rest of the population, and into which you had to play a part.

Then people started getting arrested. Adrian Leftwich[5] began to sort of name and betray people, one after the other, so over the next ten days people were being arrested. They actually wanted me to give evidence against him. The last thing they wanted was for me to stand trial — this young, pretty Afrikaner girl to stand trial while this Jewish radical student leader got off. I was far too mainstream, it offended them to find an Afrikaner woman on the wrong side of the law. They hated it. So I held out, and always in the background was Nelson Mandela. I didn't know anything about him, but he was this figure, and Rivonia had just happened and I wasn't going to stand up in court and be on the wrong side.

For all the criticism of the Liberal Party, its demise made the political landscape even more barren for whites.

Sheena Duncan, member of the women's service organization, Black Sash:[6]

In those days a whole lot of our contemporaries left. It was very like what's happening now amongst a number of people who are deciding to leave South Africa. They said, 'We cannot go on living in the apartheid society,' or alternatively they said, 'The revolution is just around the corner, this isn't a safe place for our children.'

So it was imperative to get involved, and I did. The black community was totally crushed, and the only white organization that was doing anything at all was NUSAS [National Union of South African Students][7] and I was too old to be a student. The Black Sash was the only organization in the white community, outside party politics, that was doing anything at all.

The first advice office started in Cape Town, because hundreds of black women were being arrested for refusing to apply for passes. It started just as a bail fund, to get those women out of jail while they awaited trial so that they could be with their children. After that advice centres grew all over the country.

Black Sash women were very emotionally involved about the destruction of family — this person sitting in front of you whose wife and children aren't allowed to be with him. Or this woman whose husband was arrested yesterday. Or this woman whose child was detained by the Security Police. That concern for the individual person has remained all the way through, but what has developed is the understanding of the structures and the philosophies and the forces at work in the society that have maintained that system.

Black Sash demonstrators hold placards reading, 'Justice demands a national convention of all races'.

We've moved from our naive belief that if you could convey to people, such as English-speaking businessmen, the human suffering involved in migrant labour, if you could convey that to them, they would do something to get rid of it. Our whole attitude has toughened considerably in that respect because we have discovered that people, on the whole, are not moved by human suffering, and that you therefore have to find political pressures that will start hurting them enough to make them move. If profits are threatened, that is when you get white people in this country to act. So we stopped going on deputations to Harry Oppenheimer[8] and people like that, because it was a total waste of time.

So what does move them?

What moves them is what hurts them, not what hurts other people.

The first signs of an end to the lull came from outside South Africa. Umkhonto we Sizwe had regrouped in exile and in 1967 the ANC launched its first major military campaign. Guerilla infiltration was complicated by the fact that the neighbouring states were still under colonial rule, so the ANC's army joined forces with Zimbabweans fighting the white minority regime ruling the colony of Rhodesia,[9] as a first stage in establishing routes to South Africa.

Joint press release, Zimbabwe African People's Union (ZAPU) and African National Congress (ANC-SA), 19 August 1967:

Furious fighting has been and is still taking place in various parts of Southern Rhodesia. From the thirteenth of this month, the area of Wankie [now Hwange] has been the scene of the most daring battles ever fought between freedom fighters and the white oppressors' army in Rhodesia. We wish to declare here that the fighting that is presently going on in Wankie area is indeed being carried out by a combined force of ZAPU and ANC, which marched into the country as comrades-in-arms on a common route, each bound to its destination. It is the determination of these combined forces to fight the common settler enemy to the finish, at any point of encounter, as they make their way to their respective fighting zones.

Signed,
J. R. D. Chikerema, ZAPU Vice-President
O. R. Tambo, ANC Deputy President

Ralph Mzamo, founder member of the Umkhonto we Sizwe Eastern Cape Command, who left South Africa for military training and then fought in Zimbabwe in the ANC's 'Lutuli Detachment':

I didn't want to come out of South Africa. We had already sent out some men and I took the stand that they would come back and train us inside the country. But then the chaps warned me that the Special Branch were hunting for me. So I left: to Botswana by round-about route and to Tanzania, back to Zambia, and into Zimbabwe. We went to fight there because we had no friendly borders at the time. We went to fight there because those were our brothers, they were as oppressed as we were. We had a jolly fight with the Rhodesians. We existed in the bush for a long period, nine months.

Wasn't it a problem not speaking the main language spoken in Zimbabwe, Shona?

Oh yes, it was a problem. We, the South Africans, couldn't simply go among the people unless they were already known to us. But then the Zimbabweans amongst ourselves were not so much better off. Everybody knows that you are a stranger because everybody knows each other. There's always that difficulty everywhere, so what we did was whenever we went to meet people we simply used people who came from that region, who spoke the same dialect, you see. But then there was another slight problem: there was the question of complexion. We were slightly lighter, generally.

Whenever people discovered that there were South Africans, we would explain, 'Of course, yes, but we all regard Southern Africa as oppressed. Rhodesia is as oppressed as South Africa is oppressed, so our business is to liberate the sub-continent.' We never had any difficulties about that, we never had awkward questions. We just got cooperation. You must remember the ZAPU freedom radio in Zambia was operating full blast, twice, thrice a week, and in any case, it got to be known by the world that there were ANC people who were operating there, so it was not such a secret.

South Africa responded by deploying its 'Police Anti-Terrorist Unit' to fight the ANC-ZAPU incursions into Rhodesia: [10] *did you get any sense that the South Africans were threatened by the idea of two different groups of blacks fighting together?*

They were threatened by that. We actually suffered for that. They didn't like our participation in that struggle one bit.

What did they say to you in interrogation after you were captured?

'Why do you fight here? What business have you got here? You are an intruder, you are an invader.' Then they would take a different line, like for instance: 'Zimbabweans can't fight — you are the only people who are doing a lot of fighting here.' It's the old enemy tactic of trying to drive a wedge between you. But it didn't have effect. They didn't impress us one bit.

Those Zimbabweans, I want to tell you one thing, I bloody well respect them. We came off well in a fight, but whenever we were walking, hell, those men are strong. They are rural-orientated and it makes them used to walking long distances, and they are bloody well tough, I can assure you. I used to marvel at them, really.

With all the time you spent together, and with all the tensions and deprivations, were there not ever times when there'd be a resort to an ethnic slur?

No, not that way, not that way at all. Listen, we were mature politically. The basis of a guerilla movement, it is the political training of the cadre. We are not just fighting by pulling the trigger and releasing the bullet — no, we also have to win people. You have to know what you are fighting about, you have to be able to tell the people what we are fighting for, why we are fighting, how we are fighting, why they should contribute. I'm trying to tell you that there was no question where I'm going to start quarrelling with you because you are white, because you are Zezuru, or you are Ndebele, or you are South African — no, no, no. We disagreed occasionally over issues, but that didn't mean that we disagreed because of ethnic divisions, because I came from South Africa or because he was Ndebele. There were Ndebeles, there were Shonas, there were ourselves,[11] the Zulus, Xhosas, Sothos, Tswanas.

This joint South African-Zimbabwean offensive was subsequently criticized as a short-sighted response to agitation for action from frustrated ANC and ZAPU cadres idling in Tanzanian military camps, and indeed the 'Wankie Campaign' failed in its goal of opening infiltration routes southward. The success it did achieve was rather in signalling — at the height of the demoralizing lull in popular resistance inside the country — that the struggle was alive and continuing from outside.

While mass political organization was at an all-time low in the 1960s, there was less inertia on other levels. This was a time of analysis and reassessment, and one of the key debates concerned the position of non-Africans in the exclusively African ANC. Following the decision by the Congress Alliance that the Indian Congresses, CPC and COD would not open missions outside South Africa, some ANC members opposed the inclusion of non-Africans in their organization. They argued that minority groups should mobilize within their own communities, and that only when Indians, coloureds and whites were politically engaged in confrontation with the regime and could be found in corresponding numbers within Umkhonto we Sizwe would the time be ripe to consider the question of 'open membership'. The 'London Debates', as the controversy that erupted in London was known, made a consultative conference imperative in order to resolve the issue once and for all.

More than seventy delegates[12] met in Morogoro, Tanzania in 1969 for the ANC's first big conclave outside South Africa. The consensus at Morogoro was that non-Africans should be integrated into the ANC's External Mission and serve for the first time as full members of the ANC, but that only Africans could be elected to its top policy-making body, the National Executive Committee (NEC).[13]

'Strategy and Tactics of the ANC', the central policy document adopted by the Morogoro conference:

The main content of the present stage of the South African revolution is the national liberation of the largest and most oppressed group: the African people. This strategic aim must govern every aspect of the conduct of our struggle, whether it be the formulation of policy or the creation of structures. Amongst other things, it demands in the first place the maximum mobilization of the African people as a dispossessed and racially oppressed nation. This is the mainspring and it must not be weakened. It involves a stimulation and deepening of national confidence, a national pride and national assertiveness.

The national character of the struggle must dominate our approach. But it is a national struggle which is taking place in a different era and in a different context from those which characterized the early struggles against colonialism. Thus our nationalism must not be confused with chauvinism or the narrow nationalism of a previous epoch. It must not be confused with the classical drive by an elitist group among the oppressed people to gain ascendancy so that they can replace the oppressor in the exploitation of the mass.

But none of this detracts from the basically national context of our liberation drive. In the last resort it is only the success of the national democratic revolution which — by destroying the existing social and economic relationships — will bring with it a correction of the historical injustices perpetrated against the indigenous majority and lay the basis for a new and deeper internationalist approach. Until then, the national sense of grievance is the most potent revolutionary force which must be harnessed.

How can we strengthen and make effective the cooperation between the communities, and how can we integrate committed revolutionaries, irrespective of their racial background? Whatever instruments are created to give expression to the unity of the liberation drive, they must accommodate two fundamental propositions. Firstly, they must not be ambiguous on the question of the primary role of the most oppressed African mass, and secondly, those belonging to the other oppressed groups and those few white revolutionaries who show themselves ready to make common cause with our aspirations must be fully integrated on the basis of individual equality.

Approached in the right spirit, these two propositions do not stand in conflict but reinforce one another. Equality of participation in our national front does not mean a mechanical parity between the various national groups. Not only would this in practice amount to inequality (again at the expense of the majority), but it would lend flavour to the slander which our enemies are ever ready to spread of a multi-racial alliance dominated by minority groups.

News of the joint ANC-ZAPU military activity in Zimbabwe served as an important morale-booster: since the government censored reports of 'terrorist activity', the ANC's media was the main source of such news.

Opposition to the policies adopted at Morogoro continued even after the conference. A dissident faction representing the rump of the Africanist camp — such as it still existed within the ANC following the formation of the PAC — began denouncing even the limited involvement of non-Africans. The faction focussed its attacks on the ANC's London office, headed by a coloured (Reg September) and including a number of Indians and whites. In 1975 a group of eight Africanists issued a statement charging that a 'non-African clique' had 'hijacked the ANC', and was attempting 'to substitute a class approach for the national approach to our struggle'. The ANC expelled the Africanist group,[14] but the movement was well aware that the resentments and fears that lay beneath this controversy were not so easy to dismiss.

Frene Ginwala, a senior representative in the ANC's London office since the 1960s:

Now when you have very physically divided groups with different economic and other status, if you suddenly imply a blanket society with pure merit and nothing else, the whole history of acquired skills, of acculturation into a modern technological world and so on will mean that the people not of the majority will have the skills and just on pure merit they will dominate. So how then are you going to help the other group, given a long history of racism?

One way is parallel development: saying we keep the leadership of this group, we teach ourselves a self-awareness and political consciousness. That's why in the first instance the ANC's doors were closed, this is why all these things had to go in stages. You know, merit can be technical, but if you talk in terms of the ability to mobilize, then all sorts of other forces come into play: the ability to communicate, language and so on. The tendency is that because you operate in a modern technological world, people see the need for leadership qualifications to come out of the ability to operate in that world — the fact that that ability doesn't necessarily go with an ability to operate in the world of the oppressed is not often recognized. They're different value systems. So perhaps the best way is to close that society for a while.

This is where the question of positive discrimination would come in — it's a question that we argue about in the women's movement. I personally would not oppose positive discrimination in principle. It's got to be done consciously, with an awareness of what we're doing, and it's got to be done for a limited time. I would say that for women, and for all racial groups.

If women stay out of the struggle, how then do we get women's issues put on the agenda? You do it by participation now, by raising the issues now, and in the process of the struggle you fight those things out. You don't, after one kind of liberation, put the question of how you protect minorities on the agenda — you sort it out now. That's why you've got to get at the grassroots and you've got to address the fears.

With all minorities — it doesn't matter whether you're talking of the Southern Sotho or of the protection of the Tswana against the Zulu — you first establish a national objective of a non-racial society, a recognition that rights and privileges or disabilities and whatever else don't accrue because of race or ethnicity. The second step is that these groups then have to pitch in and put what concerns them onto the agenda, because by working together is how you will resolve these problems.

Now if whites or Indians or coloureds are not there to be seen, there's no way the ANC's going to convince the African people that we want to be a non-racial society. You've got to be seen there, within the movement. Non-racialism has got to be seen to be there, in practical terms. It requires a degree of sensitivity on the part of the non-Africans, because we do have skills, we do have a history of privilege, which affects us in all kinds of undefinable ways which we're most unconscious of. And it requires a tremendous sensitivity on the part of the leadership of the ANC, so that you can defuse the problems as you go.

The irony of 'the lull' lay in the lack of cross-fertilization between the ideas that emerged from this re-think outside South Africa and from the re-evaluation taking place inside the country, for the links between the exiled movement and its internal supporters were still under reconstruction. Young South Africans coming of age during this period were deprived of the history of the ANC, and few had studied the documents reflecting its revitalization. It was no wonder, then, that so many dismissed the ANC as moribund and saw their own generation as the vanguard of change. The black student movement that did so much to rekindle mass resistance in the 1960s and 1970s owed a great debt to a tradition it was still to discover.

Notes

1. Legislation which criminalized political parties embracing both black and white.
2. Internationally famous for his 1948 book, *Cry the Beloved Country*, which propounded quite liberal views in the context of the time, Paton moved rightward in his later years. In the decade before his death in 1988, he opposed sanctions, supported Zulu homeland Chief Buthelezi, and endorsed a federal, multi-racial solution for a post-apartheid South Africa.
3. The Progressive Party was founded in 1959 with the support of liberal big business (mainly the Anglo American Corporation), and its sole parliamentary representative throughout most of the 1960s was Helen Suzman.
4. The ARM arrests and trials involved only a handful of blacks, but it was a coloured man, Eddie Daniels, who received the stiffest prison sentence of fifteen years.
5. The National Union of South African Students (NUSAS) president at the University of Cape Town who helped found ARM, and then gave state's evidence against those he had recruited in order to win immunity from prosecution.
6. Founded in 1955 as the Defence of the Constitution League by a group of women that included Duncan's mother, Jean Sinclair, initially to protest the gerrymandering of the South African constitution to effect the removal of the coloureds from the common voters' roll.

7. NUSAS was formed in 1924 by the white universities and focussed on forging English-Afrikaans student unity, but all the Afrikaans campuses had disaffiliated by 1936. In 1945 NUSAS admitted the black campus of Fort Hare, and by the mid-1960s it had become the most radical and outspokenly non-racial of the legal organizations.

8. Then chairman of the Anglo American multi-national and an important source of finance for the Progressive Federal Party (PFP), as the Progressive Party was known after a 1977 merger with former United Party members of parliament.

9. After the white leaders of the British colony of Southern Rhodesia illegally declared independence in 1965, the two wings of the Zimbabwean liberation movement launched an armed struggle to win back their country. The ANC formed an alliance with the Zimbabwe African People's Union (ZAPU), for at that time the ANC (like the leading liberation movements of Mozambique and Angola) regarded the Zimbabwe African National Union (ZANU) as a break-away, Africanist grouping in the mould of the PAC. The ANC was also drawn closer to ZAPU by the fact that ZAPU's guerillas were based in neighbouring Zambia, infiltrating from the southwest, so its supporters tended to come from southwestern Zimbabwe's Ndebele minority, which has a language and culture similar to that of South Africa's Zulu. In addition, like the ANC, ZAPU was supported by the Soviet Union and the Eastern socialist countries.

10. South Africa continued to deploy its paramilitary forces in Rhodesia for the next seven years, until the troop withdrawal of the detente era, and at a less publicized level it maintained 'logistical support' up until the 1979 ceasefire that led to Zimbabwe's independence in 1980. The South African military took advantage of the Rhodesian training ground: from 1989 revelations about Security Police and military involvement in 'death squads' formed to assassinate anti-apartheid activists it emerged that former death squad commander Major Eugene de Kock had trained under the 'anti-terrorist' Rhodesian Special Air Services from 1968 to 1972.

11. Several coloured cadres played important roles in early Umkhonto campaigns, a fact not well known in South Africa at the time, but by the mid-1980s awareness was such that students at the University of the Western Cape renamed a residence after Basil February, and MK cadre James April was feted upon his release from Robben Island after serving fifteen years.

12. The overwhelming majority were African, but conference delegates also included three coloureds, five Indians and three whites.

13. The ANC's Revolutionary Council, formed in response to a resolution taken at the conference and later renamed the Political-Military Council (PMC), included non-Africans: an Indian, a coloured and a white.

14. The 'Gang of Eight', as the ANC disparagingly referred to those it expelled, included George Mbele, Pascal Ngakane and Thami Bonga (who all later rejoined the ANC), Jonas Matlou, O. K. Setlapelo and Alfred Kgokong Mqota (who have remained politically non-aligned since then), Tennyson Makiwane (who was shot dead after his return to Transkei in 1980 in what was widely seen as an assassination, although Umkhonto we Sizwe never claimed credit for the deed), and Makiwane's brother, Ambrose (whose current whereabouts are unknown).

PART THREE
1969—1976

Steve Biko speaking at the second General Students Council of the South African Students Organization (SASO), held at the University of Natal, July 1971.

13 Black Man, You're on Your Own

'Ofay-Watcher, Throbs-Phase', poem by Mongane Wally Serote, 1972:[1]

White people are white people
They are burning the world.
Black people are black people
They are the fuel.
White people are white people
They must learn to listen.
Black people are black people
They must learn to talk.

'Black Souls in White Skins?', inaugural article in the 'I Write What I Like'
series by 'Frank Talk', South African Students Organization (SASO)
Newsletter, *August 1970, later revealed to have been authored by SASO*
President Steve Biko:

Basically, the South African white community is a homogeneous
community. It is a community of people who sit to enjoy a privileged
position that they do not deserve, are aware of this, and therefore spend
their time trying to justify why they are doing so. Where differences in
political opinion exist, they are in the process of trying to justify their
position of privilege and their usurpation of power.

The role of the white liberal in the black man's history in South Africa
is a curious one. Very few black organizations were not under white
direction. True to their image, the white liberals always knew what was
good for the blacks and told them so. The wonder of it all is that the black
people have believed in them for so long.

Nowhere is the arrogance of the liberal ideology demonstrated so well
as in their insistence that the problems of the country can only be solved
by a bilateral approach involving both black and white. This has, by and
large, come to be taken in all seriousness as the modus operandi in South
Africa by all those who claim they would like a change in the status quo.
Hence the multi-racial political organizations and parties and the
'non-racial' student organizations – all of which insist on integration not
only as an end goal, but also as a means.

Does this mean that I am against integration? If by integration you
understand a breakthrough into white society by blacks, an assimilation
and acceptance of blacks into an already established set of norms and
code of behaviour set up by and maintained by whites, then yes, I am
against it. I am against the superior-inferior white-black stratification
that makes the white a perpetual teacher and the black a perpetual pupil.

I am against the fact that a settler minority should impose an entire system of values on an indigenous people.

From this it becomes clear that as long as blacks are suffering from an inferiority complex — a result of 300 years of deliberate oppression, denigration and derision — they will be useless as co-architects of a normal society where man is nothing else but man for his own sake. Hence what is necessary as a prelude to anything else that may come is a very strong grassroots build-up of black consciousness, such that blacks can learn to assert themselves and stake their rightful claim.

Black Consciousness (BC) was an angry blow against the frustration and impotence of 'the lull'. The walk-out of black students led by Steve Biko from the white liberal-dominated NUSAS in 1968 heralded the demise of the era of fear and submissiveness and the birth of a psychology of liberation. The rebellious founders of SASO rejected the label of 'non-white' and pioneered the unity of African, coloured and Indian as blacks against the white oppressor.

Pandelani Nefolovhodwe, SASO member from its inception, active at the University of the North:

From 1960 up to about 1966 there was a lull in this country, but as early as about 1967 some people got involved in trying to shape a new direction. We were debating issues like the disaffiliation from NUSAS, as part of this new mood which wanted to get away from liberalism as a form of struggle.

At that stage we were in a state where we were searching for our own identity. We had to liberate ourselves from this psychological oppression, and to do so the argument was that you have got to be away from the people who on a daily basis infuse you with an idea of their superiority, because if you continue to be with them you will forever not be able to extricate yourself.

It's a question of oppressor and oppressed, so we had to galvanize ourselves, and that's why we came with the concept of black solidarity: to bargain from a position of strength. The first thing that we sought to do was just to extricate ourselves from the oppressor and all the agents of oppression — which needed us to run away from multi-racial organization. We needed to inculcate into the minds of our people that they are not inferior to any person, and secondly, that we all belong to one human race.

'SASO Policy Manifesto', SASO on the Attack: An Introduction to the South African Student Organization, *1973:*

1. SASO is a black student organization working for the liberation of the black man,[2] first from psychological oppression by themselves through inferiority complex, and secondly from the physical one accruing out of living in a white racist society.

2. We define black people as those who are by law or tradition politically, economically and socially discriminated against as a group in the South African society and identifying themselves as a unit in the struggle towards the realization of their aspirations.

3. SASO believes that:

a) South Africa is a country in which both black and white live and shall continue to live together;

b) That the white man must be made aware that one is either part of the solution or part of the problem;[3]

c) That in this context, because of the privileges accorded to them by legislation, and because of their continual maintenance of an oppressive regime, whites have defined themselves as part of the problem;

d) That therefore we believe that in all matters relating to the struggle towards realizing our aspirations, whites must be excluded;

e) That this attitude must not be interpreted by blacks to imply 'anti-whitism', but merely a more positive way of attaining a normal situation in South Africa;

f) That in pursuit of this direction, therefore, personal contact with whites, though it should not be legislated against, must be discouraged, especially where it tends to militate against the beliefs we hold dear.

4. a) SASO upholds the concept of Black Consciousness and the drive towards black awareness as the most logical and significant means of ridding ourselves of the shackles that bind us to perpetual servitude.

b) SASO defines Black Consciousness as follows:

(i) Black Consciousness is an attitude of mind, a way of life;

(ii) The basic tenet of Black Consciousness is that the black man must reject all value systems that seek to make him a foreigner in the country of his birth and reduce his basic human dignity;

(iii) The black man must build up his own value systems, see himself as self-defined and not defined by others;

(iv) The concept of Black Consciousness implies the awareness by the black people of the power they wield as a group, both economically and politically, and hence group cohesion and solidarity are important facets of Black Consciousness;

(v) The message of Black Consciousness has to be spread to reach all sections of the black community.

5. SASO believes that all groups allegedly working for 'integration' in South Africa — and here we note in particular the Progressive Party and other liberal institutions — are not working for the kind of integration that would be acceptable to the black man. Their attempts are directed merely at relaxing certain oppressive legislations and to allow blacks into a white-type society.

Although supporters of Black Consciousness claimed political non-alignment, the rhetoric associated with the new ideology was derivative of the American Black Power movement[4] and reminiscent of the PAC.

Thus the slogans of the day became 'Black is Beautiful', a reference to the 'Afro' look of unstraightened hair and unlightened skin,[5] and 'Azania Shall be Free!', from the name the PAC advocated for a liberated South Africa.[6]

Masterpiece Gumede, who joined SASO at the University of Zululand (Ngoye) in 1972:

When we came to Ngoye we were immediately grabbed by SASO. All my university days I was SASO. I know some people come into the struggle because they are workers and they feel the exploitation at the factory place – this is not my experience. I only got into politics through the student movement at university.

What was your view of the PAC at that time?

I knew very little to begin with. I remember one old man I talked with at home when I was a very strong BC advocate, and he looked at me and said, 'You boys, I'm sure if you were around in the '50s you would have joined the PAC, you would have been Sobukwe people.' In terms of rhetoric, I think we were close to the PAC, but the people we wanted to be with were people like Mandela and Lutuli and ANC people. You know, this whole question of BC being PAC-leaning, it wasn't a reality when we were at home.

The South African government initially interpreted the formation of SASO as a vindication of its policy of 'separate development', while white liberals felt threatened by the rise of Black Consciousness.

'Sad About SASO', Daily Dispatch, a liberal English-language newspaper edited by Donald Woods in East London, 10 August 1971:

The emergence of SASO is one of the sad manifestations of racist policy at government level. The cornerstone of apartheid is the bantustan policy, through which blacks are compelled to regard themselves as separate people – a people set apart – who can aspire to progress only on the basis of exclusivity. The result is the emergence of a 'blacks only' mentality among blacks. The promoters of SASO are wrong in what they are doing. They are promoting apartheid. They are entrenching the idea of racial exclusivity and therefore doing the government's work. Fortunately, they represent only a small minority of black students.

Revd Francois Bill, who served from 1971 to 1974 as chaplain at Fort Hare University and lecturer at Federal Theological Seminary, both blacks-only institutions in the Eastern Cape:

Did you experience any anti-white attitudes from blacks in that period?

Yes, I went through that. The SASO president at the time, Temba Sono, I knew very well because I had been his chaplain when he was in high school at Lemana in the Northern Transvaal, and I went to listen to him. He

The Black Consciousness Movement was inspired in part by the US Black Power movement of the late 1960s. The writings of African-American leaders, though banned in South Africa, were smuggled into the country and widely circulated in university circles.

expounded the whole BC philosophy and said, 'The time has come where we've got to say, "White man, get off our backs, we're going to do it on our own and we reject you. If you want to go and do something, do it in your own community." '[7]

And I got up at the end and I said, 'How do you think that the white man is ever going to find out what the hell he's got to do unless he's challenged by black people?' And he took the opportunity of saying, 'You know, you are my old chaplain, but this is where you reveal just what a bloody racist you are.' He just lashed out at me — it hurt.

Eventually I came to understand how important it was for black people to undergo that process of psychological liberation. I came to realize that we, as whites, were actually projecting our guilt onto blacks. You know, I have been involved in all these multi-racial efforts within the church and I've been extremely upset by the insensitivity of whites. White people are not good at listening — they are very good at telling other people what to do. So that when black people are articulating — and don't forget that they articulate in the language which is not their mother tongue — white people somehow just ride roughshod over that kind of expression of black feelings.

So that's why I say that my first exposure to BC was a traumatic experience in one way, but it was also a very salutary experience. And that was confirmed to me when I went to Biko's funeral,[8] because there were 30,000 people in that football ground, with a sprinkling of whites, and I'll never forget standing with a friend of mine in this sea of black people. The one particular song they were singing was '*Abelungu Bayizinja*', which means 'Whites are dogs', and there was this guy standing next to me singing for all he was worth, and then he turned to me with a beautiful smile and he said, 'Ja, they are dogs – I don't mean you.'

And this is where I believe that blacks have a hell of a lesson to teach us. We've got some bloody obsession about race – they just look at a person as a person, as a human being. If only white people in South Africa could know that. Whites say to me, 'Aren't you scared of going into Soweto? Won't they do something to you?' I've never felt scared.

It was in part to combat white fears that the Christian Institute of Southern Africa (CI)[9] set up Spro-cas, the 'Study Project on Christianity in Apartheid Society',[10] which answered Black Consciousness with 'white consciousness'.

Richard Turner, The Eye of the Needle, *a Spro-cas publication, 1972:*

To maintain political control of South Africa a certain type of government is required, and it is impossible to separate completely what it must do to blacks from what it does to whites. A minority cannot rule a majority by consent. It must therefore be prepared to use force to maintain control, and this in turn requires a cultural climate that sanctions killing. It must be continually on its guard against 'subversion' and be prepared to react to it rapidly. A climate develops in which people who are not even white dissenters fear to speak of politics or to openly criticize government policy. Thus the political cost to whites of maintaining economic privilege is that they lose control over many other areas of their lives and become subject to an external authority.

The political fear and loss of freedom is accompanied by an even more insidious cultural unfreedom. Psychologically insecure individuals are threatened by change. They turn in upon themselves, blindly assert their importance, their own identity and their own cultural traditions, but are not capable of opening themselves out towards the future. Race prejudice prevents intelligent thought about the nature and functioning of society.

But these patterns can be broken. And it is important to try to break them. It is important to show the whites what they have to gain from a free, democratic society. Until white South Africans come to understand that their present society and their present position is a result not of their own virtues but of their vices; until they come to see world history over the last five hundred years not as the 'triumph of white civilization', but simply as the bloody and ambiguous birth of a new technology; and until they come to see these things not in guilt for the past but in hope for the future, they will not be able to communicate with black people, nor ultimately with one another.

Horst Kleinschmidt, a NUSAS leader in the late 1960s who worked for the Christian Institute in the early 1970s:

Through Spro-cas, the white programme [the counterpart of a programme for blacks], we were to find ways of translating a non-racial society into an active programme by cooperating with white groups, student or church or anything. We didn't fare very well because it was a heyday for SASO and so on, while in white politics it was a very fruitless period. In fact, after a two-year period we closed the white programme down and expanded the black programme, simply because we had not made any serious impact in the white community.

I think BC had an impact on the liberal white who was plagued by guilt, but I don't think that that moved whites to action or to resistance or to a clarity about their position. The tension expressed itself very much when, for example, SASO and Black Community Programmes (BCP)[11] would regularly need the resources of the Christian Institute. There was a fleet of cars that we constantly loaned out, and there was an attitude in the BC structures that because it was provided for by whites it need not be respected. And that resulted in there being a preponderance of cars being wrecked.

It was the black CI staff who then demanded of the white staff that they should cease giving cars or anything to SASO until SASO had rethought their position, and that really we were providing at the level of our own guilt — which was just nonsensical. And shortly after this decision was taken, unanimously by the staff, I was approached and I said, 'Sorry, no car.' And I was immediately told, 'Oh, you bloody racist.'

But the point I'm making is that I learned in that situation to know that if my motive is guilt, it is merely another form of patronage of the black person. And therefore I cannot be a political person in the South African struggle and refuse to accept that I can have arguments, disputes — and for that matter, break-ups — with black people whom I'm closely relating to. The colour of their skin cannot determine the nature of that relationship.

The Black Consciousness philosophy evolved over time beyond its initial social and cultural focus, and by the mid-1970s a critique of BC which stressed economic issues was beginning to emerge from the youth and students. This development sowed the seeds of an eventual rift between the more left-wing SASO and the BC veterans who went on to found the movement's non-student wing, Black People's Convention (BPC).

Papi Mokoena, SASO activist expelled from Fort Hare University in 1973 for leading a student strike:

The two political trends have always been struggling against each other: the non-racial attitude that the whites have got a role to play, and that the whites do not have a role to play: 'Black man you are on your own,[12] you must free yourself.' There were people I met — who I only later came to discover were ANC members — who were putting across this line that we cannot define ourselves only in terms of blackness, that oppression has never been a political vehicle. They argued that we should move out of this social identity to one which is much more dynamic, which sets forth perspectives for the future.

I think contact with the ANC was growing. More people from outside were coming into the country, books were coming from outside. There was a dearth of material at that time: published material of the ANC was particularly valuable and one treasured it as if it was gold. We even had a 'mobile library' — books which moved from hand to hand amongst selected people. You see, we knew the ANC was underground, but the problem was finding the underground members of the ANC. At that time more and more of them were coming out of prison and coming to see us, SASO, to see who we were. We used to listen to Radio Freedom every day when there was a broadcast.

We were not anti ANC's political ideas at that time — never — because we felt that it is a liberation movement, we are a students' movement, and these are the people we need, we want to have the material they are giving us. That is why SASO became so receptive to ANC ideas later on. The situation was constantly developing, we were meeting hard practice which could not be fitted onto those ideas which we had developed in college.

Let me just inform you: we had a national executive committee meeting in 1973 in which we had sent out people to go and meet the liberation movements, to talk to them and say, 'In what way can we work together?' We wanted contact with these people. SASO people were sent to the two movements, and the only movement which replied positively was the ANC.

As a SASO leader you had been supportive of a decision to avoid contact with whites; did it then surprise or disturb you to see whites accepted in the ANC?

This time I knew that I am not meeting whites who are going to push me around — this time I was meeting whites who were comrades. We could think together, work together, act together, and plan together for the future — it's quite a different thing. The non-racialism of the ANC was positive because it involved a very clear analysis. It was not just theory, but it came from the nitty-gritty analysis of the contradictions which are existing in the South African situation: how is race a factor? Why is non-racialism a policy position which is the only way forward to bring about a situation where apartheid can be eliminated? One cannot eliminate apartheid with apartheid.

Nkosazana Dlamini, a BC supporter recruited to the ANC while visiting Swaziland in 1975, then elected SASO vice-president in 1976: [13]

I did not understand BC as an end in itself. At that time I think it was important for people inside the country to find something which could motivate and rally people and put confidence again in themselves as black people. But it was very clear to me that there's a limit to which BC can take you, and you had to find the next step up, because it was very clear to me from the beginning that BC was not going to bring the government down. From an historical point of view, it was clear that no amount of talking and no amount of conscientizing people will do that. I would say it was like a growing child:

you need to crawl before you can walk, and so BC was just one of those stages that you needed to grow up in politics. But you couldn't be BC forever — and there was no other alternative except the ANC.

Was the ANC's non-racialism an issue for you before you joined?

Well, the ANC had an alliance with different racial groups, but the issue really was to fight for the rights of the Africans — it was not to fight to get rid of the whites. The whites were just a fact of history: they were there and there was nothing much to do about them. To be honest with you, at that time I didn't think there were enough progressive whites to make a difference. I didn't think that all whites were bad, but I just thought there weren't enough whites who were prepared to stick their necks out for us.

So what kind of work did you do as an underground ANC member?

They didn't want us to talk overtly — I mean, that would have been disastrous because I don't think at the time there was anyone who was talking overtly about the ANC. But they did want us to influence other people that we are in contact with, those who we thought had reached a stage in BC where they wanted something else, like us.

We felt that it was our task to try and influence the debates and the discussions in BC to have more leanings towards ANC policies — without saying they were ANC policies, if you see what I mean. You would talk about things that are in the Freedom Charter, what kind of education people should fight for, what sort of land policies. And also influencing people towards not seeing the struggle as waged only by Africans, coloureds and Indians, but that other people should also have a role to play.

And more so, to influence people that when they left South Africa they should join the ANC. Because there was quite a big group of BC people which was just being wasted in Botswana. They were not part of any liberation movement, they were keeping themselves as a BC group. Obviously there was no way forward for them, and some of them were even discussing forming their own army wing.[14]

So what was the reaction you got?

Well, some thought that the ANC hadn't done enough. It's very easy when you are in South Africa to think you can just go out and get trained and come back and fight, because it's very difficult to come to grips with all the problems and complications of training people and infiltrating them back to the country.

You didn't get questions or criticism about the ANC's working relationship with whites?

I would say that there were a few — but not really many — who just wanted to know what sort of role they had in the ANC, because everyone, including me, had the idea that it's the Africans who should be in the frontline and who should be in the leadership.

When I say we wanted to meet the ANC, we wanted to join the ANC, it does not mean that we didn't have any reservations — we did think they were a bit slow. Even after having spoken to them and appreciating the problems they were facing, we still felt that. But we felt that to make them fast we had to actually help them: join the ANC and try and put our enthusiasm into the ANC.

Do you think there was any re-directing of SASO as a result of your ANC

I think so. Having met with the ANC and got a better
ourselves, we did try to get SASO to think about things in a r
way, and to try and introduce the subject of ANC — maybe
but by inviting known ANC people like Winnie Mandela
ference to be the guest speaker, and so on. And there was s
actually introduce the subject of class and an economic p
SASO.

Some people were quite positive about it and thought w
explore this kind of thinking, because they were feeling th
the ceiling of BC and the ANC was going to open other avenues
were other people who actually said, 'You must be very careful.
people are known to be tomatoes.' And 'tomatoes' was meaning 'red', and
'red' was meaning communist. I think that comes from the fact that South
Africans — at least our generation — have never been allowed to know what
communism is. We've been told how bad it is without being told what it is.
Now things have changed: in the same way that people are much more open
to carrying the ANC flag, they're probably much more open to the
Communist Party. It was ignorance and state propaganda.

The watershed marking this shift in Black Consciousness away from a
colour-based analysis came in 1976, with the outgoing address of the last
SASO president to serve out his full term of office, Diliza Mji.[16] He argued
that if BC was to survive as a viable philosophy it needed to 'start interpreting our situation from an economic class point of view' informed by
'an accurate perception of who the enemy is'. This 'late SASO line'
characterized the government's agenda as the promotion of an aspiring
black middle class with a stake in the free enterprise system, concluding
that, 'All they are saying is that blacks should be exploited by blacks.'[17]

Diliza Mji, SASO National President, 1975–76:

Funnily enough, BC, when it started off, had as one of its central principles
that it recognizes the validity of the older liberation movements, and some
of us truly believed that we were taking over from people who had gone on
before us. But that was exactly where the mistake was, I think. It was a very
romantic situation, where we looked at the ANC and the PAC as
organizations of equal credibility, equal contribution, and I wouldn't think
that a lot of us were clear about the differences that lay behind ANC and
PAC, beyond just saying that there were white communists in the ANC and
that the PAC was objecting to the hijacking of the black people's struggles
by white people, and so on.

During that time we did not have any exposure to any other political
forces. In trying to analyze you used the BC framework, and sometimes one
just found oneself frustrated, not able to answer questions. I'll give you some
examples. What used to really worry me was the fact that a lot of the

oppression in this country was actually perpetuated by black people like ourselves — Transkei's Chief Matanzima and so on. Security Police surveillance of our movements was very, very obvious and a lot of this was done by black Security Policemen. So through those sort of tangible experiences one began searching for an answer to some of these obvious questions, and it was clear that an answer lay outside the BC framework.

When did you start searching beyond BC?

Around '74, '75, BC was under heavy questioning. We were challenged to answer questions like: how can we bring about change in the society? This in itself made us aware of the class nature of society. It led us on to realize that students are just a part of it — in fact, not even the most important part. We became aware that there are workers and trade unions which were emerging around that same time. The strikes here in Natal in '73 were very important events that one could not just ignore.[18]

We tried to conscientize people through educational projects, literacy projects, and things like that, but in implementing those projects, it was quite clear that we were only reaching a few selected groups of people, and not in any systematic way. It was quite clear that we were not making any impact outside the student movement.

Then there was a BPC conference that was held in Mafeking in 1976. Personally, I must say that that was my turning point, because the document that was supposed to be the economic policy of BC was no different than the present sort of capitalist nature of the society.[19] It was not an alternative at all, and although I did not have a clear understanding of an alternative society, I knew at that time that the answer to the problems of the society lies not only in a different political order, but also in an alternative economic system. I must say that at that conference, purely around this document, it became quite clear that there were two main trends within BC itself: there were people who were questioning the nature of society in a broader sense, and then there were those who were vehemently defending the racial way of interpreting our own society.[20]

I remember very clearly what happened after that: in June of '76, at the SASO congress which was held in Hammanskraal, most of the campuses in Natal and Jo'burg were said to belong to the camp that has sort of betrayed BC, because they were beginning to raise more fundamental questions. People in Cape Town, Natal, and some people in Jo'burg were together in interpreting things differently. But people in the Cape, and some people in Jo'burg — these were mainly people around Steve Biko — they were very unhappy about the direction that SASO was taking.[21]

In fact, when I got detained in '76 in the aftermath of the [Soweto] uprisings, that, I think, was the breakthrough, because one got in touch with people who were returning from the Island. So that in talking to such people, one then was able to reconnect the pieces that were missing about our history, the history of the struggle in South Africa. You must remember that our political development was not from a textbook: it was from participating in events that were happening at the time, and having developed in a period whereby the movements had been banned and people who belonged to those movements had been silenced.

I like to look at that period of BC as a period in which there was a disconnection between the historical evolution of the struggle. I really don't think that anything new has happened now — it's just that people have rediscovered the period that they, unfortunately, had missed because of the repression and so on.

In October 1977, the government finally banned the Black Consciousness movement, issuing the first organizational restrictions since the 1960s against seventeen BC bodies.[22] Many analyzed this delayed state response — nearly a decade after BC first emerged — as evidence that it was the decline of the conservative Black Consciousness tradition that had prompted the bannings. Pretoria had tolerated the Black Consciousness era: what it would not abide was the reconnection with the history that had gone before it. But the bans came too late. The new trend toward non-racialism was now firmly entrenched, and the revival of the Congress tradition had already begun to eclipse Black Consciousness.

Notes

1. From Mongane Wally Serote, *Yakhal'nkomo*, Renoster Books, 1972. 'Ofay' is African-American slang from the 'Harlem Renaissance' era (1920s): a derogatory word for a white person, derived from Pig Latin for 'foe', pronounced oe-fay.
2. The sexist language and ethos of the Black Consciousness Movement was grounded in a number of factors. BC's base among the black middle class meant that its influence was largely confined to university students and the intelligentsia, a male-dominated sphere in that period. Feminism had not yet made the impact on South Africa that it had in the US and Europe. By the early 1980s, black political organizations like the Congress of South African Students (COSAS) were responding positively to criticism of their sexism (epitomized by the common call to order in meetings: 'Gents...'). As of the mid-1980s, the United Democratic Front and the Congress of South African Trade Unions included far more women in their leadership than the political groupings of the previous decades, with greater prominence given to women's issues. By the late 1980s, political activists commonly featured a call for a 'non-sexist' South Africa in their demands for a democratic and non-racial society.
3. A paraphrasing of an aphorism from American Black Panther Eldridge Cleaver.
4. This is not to imply that the only international influence on BC was from the US. The evolving ideology was also influenced by news of the liberation movements active in the neighbouring states, the student uprisings in Europe, and the death of Che Guevara in Bolivia. However, black South Africans learned of these developments via mainstream media reports. The little socialist analysis that filtered into South Africa in this period came mainly via Western books and journals, e.g., analysis of Tanzanian President Julius Nyerere's '*ujamaa*' village model of socialism.
5. Yet at the same time, other aspects of the BC image were the use of English and a great concern for dress and appearance. Furthermore, the Afro look was later co-opted by both white capital and black small businesses to market Afro-style

designer clothes, hair care products and salons specializing in American-style perms.

6. A contentious term deriving from the Arabic word for a black person, '*zanj*', thus loosely interpreted as 'the land of black people'. The ANC rejects the word as historically and geographically incorrect, and etymologically derogatory because of its association with the East African coastal slave trade. While the term was originally proposed by the PAC in the early 1960s, it only gained currency a decade later, in Black Consciousness circles.

7. Sono later changed his views, advocating closer cooperation with whites in a controversial speech to the 1973 SASO General Students Council. This resulted in his ouster from the SASO presidency by BC militants.

8. Steve Biko died in detention in September 1977; an inquest exonerated the Security Police despite evidence that he died after torture, and the doctor charged with Biko's care was penalized for misconduct by the Medical Association of South Africa.

9. Based in Johannesburg and formed in 1963 (a result of the Cottlesloe Consultation, convened by the World Council of Churches following the Sharpeville massacre), the CI was headed by Dr Beyers Naude of the Dutch Reformed Church. Spro-cas was also sponsored by the South African Council of Churches (SACC), but the CI did most of the administration and fund-raising for the project.

10. The project gave rise to six commissions under the Special Programme for Christian Action in Society, which published material such as *Power, Privilege and Poverty: A Spro-cas Report, 1972.*

11. Part of BC's national umbrella body, Black People's Convention (BPC), BCP ran clinics, literacy training, creches, etc. in black communities.

12. The first time this slogan appeared in print was in Barney Pityana, 'Priorities in Community Development', *SASO Newsletter*, September 1971.

13. Following note 2 (above), it is worth mentioning that Dlamini is female. While the underrepresentation of women in legal opposition politics has been frequently noted, obvious security concerns have so far precluded an analysis of the role of women in underground structures.

14. Some governments and non-governmental agencies made concerted attempts to build a 'third force' to counter the ANC and the PAC, especially in the period immediately following the 1976 Soweto uprisings. For example, the then-Nigerian government feted Soweto student leader Tsitsi Mashinini and supported an abortive effort to form a military wing of the Black Consciousness Movement, the South African Youth Revolutionary Council (SAYRCO), while some Western governments and organizations favoured 'non-aligned' South African exiles in scholarship applications.

15. The wife of Nelson Mandela, and in her own right a leading member of the ANC Women's League and FedSAW in the 1950s, as well as chair of the ANC's Orlando branch. Banned and restricted from 1962 to 1975 and tried under the Terrorism Act in 1970, she was detained in 1976 upon her reinvolvement in politics, banned again, and then banished to a small town in the Orange Free State in 1977. A prominent symbol of the ANC who made a point of attending ANC trials (of blacks and whites) during her few months of freedom, her presence at BC events was significant.

16. Mji was elected in December 1974, following the arrest of the entire SASO executive (later prosecuted in the SASO-BPC trial). He was re-elected in June 1975 and served a full year's term of office. Mongezi Stofile was elected SASO president in June 1976, but was detained two months afterwards, released in February 1977, and then banned in June 1977. The last SASO president, Faith Matlaopane, served from June 1977 until SASO was banned in October of that year.

17. 'Presidential Address to 8th General Student Council', reprinted in *SASO News Bulletin*, June 1977. The dearth of other historical documents marking the shift in

SASO policy is the result of two key factors: the discovery of a suspected Security Police agent at the 1976 SASO General Student Council, which prompted the withdrawal of most other documents from the record; and state pressure on SASO in the eighteen months preceding its banning (e.g., via prosecution of SASO leaders and tighter monitoring of its international funding), which meant that there was less time and money for the production of SASO publications that could have highlighted these ideological developments.

18. Some 61,000 workers were involved in a series of strikes in Durban in early 1973, the first major labour unrest in South Africa in more than a decade.

19. In this document, also known as '31 Points', BPC adopted 'black communalism' as its economic policy, defined as 'a modified version of the traditional African economic lifestyle' and 'an economic system which is based on the principle of sharing, lays emphasis on community ownership of land and its wealth and riches, and which strikes a healthy balance between what may legitimately be owned by individuals and what ought to be owned by the community as a whole'.

20. Another point of contention concerned BPC's lack of consultation with SASO in the preparation of the document, a departure from the cooperation of the past that signalled to SASO that the BC old guard was starting to regard itself as a 'third force' vis-à-vis the existing liberation movements, and no longer simply as a caretaker body. After a threat by the SASO executive to break relations with BPC over the issue, SASO presented an alternative economic policy — which was rejected by BPC as 'red'. The dispute was compounded, in the view of SASO, by BPC's appointment of Biko as 'life-president' at the 1977 Mafeking conference, followed by his release from detention timed to facilitate an unmandated meeting with an aide to a visiting American politician, Senator Dick Clark.

21. An indication of the depth of the SASO-BPC divide was revealed with the detentions that followed the October bannings. Some forty leading activists were divided into four tellingly nicknamed cells in the Transvaal's Modder Bee prison: the mainly SASO contingent (plus a group of ANC prisoners) that supported a class analysis was in 'Vietnam' and 'University' (after Moscow's Patrice Lumumba University, which catered for African and Third World students), while the mainly BPC grouping that continued to emphasize race (including prominent older leaders from the Soweto Committee of Ten thrown up by the 1976 uprisings) was confined to cells dubbed 'America' and 'Britain'.

22. The BC-supporting Christian Institute was also banned.

14 Then Who is Our Enemy?

The rise of Black Consciousness did not mean the decline of non-racialism. Even during the height of the Black Consciousness era, ANC underground structures were slowly being rebuilt, and those involved in this clandestine process were both black and white.

Tony Holiday, reporter on Johannesburg's Rand Daily Mail *who clandestinely produced ANC literature in the early to mid-1970s:*

The time that I was working was a very important period and we still need to understand it, because it was the period where the movement reconstructed, and of course, in a renewal like that things change. The movement had new content to it, new people. Young people were coming in and the movement had to adapt to it, and they had to adapt to the movement, you know. There were all those challenges, but I think that the seeds of the thing were there. They were there before Rivonia, when the movement sat down and said, 'We are going to have to continue illegally and we are going to have to undertake armed struggle.' So that in a certain sense there was a thread. People think the thread snapped — I'm trying to say it may have looked very thin, but it was there, and it was unbreakable.

In 1972, I was expelled from a SASO meeting because my newspaper used the term 'non-white' instead of the term 'black'. In fact, a whole crisis had been going on: SASO had written a letter complaining about the use of the term 'non-white' in the paper. I thought that it was time for a change, and I wrote a long memo to the editor, Allister Sparks, about it. The next day I went back and was expelled from the conference because the newspaper was wavering. I went on with the fight and Allister changed the policy of the paper. The *Rand Daily Mail* had been the first newspaper to use the term 'African' instead of 'native', so then the *RDM* started referring to people as 'black', and I actually pride myself that I helped to persuade them to do it. I remember writing a story about it, what it felt like being ostracized by these black students.

'A Lesson in Discrimination', Tony Holiday, Rand Daily Mail, *10 July 1972:*

Spending a day at the conference of the South African Students Organization was instructive. It was informative and stimulating to watch young people of colour — African, Indian and coloured — trying to come to grips with the gut-problems of racial discrimination in South

Africa. But what really taught me something was the brief experience of being the actual object of that discrimination, and the feeling of utter loneliness and resentment that goes with it.

The delegates, with a few exceptions, made it quite plain that they did not want a white reporter covering their conference, and that whites were permitted only under special conditions and under heavy sufferance. What sharpened the edge of the feeling of rejection was the uncomfortable awareness that the experience one was going through was part of the daily lot of people of colour throughout South Africa.

The reconstruction of the ANC's underground concentrated less on black intellectuals — the focus of the Black Consciousness movement — than on the working class communities that BC had bypassed.

Themba Nxumalo, who worked underground recruiting for Umkhonto we Sizwe in Durban in the mid-1970s:

Well, in the '70s it was a period of Black Consciousness, but I personally did not get into contact with the Black Consciousness Movement as such. Their meetings used to concentrate on people who were in the universities. Hey, you found those people actually conversing in English — and really big English, you know. We could not just understand. Because of the level, I think there was a communication breakdown, so to say, between these organizations and the normal person. I remember at one stage I went to their offices, but even then I didn't know what to say, so I just was around and then I left.

But BC was all right: somehow people had to be revived and the Black Consciousness really contributed towards that, because after BC there was no longer that tranquillity period like the '60s and '70s, where there was completely a lull, when some people were saying, 'Look, these people, they ran away' — referring to Tambo — 'the Mandelas, they got themselves arrested' and things like that.

I would say the turning point was really at one of the places that I worked, this municipality police — they are popularly called the 'blackjacks' and they are really brutal, those people. Actually, even the captain who was the head, he asked me, 'But why do you want to be a security cop? Your friends will despise you.' I said, 'Oh well, that's true, but at the same time I have to live.' So I worked there for five years, at the same time collecting in my mind evidence of what actually we are doing, and linking this up with the general condition, the oppression of the African people. Then I came to the conclusion that by being part of the whole machinery, actually I am directly suppressing and oppressing our own people.

There was something developing in me. By then I was very good in reading. I could simply close myself there in the bedroom and read the whole damn day, not going out: history, political books. There was one actually by an American, on Black Consciousness. Who is this chap, man?

Malcolm X.[1] I just looked at reality and saw that what this chap is talking about are things that are actually happening right now. Whom to blame? I know it's whites. It was just like that.

Did you also go beyond Black Consciousness, had you heard of the ANC or the PAC?

No, unfortunately about the PAC, here in Natal it has never been actually known or popular. So as a result, you find that if you discuss with old people, they will tell you about the ANC. So I actually never even knew about the existence of PAC until I got it from the books very, very late. Then it was just a dead thing, something far removed from me. By then I had read enough, I had known that there was an ANC, there was a Freedom Charter, and my sympathies personally were now with the ANC. That was through material, reading books and getting this and that from the ANC. Some had to be used in very clandestine ways, otherwise you get yourself in trouble.

I left my job with the municipal police in 1975, and then I became a seaman. We used to travel all over Africa and Latin America. That's when the contact with the ANC was made, during that period, through one friend of ours in Chesterville [Durban African township] who actually went out for about a year or so and then came back about '72. Then he worked in a factory up until '77. Through him I was able to actively be involved in the struggle.

Was your motivation one of wanting to fight the whites?

No, actually, the person who really grounded me about the ANC made it clear to me about the racial question. He used to make examples, like saying, 'Okay, if you say whites are wrong, they should be killed, what do you say about Slovo?'[2] The only white person in the struggle that I knew at the time was Slovo, because he used to refer to him: he was an advocate, he could be making money and living well, but he chose to forego all that and decided to live as he's living now. So I was very clear in my mind and there was no longer any problem with whites.

When you were doing underground work, were you involved only with Africans, or did you also come into contact with ANC members of other race groups?

There was that contact between all the different races, we used to work together on some issues. But the Indians were more of a surprise than the whites. Initially I was really puzzled, because there was the feeling that Indians, man, are sell-outs. On the factory floor level you will find that as far as Indians are concerned — I'm saying this with no ill feeling, because actually right now I regard Indians, coloureds and everything as my comrades — you'll find that it's them who will harass, rather than the white foreman or supervisor. At least with the whites, I had heard about this Joe Slovo. Now, Indians was something that came very late, when I started to have certain contact with them while working.

Jacob Zuma, a former ANC Youth League member from Natal who spent 1963–73 on Robben Island for his Umkhonto we Sizwe activities:

BC emerged very strongly whilst I was in prison, so by the time I came out we were fully aware of the BC's presence, and we had done our own analysis about the BC at the time. We viewed it as an important development, and we were clear that there was new, serious political activity that would take place in South Africa, and we saw our influence as being clear.

Though the BC movement said there was a lull, there had been political happenings — I don't think there was any stretch of two to three years that there was no ANC trial. I think some of these things need to be put into proper perspective, so that people shouldn't think that there were then people who just emerged out of no influence at all. After all, you had a lot of ANC people who were not arrested or sent to prison, who were lying low — many of them were the fathers of these comrades who were emerging, who had been whispering and talking to them about the good old days.[3] So when the BC movement emerged, in so far as our analysis was concerned, it could not escape the influence of the deep rooting of the ANC.

As a person who came out of prison, I immediately made contact with the other comrades and said, 'A luta continua!' [The struggle continues] and we regrouped and started operating again, and they actually received us with enthusiasm. They wanted to help politically. Some of them began to belong to the ANC underground inside South Africa whilst they were in the BCM — they were actually in ANC units inside the country. And some had to leave the country because the police were looking for them, because they'd come to find out that they were, in actual fact, ANC people. It is an open secret now that in some meetings of the BCM some of the people actually produced the Freedom Charter and said, 'Here are the solutions of this country.'

In 1975 we actually, as an underground ANC structure inside, analyzed the situation and realized that there was a political explosion coming, and our thinking was that it will come from the workers' front. To me, by the time the KwaThema bus boycott took place, in early '76 in the Transvaal, it was proving our analysis, because people were just ready to challenge the enemy. And it moved to the students — then it burst out. I must say, we did not think the explosion will occur on the student front — we missed just the sector where it was going to occur in the end. But I think we were almost on the ball.

That's the reason why, in fact, it is not a correct assertion to say 1976 just happened on its own, and that you could exclude the ANC from 1976. Certainly the students were demonstrating, but the students had had contact, and they always went back to the ANC to say, 'What do we do?' The ANC people, people like Joe Gqabi[4] at the time, were actually playing a key role in that struggle.

The explosion in South Africa's largest black township of Soweto on 16 June 1976 was sparked by a range of factors, from mandatory instruction in Afrikaans to the advent of majority rule in neighbouring Mozambique and Angola. As the unrest spread throughout the country over the next few months, seasoned ANC members offered advice and support to the inexperienced student activists.[5]

White students from Johannesburg's University of the Witwatersrand demonstrated against the killing of Soweto students by police in June 1976, carrying banners with 'krag', the Afrikaans word for power, replaced by the Zulu 'amandla'. Black workers joined in the protest while white workers attacked the demonstrators.

Sacky Madi, a member of the Soweto Students Representative Council (SSRC) who was involved in the uprising:

That was when we started knowing ANC stalwarts, during the events of June 16th. Before I left South Africa I already had serious contacts with people of the ANC. Somewhere around September I met a friend — he was a long-time friend of mine, but I was not aware that he was an ANC activist. We used to share ideas, we were together in the SSRC, but he never mentioned anything about his outside connection until the day when he decided to reveal some of his secrets. Then, well, he gave me some small duties to carry out for the ANC. During that period I was active, but not like before — I was somehow operating a little bit underground until I left the country.

When you were first exposed to the ANC point of view, was the issue of non-racialism ever raised?

I think within the ANC I learned that non-racialism should be a concept in the revolution. If I remember well, they never sat down and said, 'Now we are discussing non-racialism,' but while we discussed ANC politics you find that you are always talking about non-racialism. We used to have very serious debates about this issue. The point was, okay, if you are saying South

Africa belongs to both black and white, people used to ask the question, 'Then who is our enemy?' That was when experienced ANC stalwarts would come up and explain exactly what we mean in the ANC by non-racialism.

There were those who believed that the ANC was too liberal: why do we accept whites in our ranks? But everything was explained, that we had people like Ruth First [Slovo] – she believed in non-racialism, she was our comrade. The explanation which we got from the ANC was that the ANC, it's a movement of all genuine freedom fighters, black or white. Those who are opposed to racial discrimination and the apartheid system are welcome to participate in the ANC.

That was the theory, but in practice, those few whites who tried to get politically involved often found that the racially polarized mood of the 1970s made it hard for them to believe that they were really welcome.

Jeremy Cronin, who worked underground producing ANC literature in Cape Town from 1974 to 1976:

In the course of the early '70s I became increasingly aware of the need to link up with the underground organizations, and slowly, slowly, there were beginning to be pamphlets circulating which were produced inside the country by the ANC which made one aware of their existence underground – but in a very tenuous way, at that stage. I still remember going through the pamphlets and always being helluva relieved to find that down on the sort of third-to-last paragraph there would normally be a sentence or two saying that whites also have a role in the struggle. So in a sense, one did have a place in the struggle, one believed in it, but it was something of an abstract belief.

I found myself being in quite a lot of sympathy with Black Consciousness ideology, because at least some of what SASO was saying corresponded with my view that NUSAS was often rather liberal, rather patronizing, rather forgetful of the fact that the struggle was going to have to be led largely by black people – and thus the need to mobilize black people. But the Black Consciousness leaders were often conflating liberalism with socialism and communism and 'foreign ideologies' or whatever, and that seemed to rule us whites out.

When you first made contact with the ANC, was race an issue?

Knocking in my head was certainly that kind of motivation: to put myself on side with the broad majority of South Africans, and to throw myself in, shoulder to shoulder with them in their struggle. I think that the first thing I picked up in making the approaches that I did when I was overseas was that the ANC people were very keen to sort out and be clear that my motivations weren't primarily of that kind, that they were political motivations. They were very insistent that my task was to go back and be effective – not go back and be caught. That happened a bit in the '60s with some people, probably considerably with ARM people. There was a bit of a martyr thing: throw ourselves into the jaws of the monster, get caught, never mind, it'll show that white people are prepared to suffer and sacrifice.

Now that symbolic dimension is important, clearly, and figures like Bram Fisher and Denis Goldberg had that kind of symbolic impact on people: that whites, too, were in jail and were prepared to die, if necessary. But my major task was to be politically effective, to take the struggle forward in small ways, in so far as I was able to do it, and not to get caught and not to be a symbol.

I was instructed not to have any contact with black people — which was terrible, because I hadn't really had that possibility beforehand, and now I was being told not to do it. Now, with the development of non-racial mass organizations, contacts between blacks and whites on the left are frequent and daily, but at that stage they weren't, and to be going into townships or whatever would have marked one out and could have led to one's detection and capture. It was quite a lonely experience. Underground operatives do have the temptation of getting caught, because then all the mysteries can be revealed: friends that you've annoyed or hurt will understand all those uncomfortable kinds of psychological dynamics.

What was the reaction of the Security Police to you when you were arrested?

One of the first questions they asked me was: was I Jewish? Because that would have explained things to them. And I had quite a lot of fun evading the question, keeping them guessing and refusing to see the importance of it. And a second question they asked me, which obviously related to the first, was: was I born a communist? Because, I presume, if you're a racist the biological explains everything to you — in some way or other you must have somehow genetically inherited the predisposition. It's all rather difficult to work out if you're white. So obviously this was a question which bothered them, this business of were you born a communist. Quite how one gets to be born that, I don't know. I certainly wasn't. I was born in Durban in a naval base.

Then they were quite anxious to turn it into a bit of a show trial and to demonstrate that there were white communists behind the June 16th uprisings, the old story that blacks are contented until whites come along — white politicos with their own motivations who stir up an otherwise contented black grouping. Particularly in the Afrikaans press, there was an aura surrounding the trial that here are the arch-white fiends behind the thing, the white agitators, '*opstokers*' [instigators], Moscow's agents and that sort of thing.

Vukani — Awake, '*Published in Support of the National Liberation Movement*', *ANC pamphlet distributed inside South Africa, July 1976:*

Our freedom struggle is being waged on many fronts — one of the most important is in the field of propaganda. Propaganda counters the lies of the enemy, it develops political awareness, it inspires our people to greater efforts and it shows by concrete example that the fascist police can be outwitted in their own backyard. Each of us can play a role in distributing and making propaganda. You can help distribute by showing the revolutionary pamphlets you receive to your trusted friends. You can also leave these pamphlets in public places where others will find and read them.

Slogans are a simple but highly effective way of making propaganda. A well-placed slogan can reach hundreds of people. Slogans can be spray-painted or chalked onto walls in places where people come together — in subways and bus shelters, in trains, factories and schoolrooms. If you use spray paint, wipe the can clean of your fingerprints afterwards and throw it away, but not near to the place where you've used it.

[Jimmy] Kruger, the Minister of Police, is alarmed at the growth of our underground movement. He has boasted, like others before him, that he will root out every freedom fighter. With each slogan and sticker, with each act of propaganda, you will make Kruger's boast ring more hollow!

Revd Fumanekile Gqiba, who recalled the dissemination of ANC pamphlets in Cape Town in 1975 and 1976:

I remember some of them at Mowbray bus stop. They used to refer to them as 'bucket bombs', pamphlets that were just blown during the pick-up hour, right in the heart of town, in the main streets. They did a good work, I must say it — they really worked. There was also a heavy publicity on it, press and the like, and blacks again discover, look, the ANC's alive. And the method which was used was really sophisticated — as a result, it was said these are well-trained people. People said, 'Ah, our boys have come back,' because we were told that there are some people who went outside to train and they'll be back one day.

I had no political direction then, I just had hatred for the white man — until I met this old man, one of the greatest trade unionists of our times in that part of the world, the late Elijah Loza.[6] That hatred needed some kind of a guidance, and it was through him that the right politics were instilled in me. And then I got direction — I became a fully-fledged ANC member.

After that I stopped hating the white man just because he happened to be white. Loza taught me that that is a starting point — it's a process. You must hate, and then out of that hatred you'll build something out of it. You'll hate the system, the apartheid system — but not the man, just because he happens to be white. Being anti-white is a stage which I feel each and every individual should go through, but it's not an end it itself. We have to overcome it.

Loza used our history as our guide. He said, 'You'll find those whites from Holland who came to South Africa have nowhere to go — we have got to face that reality. Do you want to chase them to the sea?' And then he said, secondly, 'Look at South Africa, compare it with other African countries. It is well-developed. If we get rid of these people, who's going to man the infrastructure of this country? Are we not going to destroy what has been produced by both black and white?' That's why ultimately I realized that these people really belong to our country and we have to learn to live side by side with them.

When you were with Loza, did he ever use the word 'non-racialism'?

You know, Loza was a worker, he never used such terms. He would just tell you straight, 'Look, the country we are fighting for is the country where black and white will live side by side' — simple language, not this academic language.

Had you not heard much of the ANC before you met Loza?

No, there was talk about the ANC, but it was a secret for the few during that lull. Everything was crushed, it was dangerous to talk about the ANC. Even those who were involved were very suspicious of anybody. They were not prepared to dish out their political knowledge. But later, certain individuals within those cells started to reach out, and fortunately people like Loza reached out to people like us.

Did you debate political issues with friends who supported Black Consciousness?

We discussed with them, but the problem with BC people was they had no alternative. They took it as if this is an end in itself, which was not the case. The problem with the BC was that they had no programme of action. Unlike the ANC: we had the programme of action.

Ilva Mackay, a SASO activist at the University of the Western Cape who received some of the pamphlets that internal ANC units were disseminating in the mid-1970s:

I did realize that there was something more to the struggle. BC never had any political programme for how we'd work out things in the future. And I thought that once we had reached that point of cementing the unity, making black people more positive, from there we would have to move. And I think that's how a lot of people saw it as well — which is why there was no contradiction for people to join ANC from the BC organizations, because we thought it was a very natural step. I mean, here was an organization that does have a programme, and it is carrying out armed struggle.

Then at the beginning of '77 I received these ANC leaflets through the post that they were sending from inside the country. They were speaking about armed struggle, calling on people to join the people's army. My friend and I just decided, right, by the end of this year we are going to leave the country and we are going to join MK — I mean, as a direct response to what we had been receiving through the mail.

By the late 1970s, popular support for the ANC was growing to such a degree that Black Consciousness leaders began investigating the potential for forging more tangible links with the movement. The catalyst for the arrest of Steve Biko by the Security Police in 1977 — and his subsequent torture and death — was the government's fear of this impending rapprochement with the ANC.[7]

Barney Pityana, one of Biko's closest colleagues, SASO president in 1970 and then banned from 1973 until 1978, when he fled South Africa:

It was obvious by 1976 that many members of the BC — who by then were beginning to say, 'Where is this BC taking us to?' — had rightly felt that when they left the country they would become members of MK or ANC. Already as long ago as 1972, that's when for the first time chaps from SASO left the country and joined ANC. And so the moves that Steve Biko and I and others were making in 1977 towards ANC were really the beginnings of a wider process of seeding alliances between the ongoing struggle at home and how the resources and the expertise and the infiltration from overseas were to work with that.

What actually caused this move in the first place was the fact that many of our chaps who left the country in '75, '76 didn't join PAC – at that stage they went to join ANC. So that within ANC there were many people in BC who were beginning to find a different way of working, with a commitment to coming back home. There was a link there. But the second thing is that ANC was demonstrably, visibly, the more viable of the two organizations. It seemed to be the one anyone who was serious about liberation would talk to.

In fact, in 1976 guys were sent to Robben Island[8] and in large measure the evidence against them was actually drawn from this ongoing debate. That's where the system appears to have got the idea that they were preparing to be engaged in subversive activity, and that the Viva Frelimo rallies were the first step in this major campaign that was about to be launched. As it happened, that was premature, because actually it was just an internal debate at that time. I don't think there were any big plans.

After you left South Africa, why did you then get involved with an external BC grouping?

In the early '80s, the BCM was calling together all the people who were abroad who were actively engaged in and committed to the BC movement and ideals. This was really working towards a major conference, which I was involved in planning for, which would help articulate where these BC people abroad saw their future and how they saw BC proceeding. Some of us had had a meeting with ANC in December 1979 in Lusaka, and we were hoping to proceed to Lesotho and brief people about possible moves and discussions that had taken place with ANC.

I wasn't pro-BCM because I had rejected ANC. I desired that we find a way, a vision of enabling BC people to work with ANC. At this time, BCM was not an organization as such – we were just working out certain lines for the future. So we had what I thought was an excellent meeting with ANC. We were extremely well received and ANC outlined very clearly what their position was towards BCM. But going back to report this to the BC people, I felt an amazing and unacceptable level of hostility to ANC as such – which I felt was totally unacceptable, because it seemed to me it was totally irrational. And it seemed to me that several people who called themselves BCM had moved, and now had political ideals that I wasn't part of any more. So that's when I left BCM and said I wouldn't have any more to do with it. I felt it was unacceptable to be opposed to the ANC just for the sake of it.

And then did you join ANC?

I didn't join ANC because I felt I never un-joined ANC. From the time I was in Lesotho [after fleeing South Africa], I'd always been in touch and contact and participating in the work of ANC. I don't think ANC – and to their credit – ever wanted to badger everybody to become ANC, but they wanted to find a working relationship.

Of the Black Consciousness activists who remained politically active after leaving South Africa, most eventually joined the ANC. Others maintained their BC ideology and identity without any further alignment, and a small minority linked up with the PAC.

Excerpts from PAC publications.

Henry Isaacs, a SASO leader who left South Africa in 1974 and studied in New Zealand, then joined the PAC in 1976, becoming its Foreign Affairs representative in the US from 1978 until his resignation in 1982:

The BC movement, in a sense, revived the PAC. We in the BC movement were critical of the ANC, mainly because the organization had been in existence for so long, but had failed to effect any meaningful change in South Africa. We appreciated the difficulties under which they operated, but our major criticism was that the leadership of the ANC had restrained the membership, and throughout the history of the ANC, as we interpreted it, the leadership was really afraid of preparing or mobilizing the masses for confrontation with the system. For this reason, I think that amongst very many of the early activists within the BC movement there was greater sympathy for the PAC, which within a short period of its existence had precipitated a confrontation which resulted in the Sharpeville massacre.

This did not mean that we blindly supported the PAC or accepted very many of its basic premises. For one, we were aware of the black racism of the PAC and the fact that in so far as the PAC was concerned, it regarded so-called coloureds, Asians, and whites as foreign minorities, despite whatever occasional rhetoric there might be from one or two individual leaders within the PAC.

The major criticism of the PAC was the fact that it provoked a confrontation without sufficient political preparation having been done, so that after the detention of the major leadership and the proscription of the organization, it in fact ceased to exist. But I think that the major attraction that the PAC offered at the time was the whole emphasis of black leadership in the liberation struggle, and the need to free blacks psychologically from the feelings of inferiority.

Was your analysis of ANC versus PAC influenced by a rejection of white involvement?

Yes, the whole question of white involvement in the struggle did play a major role in our thinking at that particular time. The perception we had of the ANC was of white leadership and behind-the-scenes influence far out of proportion to the small number of whites who were actually involved in the struggle. I think it was exaggerated — I'd be the first to admit that.

By then we all recognized the fact that the PAC was weak, but then we had this mistaken belief that if the PAC could be injected with young blood and talent from the BC movement, the organization might be revived, so that it would once more become a viable factor in the liberation struggle. When I met the de facto representative of the PAC in Swaziland, where he was working for Coca Cola, he told me, 'Oh, we have about 20,000 men in training right now.' I was immediately sceptical, but I genuinely believed that the PAC had a sizeable number of people, waiting for the opportunity to return.

I think the PAC tried very hard at that particular time to recruit BCM people, because they saw in the ideas that were being propagated by BCM people an ideological affinity with what they were themselves saying. But then later on they began to argue that the BCM was really a continuation of the work that they had started — which was again both historically and academically untrue.

Well, I continued in the leadership of the PAC for several years, and I became very, very much aware of the fact that the organization existed purely as a small number of people in exile who had no connection whatsoever to what was going on inside the country and that there was no programme for the execution of armed struggle, despite the rhetoric. One legacy of the PAC's short history within the country was the fact that it had failed to develop any organizational structures in the country or in exile. It existed basically as a conglomerate of individuals, and I think that that largely explains the perennial problems within the PAC, and also its ineffectiveness.

What I underestimated was the capacity of an organization that had existed for so long in that state of confusion to resist any change, particularly by older leaders who had no means of support but the continued existence of the organization. They resisted any effort, particularly by the younger members, to bring about any changes that would threaten their positions.

The majority of Black Consciousness supporters who remained in South Africa after the 1977 crackdown eventually moved beyond BC to embrace non-racialism. The transformation was most profound for those arrested, tried and sentenced to serve time on Robben Island,[9] for there they encountered the imprisoned ANC leadership.

Ebrahim Ebrahim, who spent from 1964 to 1979 on Robben Island for Umkhonto we Sizwe activities, recalled the political debates that ensued when new prisoners came in following the 1976 uprising:

The authorities decided to separate them from us, the ANC — we were expected to have a bad influence on them — but the warders couldn't handle these young boys, you see, so they decided then to mix them with us. They were fascinating, they had very sharp minds, were very keen to learn, but they had adopted an outspoken non-historical approach to the struggle. We had to clarify their ideas on a number of issues: on the nature of our struggle, on national liberation, liberation of other groups, and so on. Most of them did not know the history of the Congress movement — they had just been caught up in these uprisings. Many of them were able to pick up very fast the revolutionary thinking and the historical background of the struggle.

When they left prison they became the leaders of the struggle today. So what was the purpose of this imprisonment? It was not a deterrent — it became a school of revolution. It hardened you, it made you more conscious, it matured you. People came in with a lot of funny ideas, but when they left prison they were in a position to give leadership and direction to the struggle. As more and more people returned from the Island, the whole struggle was strengthened.

Patrick Lekota, a SASO founder member who was sentenced in 1976, along with eight other Black Consciousness leaders, to six years on Robben Island:

I regard my days in SASO as my formative years, politically. We saw the struggle strictly in terms of one race versus another race. We were deprived of the wealth of the heritage of struggle which others who had gone before us had already amassed. We moved into this as virgins, completely. We were bound, therefore, to commit mistakes, in terms of judgment.

So how did your views change such that you now support non-racialism?

That began to happen, in particular, in the period of my arrest. We were arrested with men who were blacks like ourselves, men with whom we had shared platforms and campaigned together against apartheid. But it was precisely from among those men that some of them took the witness stand, side by side with the South African Security Police, and condemned us and sent us to jail. And then there was also the case of Anthony Holiday, who happened to have been arrested at the same time we were on trial in '76, with a black man. The irony of that case is that Holiday, a white man, stuck to his opposition to apartheid to the end, and the black man abandoned him, joined sides with the Security Police, and testified against him.

And then there were men like Bram Fischer, who at the time was serving a life sentence. And he died a prisoner for opposing apartheid because he did not approve of what his own people were doing to us. There was Beyers Naude, himself an outstanding Afrikaner, a man who had reached very high positions within the NGK [Dutch Reformed Church] and then the Broeder-bond. He had been ostracized by his own people — they had actually banned and restricted him.

Now I felt it was high time that one really reflected carefully as to whether the struggle for justice in this country can be pursued only by people of dark skin colour, or whether, in fact, this was a struggle of those who were committed to justice — never mind the colour of their skin — and those who were committed to injustice. And then later on I was to come across a statement which Mandela read to the Rivonia trial in '64, in which he made it quite clear that he was committed to a struggle against white domination and black domination. That was quite intriguing.

Was your acceptance of non-racialism also related to your adoption of a class analysis of the South African situation?

Oh yes, quite definitely. It is true that the majority of capitalists in our country would come from the white grouping, just as it is true that the majority of the working class will come from the African section of the population of our country — but it is also true that within the African grouping itself there are people who are middle-class elements.

Every one of the racial groupings in our country actually has a number of classes, and within those classes you'll find stratification. Capital in our country has won to its side a number of people from within the working class, and even from amongst our own people, who would make common cause with capitalism. One would be unrealistic to imagine that all white people are capitalists and all black people are workers — it's a distortion of the reality that is in front of us.

Fortunately for me, I was sentenced, and that gave me an opportunity in the period I spent on Robben Island to meet Mandela and to question him a little bit more deeply. It was from discussions with the freedom fighters of our people, who are committed to a free, non-racial and democratic South Africa, that I broadened my understanding of the issues involved.

All of us who embrace the non-racial line do so not because there are some white people participating in the struggle — we embrace the non-racial line, first and foremost, because we consider it to be right. So that even if there were not white people participating in the struggle, even if there were no Bram Fischers, we would still say it is wrong to judge any man by the colour of his skin. The participation of white democrats in the struggle in our country is only evidence of the correctness of our non-racial approach — not that the correctness of non-racialism is predicated upon them participating.

Notes

1. A leader of the Nation of Islam and the US Black Power movement who was assassinated in 1964.
2. Joe Slovo, exiled leader of high rank in the ANC, Umkhonto we Sizwe and SACP, a member of the liberation movement from the 1950s to the present.
3. For example, SASO leader Diliza Mji's father (of the same name) had been president of the Transvaal ANC Youth League.
4. An ANC activist from the 1950s who immediately got involved with the Soweto students when he was released from Robben Island, Gqabi was tried for his alleged role in the 1976 uprising, acquitted, and fled into exile. In 1981 he was assassinated in Zimbabwe, where he was the ANC's chief representative.
5. The Soweto student leadership also comprised elements not aligned with the ANC: a press release issued by SSRC leader Khotso Seatlholo, 29 October 1976, describes whites as 'sadists who derive satisfaction in the shedding of human blood — they are worse than communists'.
6. A former Western Cape SACTU leader who died in Security Police custody in 1977.
7. ANC President Tambo's NEC report to the ANC's 1985 Consultative Conference cited Biko's contact with the ANC as a contributing factor to his detention and death. In an interview with *Wits Student*, April 1987, exposed Security Police spy Craig Williamson admitted that his tip-off to the authorities about a planned meeting between Biko and the ANC (which Williamson was involved in organizing) probably prompted Biko's arrest. Williamson said he regretted the 'debacle' of Biko's detention and death because it 'was something that closed doors earlier than they should have been closed'.
8. The nine key SASO and BPC leaders arrested with the banning of the 1974 pro-Frelimo rallies and convicted under the Terrorism Act for 'creating and fostering feelings of racial hatred, hostility and antipathy by the blacks toward the white population group of the Republic' were: Patrick Lekota, Pandelani Nefolovhodwe (both interviewed in this book), Saths Cooper, Zithulele Cindi, Aubrey Mokoape, Strini Moodley, Muntu Myeza, Nkwenke Nkomo and Kaborane Sedibe.
9. In addition to the older BC leaders, who were mainly university students, many young blacks, largely secondary school students with only tenuous political affiliations, were jailed for several years for 'public violence' during the 1976 unrest.

15 A Very Obvious Contradiction

A wave of strikes in Durban in early 1973 — the biggest since the Second World War — signalled the end of a decade-long lull in activity among ever-growing numbers of black urban workers.[1] The reinvigoration of the trade union movement sparked by those strikes gained valuable support from white intellectuals. In their academic writings they had challenged the traditional liberal assumption that a 'rational' capitalism would erode 'irrational' apartheid. In the unions they were drawing the crucial links between South Africa's economic, social and political structures, and introducing workers to new forms of mobilization and organization.

Alec Erwin, a former academic who taught workers at the Institute of Industrial Education (IIE),[2] established in Durban in 1973:

My feeling that workers were central arose from my realization that, in fact, you had to restructure the economy if you were going to overcome the problems of underdevelopment. The change in historiography that was initiated in the '70s — looking at South Africa not just in terms of race, but looking at the economic structures that evolved, why migrant labour was so important to gold mines and how it totally reshaped the society — made it clear to me that the only way, in the long run, that this was going to change was through worker organization. Then when it came to unions as such, what we were looking at was to try and organize workers in a different way to the existing unions — organize them on the shop floor, organize them as participating in the unions as much as possible.

With regard to whites as such, white intellectuals were accepted in the organization for what they could offer and bring to it, so people would say, 'Look, the fact that you are white mustn't block you from coming in, if you can bring something useful.' Then it became clear that in the wider arena, racism is not the answer — that we should take a non-racial position.

What was it like, moving from teaching white students to dealing with black workers?

Very definitely the worker stuff is much more exciting, more challenging. People were so keen to learn, and the problems they presented you were very much more difficult ones. Shop stewards would come and present a complaint in the factory and fairly soon it became clear that, in fact, shop stewards had as many ideas themselves, and it was possibly a mistake for them to ask you to give advice.

So the challenge, I think, was to link the answers that shop stewards had to wider perspectives. We'd talk about worker history, history of South Africa, and there I would use the information I'd gathered in reading at the university — because much of that history would also be new for black people because they had been given old, distorted history. Endless discussion was what taught you, and interaction in this discussion.

Let's take a problem about the role of supervisors, that supervisors are shits. Then you go on to ask, 'Well what is the job the supervisor's doing, why's he got to do it so strictly?' Or, 'Why are management pushing you so hard?' And from there you could work to a question of the role of profits. You can try and take workers away from just a perception that the supervisor himself as a person is a shit, and you try and move it into profits, and then from profits move it to a wider assessment of class. So instead of dealing with class in the abstract, which you would do with white students, here you would deal with concrete issues and try and elucidate those issues in terms of class.

Were there no anti-white or Black Consciousness views that hampered your interaction with black workers?

I think the first point that's very important to realize is that amongst black workers BC was not a force at all. You had a tremendous tolerance by black

The Trade Union is made up of workers	Lekhotla la Basebetsi	*iBandla laba Basebenzi ibutho laba sebenzayo*
who join together because	le etsoa ke basebetsi hobane	*bebuthana ngoba benezindingo*
they have the same needs	seo ba se hlokang sea tsoana	*nezinxakeko ezifanavo*

These educational cartoons in English, Sotho and Zulu were produced by the Urban Training Project (UTP), formed in Johannesburg in 1971 as a church-supported labour training centre by white officials fired by the segregated Trade Union Council of South Africa (TUCSA). The worker support groups formed after the 1973 Durban strikes involved a new generation of radical whites from the universities, and laid a new emphasis on grassroots organization.

workers towards whites — even though they realize that it was whites giving them a hard time. And I feel that that arises out of their position in factories, where they can see that there's something bigger than just the whites that were suppressing them. They could see in the factory the black supervisors, black personnel people starting to rise in the '70s, and I think it was very obvious to them that a factory worked more than on just whiteness. On the other hand, that kind of more assertive feeling that BC had developed amongst students wasn't there amongst black workers.

The influence of Natal University politics lecturer Rick Turner on a small circle of concerned students in the early 1970s led to the formation of a Wages and Economics Commission, a group which facilitated student involvement in labour issues.[3] NUSAS then set up Wages Commissions on other white campuses: members in Durban set up the General Factory Workers' Benefit Fund; in Johannesburg, the Industrial Aid Society; and in Cape Town, the Western Province Workers' Advice Bureau.

Zora Mehlomakhulu, a former SACTU official in Cape Town:

Well, the political organizations were crushed and they went underground, but all the same there were things like the trade unions, and that sort of remained a voice of the people. SACTU collapsed as a result of a lot of pressure from the government, but it only collapsed for a period of about three years — from 1969 to '72. In 1972 things started towards forming something for the workers, and in '73 the new union was born out of ex-trade unionists that were banned and house arrested[4] and who actually felt that workers were defenceless. Something had to take place in the line of helping workers organize, and how that was going to take place, nobody actually had the right pattern. So our beginning was starting it as a small advice bureau, that was our springboard.

And at that time as well, there was a project at University of Cape Town called the Wages Commission. Now the Wages Commission was also doing a survey on conditions of workers, and we needed a base which was actually getting workers organized and seeing to their day-to-day complaints. So we actually started the project with a lot of help from the Wages Commission, which actually had white students. And ever since then the workers I am dealing with knew nothing else but that appreciation of a white skin working and sacrificing for a black trade union struggle.

Did you ever get the feeling that the authorities thought whites were 'agitating' behind the scenes?

Yes, from the interrogations, the questioning that I used to get when I was detained. They didn't think of the people who actually said the union must be formed — they all thought it was a university move, a band of communists that were wanting to take over, and that they were using me for this. Because we were working together, black and white — we started the union together, you know.

Willie Hofmeyr, one of 26 people (more than half of whom were white)[5] banned in 1976 because of their work with the emergent trade unions:

To some extent, it was easier for white intellectuals to go in and do it, because there's always a very obvious contradiction. The white intellectuals could never pretend that they were the leaders of whatever would emerge. There was, I think, a fairly constant awareness that leadership needed to be assumed by the workers. We had certain kinds of resources that we could offer, and we wanted to try and strengthen what little there was of a union movement at that stage. The idea was that hopefully we would phase ourselves out.

I think it's important for whites to be involved in the struggle, but I think there's a real need to be aware of the problems of white domination, which can happen helluva easily. For me, domination by intellectuals is really the problem.

These various student-supported benefit and aid societies played a kind of midwife role in the birth of the 'independent' trade union movement of the 1970s — independent from statutory labour bodies and multi-racial union federations like the Trade Union Council of South Africa (TUCSA). In Cape Town, the advice bureau became the General Workers Union (GWU). In Durban, the new unions joined together as the Trade Union Advisory and Coordinating Council (TUACC), which grew into the Federation of South African Trade Unions (FOSATU) in 1979, the first national non-racial union federation since SACTU.

A basic conviction that all these new unions shared was that of non-racialism. In theory, this meant that they were open to workers of all races, but in practice, the rank-and-file membership was black, while some of the top officials were white.

'A Non-racial Trade Union Movement', from a policy resolution of the FOSATU executive, 1979:

FOSATU believes that the workers' struggle in South Africa cannot succeed without the elimination of racism, but that the elimination of racism will not by itself end the workers' struggle. FOSATU is therefore opposed to all racist legislation that denies fundamental democratic and human rights to the majority of people in our society. We are opposed to laws such as the Group Areas Act, Immorality Act, Mixed Marriages Act, pass laws, etc. FOSATU is therefore opposed to all forms of discrimination based on race, sex or creed within our movement. FOSATU is committed to building a strong independent trade union movement that can act and speak in the interests of workers. FOSATU's priority is the unionization of that great majority of unskilled and semi-skilled black workers who benefit least from our wealth and bear the greatest burden of racial oppression. Any person or organization of workers that shares our aims and objects is welcome in our ranks, irrespective of their race, sex or creed.

FOSATU
WORKER NEWS
Federation of South African Trade Unions

AUGUST 1983 NUMBER 23

AT 4.30 pm on Monday June 27 the first legal strike for many years began at Natal Thread at Hammarsdale.

Nine days later the company acknowledged its defeat and negotiated a settlement with the National Union of Textile Workers.

The Natal Thread workers not only won a 15c an hour wage increase with back pay (a wage dispute had been the cause of the strike) but they also won the effective right to strike.

In South Africa, after going through lengthy legal procedures workers can go on a legal strike.

No dismissal

This means that they do not face criminal prosecution for striking but does not protect them from being fired by the company.

In terms of the Natal Thread victory, the company agreed that in a legal strike it would 'either dismiss all such strikers or none of them'.

It also agreed that 'in the event of the company having dismissed the strikers it would only either re-employ all of them or none of them'.

This agreement is similar to British labour law where workers have won legal protection for strikers.

This agreement protects strikers from dismissal because it is highly unlikely that a company would fire the entire factory as it would have to train a completely new workforce from scratch.

Also, if the company takes back one of the strikers, it has to take back them all.

First success

This makes the Natal Thread strike the first successful legal strike in recent labour history in South Africa.

The strike was marked by the solidarity and discipline of the 400 odd workers involved.

For five hours a day machines, which usually thudded all day long in the factory, were silent.

At 4.30 in the morning and afternoon, the shift workers closed down their machines.

The machines remained silent until the next shift arrived at 7 and then began the long process of starting machines designed to run continuously.

Understanding

NUTW branch secretary, Prof Sineke said although the day shift had not been involved in the strike, there had been sufficient understanding among the workers not to cause division.

Through the strike, Natal Thread lost a full week's production — costing the company thousands of Rands.

Fair bargaining

But the workers won a significant worker right — the right to strike without the fear of selective hiring or firing.

This is surely a step towards a better and fair collective bargaining system. Let us hope that more employers follow the lead set by Natal Thread.

THE RIGHT TO STRIKE

The smile of a winner — Natal Thread workers.

THE Natal Thread agreement marks another step toward winning an effective and legal right to strike for the workers of South Africa.

As we have seen over recent years workers will strike even when the law says it is illegal if they feel they have no other choice. However a strike is very costly for workers and the decision to strike is never an easy one.

Because the strike is such an important weapon of workers in the unequal struggle with employers they have also to fight to get legal protection. We want to change the moral right to strike into a legal right to strike as well.

This legal right to strike is important because it offers greater protection to strikers and allows them to use the strike weapon with more discipline and less risk of violence.

There are certain very important matters which together would create this legal right to strike. They are:

— The right to free and independent organisation
— Effective collective bargaining procedures that quickly resolve differences and disputes
— The right to picketting during a strike i.e. the right to persuade workers not to enter the gate
— The right and ability to pay strike pay
— Protection against dismissal during a strike.

In South Africa there are two reasons why we don't yet have this right. Firstly the Labour Relations Act procedures are so slow that they encourage 'illegal' strikes. Secondly even though the Labour Relations Act provides for legal strikes in which there can be picketting and strike pay other acts such as Internal Security and Intimidation are used to prevent these provisions being effective.

Despite this gains are made. The FOSATU type recognition agreements with shop stewards, and procedures for grievances, discipline, negotiations and disputes have improved the collective bargaining position of the unions.

The Natal Thread Agreement tackled the problem of dismissal. It is the usual practice of employers in illegal and legal strikes to dismiss all workers and then selectively reemploy those that they want back which usually excludes strong members and shop stewards.

The Agreement prevents such selective dismissal and reemployment during a legal strike so management now have a choice of dismissing all workers permanently or dismissing none.

This is not such an easy choice and gives workers a fighting chance in their struggle for a more equal balance of power in collective bargaining.

In the first legal strike for many years, Natal Thread workers won a significant worker right

One of the important contributions of students and whites to the independent trade union movement was in assisting the development of worker-controlled media.

Chris Dlamini, a shop steward at a factory in Springs, on the East Rand, who was elected FOSATU president in 1982:

Was there ever any criticism of the white union officials from the black union members?

Yes, well, there were a lot of criticisms levelled onto the white leadership. Some people felt that they didn't want to address themselves to the present situation, like the community problems — they were not directly wanting to get themselves involved in that. Some of them felt that you've got to maintain your trade union identity so you cannot get yourself involved in such things. Some of the whites felt like that.[6]

When I first started working, the unions were not very strong and what I heard at that time was that the unions are going to fight against the whites. I didn't feel that whites should belong to our union because they represented the oppressor, so I didn't have anything to do with the white man.

Had you never heard of any of the whites who had been involved in building trade unions in the past?

Well, I only read about those, but to me they looked like they were sell-outs, they were in this organization in order to get information for the government. This is how I understood things at that time.

When you were detained, did you sense that the police didn't like the fact that there were white officials in your union?

Yes. In fact, the interrogation was directed at saying that I've got to change because I was being used by the ANC and that kind of stuff. They said a lot about the white officials — that they were in the unions to misdirect us and they were using the ideas of communism through us, so we've got to be careful about them.[7] Well, everybody knows that with the government, anything that is against it is communist, so immediately they start to say that we know that that is the right stuff.

So you didn't come out of detention feeling anti-white in any way?

No, I only came out of detention feeling anti-police. If you look at what is happening in the townships right now, black and white policemen are the ones assaulting children, and sometimes it's worse with the black cops.

How did your non-racial views develop?

The change came about this way: when one started to look at the envisaged society. The society that you would be looking for, if you were progressive, would be a non-racial society. If you waged the struggle on a class struggle basis then it makes things easier, and at the same time you tend to win support from other countries and you tend to build relationships with other trade unions abroad.

How did you get acquainted with concepts like class struggle?

I started reading and I started to understand: it is not apartheid that makes us suffer, but apartheid as a form, covering the whole concept of capitalism. What I'm saying is, before 1982 we still had the Black Consciousness ideology in our minds, and I believed that whites were sell-outs because they were part and parcel of the oppressor.

And how did you feel about the whites who helped start FOSATU with you?

We were very suspicious of them, in fact. Although we accepted them in the federation, I did not believe that I can expose anything that I thought was secret to any of them. I would say most of the younger guys like ourselves, they shared the view of BC. It's only now that it's diminishing, people are moving more and more on to the progressive line. It's now spread out, it's a line that has been taken by the majority of the people, and it is not only challenging the apartheid system, but it's challenging capitalism as well. So the dangers are very high in a progressive line.

The workers that we represent, they support non-racialism, but sometimes if you can sit down with an ordinary member you would find that there is still an element of BC in his kind of thinking. And one cannot blame a worker for this, because it derives from the fact that in the plant where he works or she works, she is faced with the problem of whites being supervisors or foremen and the ill-treatment that one receives would be from whites. So although they support the idea of progressive politics, the element of BC still prevails in some people's minds.

What we try to say to people is that even though your boss is a conservative kind of Afrikaner or whatever, there are whites who are progressive and who are enlightened and who are sympathetic to our struggle. So to completely close the doors and say you don't want whites, you'd be closing doors even to people who could be committed to supporting our struggle.

Alfred Temba Qabula, a former migrant worker from Pondoland who joined one of the FOSATU unions that emerged in the 1970s, the Metal and Allied Workers Union (MAWU):

It was the first time to see the whites helping the black people to their organization. Then I had to ask them carefully what they're up to — I had to satisfy myself. Then they explained carefully for me. They said this is a non-racial union, everyone is free to join. It doesn't matter if it's a white or black or coloured or Indian — everyone is free to join.

> That freedom was not without its tensions, for both the blacks and the whites who were consolidating this new, non-racial trade unionism in the 1980s. Many believed that these tensions stemmed from language and cultural barriers — inevitably race-related. Others argued that differences in class and intellectual backgrounds were at the core.

Peter Mahlangu, an organizer for the independent South African Allied Workers Union (SAAWU), formed in 1979 as a breakaway from the Black Consciousness-supporting Black Allied Workers Union (BAWU):

I think there's an unwillingness from some people to learn the languages of other people, and I think that's a hindrance. I'm saying this because we used to meet people who only could speak Zulu, because that's how they feel comfortable — yet I have these other comrades who can't hear what they are talking about. And there's no willingness from their side to learn. Those are some of the things that I used to discuss with comrades, that, 'Look here, Africans are in the majority and you better learn to relate to them.'

Again, it reflects that when people think of a future South Africa, they still think of it in their own terms — but that means an unpreparedness to change. I think there is quite a lot to be overcome. The fact is that you cannot be able to work with people if you don't want to get rid of some of your own hang-ups. I still had those hang-ups that other comrades are better off than me. Those are some of the things that can cause some kind of friction — sometimes unfounded.

Dave Lewis, GWU General-Secretary from 1980 to 1986:

How I, as a white, function is important, there's no doubt about it, and how I, as a white, relate to black workers is important, but my position as an intellectual is actually a more interesting contradiction that has to be resolved. It wouldn't make any difference if my name was Sox Quthole, who's my sidekick in the union, if you like, but also an intellectual. His role is as fraught with complexity and angst as mine is, and I think that a great problem that I have with many white intellectuals — and it arises partly as a result of the sort of guilt that we experience — is that they do not do that which they are best qualified to do, and that is to be intellectuals.

They are only too willing to toe a line, because they don't feel that it's legitimate for them, as whites, to say anything in black organizations, in black

Striking black workers in Mpophomeni, Natal being briefed by a white official of the National Union of Metalworkers of South Africa (NUMSA).

South Africa. You can't assert yourself. To my mind, that's absolutely reactionary, and there's a lot of that sort of stuff that goes around in white left-wing politics in South Africa. Some white intellectuals are embarrassed at their ability to understand, to articulate, and they don't do that which they are best qualified to do. They think that the only work that is valuable is organizing.

My ability to be able to write and articulate the way I do has been a function of the kind of privileges that have been granted to me because I'm a white South African, and I still think that my primary way of paying back some of this is to use that, is to say, 'Look, I've great respect for your organization, but I think you're heading in the wrong direction. I may be right or I may be wrong in my assessment, but nevertheless this is what I think, based on sort of ten years of reading Althusser[8] and Lenin and bloody newspapers.' I think that part of the guilt of being a white South African is that the minute you get involved in realpolitik, you feel that you can't say anything because you haven't really experienced it, and you are, after all, part of the oppressors. I don't buy that.

Notes

1. An even earlier signal came from Namibia in 1971—72, when 20,000 migrant workers staged a strike; it was crushed by the South African army, at a cost of six lives and hundreds of arrests.
2. Finally brought under union control in 1976, when it became a sub-committee of the umbrella body of the new independent unions, the IIE's most lasting success was its founding of the *South African Labour Bulletin*, a journal that (like *Work in Progress* and *Social Review*, also inspired by white intellectuals) played an important role in both academic and popular political circles.
3. It was Turner's role as a political catalyst for young whites that many believe led to his assassination by unknown gunmen in 1978, shortly before his banning order was due to expire. Veteran unionist Harriet Bolton of the Garment Workers' Industrial Union initially approached Turner with the idea of encouraging white students to assist with the organization of African workers.
4. Elijah Loza was another of the former SACTU figures who helped launch the Western Province Workers' Advice Bureau.
5. Most of those banned had been involved with TUACC, the Urban Training Project (that later led to the formation of the Council of Unions of South Africa, CUSA), the Industrial Aid Society, the incipient Metal and Allied Workers Union (MAWU-Transvaal), and the revived Food and Canning Workers Union. Hofmeyr was among six white UCT students banned for their work with the Wages Commission.
6. Note that this assessment was made by Dlamini in an interview in 1985, and since it is a view associated with the pre-COSATU era, before the 1985—86 uprisings, the comment has been put into the past tense to avoid the impression that this criticism of white intellectuals continues to be widely held.
7. Ironically, many of the whites active in the unions in the 1970s shared a political perspective that was critical of the ANC and the SACP.
8. The work of white left intellectuals in the 1970s and early 1980s was heavily influenced by the structuralist Marxism of Louis Althusser, Nicos Poulantzas and others. With the increasing involvement of whites in concrete political activity, most moved away from a preoccupation with abstract theory (useful as it was in helping to characterize the structure of the state and the political economy of South Africa) towards a more flexible, pragmatic analysis of class, power and popular struggle.

16 The Most I Can Do is Be the Least Obstruction

The government was not about to stand by and watch a small core of progressive white intellectuals link up with emerging black worker organizations. The state response came in the form of a protracted enquiry pegged to the time-worn claim that whites were inciting black revolution.

Conclusion of Schlebusch Commission Report on NUSAS, 7 December 1973: [1]

No one can deny that it is good and desirable that the standard of living of South Africa's working class should be raised so that all will be able to lead a decent life. In the case of NUSAS's actions, however, certain other considerations come into play. It is clear that the upliftment of the Bantu worker is not their principal aim. It is one of the special issues around which agitation has to be built up in accordance with the lessons in the technique of successful incitement and agitation which NUSAS leaders went to learn in Europe and the United States of America.

NUSAS's action in this connection is really a means to another end, and that is political change to overthrow the existing order in South Africa and to replace it with an anti-capitalistic system which has sometimes been described as 'black socialism'. This has to be brought about by stirring up industrial and labour unrest and by inciting black and white against each other, and eventually by inciting them to conflict, even violent conflict, against each other.

This situation is fraught with dangers to which the Commission feels constrained to draw the attention of Parliament and the government. The possibility of dangerous outbursts must always be borne in mind, and this calls for constant vigilance and readiness for quick action, coupled with sustained imaginative and determined action to eliminate unhealthy economic conditions. The Commission was convinced by the evidence that people and organizations are encouraging arms boycotts and economic boycotts against South Africa as part of an attempt to bring about radical change in the existing political order. The Commission is of the opinion that this is a form of subversion of the state and recommends that steps be taken to combat it.

The Schlebusch Commission succeeded in scaring off potential NUSAS supporters and demoralizing NUSAS members. In accordance with the commission's recommendations, student leaders were banned, detained, deprived of their passports and deported. NUSAS was declared an 'affected organization' that could receive no foreign funding, and several white campuses renounced their NUSAS affiliation.[2] Young white progressives had never felt so isolated and immobilized.

'The Fantastical History of a Useless Man', play workshopped by the Junction Avenue Theatre Company, first performed by students at the University of the Witwatersrand, 20 September 1976:[3]

(Blackout. A spot comes up on four figures representing different sectors of bourgeois society.)

FIRST FIGURE: Offer! Advertising! Position, wealth, status! A studio of your own! Provided that for our money you give us your art.

USELESS MAN: You don't want art. You want manipulation. Creating false needs in people who cannot afford to buy necessities. Reducing everything to a commodity. I reject your offer with contempt.

SECOND FIGURE: Offer! Journalism! A career! Articulate opposition to the government. Part of a young, dynamic work force.

USELESS MAN: A newspaper owned by business will not criticize business.

THIRD FIGURE: Offer! Teach in a progressive school!

USELESS MAN: Provide education for an elite to take up the reins of business and management? A progressive school presupposes a radically changed society.

FOURTH FIGURE: Offer! Law! Assist in the maintenance of the rule of law. Temper justice with mercy! Radical law!

USELESS MAN: Radical law: contradiction in terms. Maintaining the rule of law simply means that the system obeys its own rules — rules made by its rulers. Tempering justice with mercy — impossible! The system is founded on oppression and exploitation.

(The lights fade as the figures silently move aside, to reveal a machine gun.)

COMPERE: What are you prepared to do?

(Watched by the figures, the Useless Man crosses the stage. He reaches to take the gun but is unable to take it. He turns away and the group of actors collapse on to the floor in cramped, grotesque positions.)

USELESS MAN: There is going to be a war, a war between those who have power and wealth and will not relinquish it, and the broad mass of the people who live voiceless at the edge of poverty. What I have I would willingly give up to avoid that war, but I am a dreamer and a fool. The class that sheltered me from violence now leads me to violence. Many people I know are gearing themselves — willing that war. In their bloodlust they are buying guns and preparing shelters and making emergency preparations.

They will bar up their wealth and their lives rather than share them.

And there are those who wish to alleviate oppression and suffering without themselves giving. They refuse to understand the relationship between their wealth and another's deprivation. These men are White Men. White is not a colour. White is an attitude. And myself. I am a coward and a useless man — the most I can do is be the least obstruction.[4]

If radical white English-speaking students felt useless, politically aware Afrikaners experienced that alienation even more acutely.

Breyten Breytenbach, a writer and artist who left South Africa in 1960 and settled in Paris following his marriage to a Vietnamese woman, returned clandestinely in 1975 to try to recruit white progressives to a proposed white liberation movement, was arrested and served seven years in prison:

All the way through, in my own political thinking and in the translation of this thinking into forms of action, there was this one given element of being an Afrikaans writer. And I rejected that fairly early on. I could not agree to being an Afrikaner in any accepted definition of that term, because obviously if you're going to say it's only a matter of language, then it cannot be white only. If you say it's a matter of certain political beliefs, including religious beliefs, then I disagree with those so violently that I couldn't consider myself an Afrikaner.

But I couldn't stop being an Afrikaner myself. Not that there's a deep urge in me to be one — it is a condition, it is that. I express myself through that bloody language. And it is not at all the possession of those who think they control the language — it's becoming something else. For me, Afrikaans is a very beautiful tool and I watch it with great interest to see how it's moving. It's a creole language. It'll keep on being bastardized, and developing. Fine.

Part of my contradiction is concretely reflected in the type of confrontation I had with the Security Police: being interrogated in Afrikaans, for instance, with the complicity that that immediately implies. They don't see me as an opponent — they see me as a traitor. If they have a black activist in their hands, he's an opponent. He cannot possibly be a traitor. They would do the same thing if they were black.

If they have an English-speaking white, they can justify or understand his being in opposition through many other reasons. He's probably of Jewish descent, therefore he's, as far as they are concerned, genetically against them — you know all the justifications. Then even the Boer War would come in, all the rest of it. It's the class distinction. 'He's a rich bloody Englishman. He's a spoilt city brat. He's gone to university. He's a cosmopolitan. He's been exposed to international ideas. He's not one of us. We grew up the hard way, in a small town, on a farm' — whatever the case may be. But in my case, no. It is really being a traitor from within. And sensing this from them also gives me a peculiar relationship to them.

Gerhard Maré, a NUSAS activist who was writing his masters thesis at the University of Cape Town on the literature of Breytenbach in 1975:

I got a phone call from Johannesburg: 'I've got something I'm sending down with a friend, could you meet him on the steps of UCT tonight at eight o'clock?' I arrive, and it turns out to be Breyten, calling himself 'Christian Galaske' — I remember the pseudonym on the passport that he had forged for himself. I was very excited to see him, first of all, because of the academic importance that he had for me, and also I had been very impressed with his poetry, with what he stood for in a whole range of ways. So he arrives with this scheme, this organization called 'Okhela' that was going to be started and that he claimed had a lot of support. He had this document with him called the Manifesto. It was a document for white activists to define themselves, because of the reality of South Africa, a separate existence — and yet a supportive existence to the ANC. That's how he presented it.[5] And then the shit hit the fan, and we were followed and ultimately all picked up after a fiasco all round, because what the Security Police then did, they made use of that opportunity and the lack of knowledge around it to pick up a whole range of white activists.

The Africanization Campaign was preceded by a debate over related concepts like 'White Consciousness', which was criticized as 'a form of nationalism which blurs class distinctions'.[6] The next campaign, 'Education for an African Future', encouraged students to make their education relevant. The campaign influenced young men who were leaving the country to avoid military service to remain within the region. As a result, some went to Botswana, a few to Mozambique, and with Zimbabwe's independence in 1980, even more settled there.

So did that experience clarify anything for you about white South Africans' political role?

It's a very difficult question to answer, I think partly because so few people have been willing to talk about the Okhela experience. In a way, it was so badly done that it was easy to just write it off. I think one thing that it did do was that it cast doubt on any white-initiated separate activity, and I think it forced whites into very much a secondary role. Remember, there was the total gap of 1960s politics. There was a tradition of way back, of the older people — what had we got? We had nobody to refer to. I don't think there was ever an awareness that there was a role within or in very close proximity to the ANC. So that was part of it: our activity had to be in relation to the ANC.

I think what I took from that is, first of all, that a white leftist, at that point in time, did not have any organizational discipline. It might not be the case now, but organizational discipline was foreign to the experience of one generation of white leftists. I don't know whether it was the correct perception or not, but that came out for me — that I was in detention as an individual.

And that individual politics isn't on?

Individual politics isn't on, ja.

It took the 1976 Soweto uprisings to dissipate the widespread disaffection among white progressives. By the end of the year, NUSAS had adopted a theme for its revival: the 'Africanization Campaign'.

Fink Haysom, NUSAS Wages Commission member in Durban from 1973 to 1975, UCT Student Representative Council (SRC) president in 1976, and NUSAS president in 1977:

One of the things we were attempting to respond to was the negative aspect of the BC movement. People had been saying, 'Whites have got no role to play, it's a black struggle.' They would use that as a justification either for doing nothing or for leaving the country. So the Africanization Campaign was a way of saying, 'Listen, this is your country as well and you've got just as much right — in fact, as much duty — to see it work as a democratic and non-racial country and to expect of it as secure and happy a place for your children as anybody.'

The campaign reflected the development of the move away from protest politics towards more of an orientation by white students towards a long-term political commitment, towards non-racial democracy, to finding the structures which would incorporate their activities. We were redefining a person's conception of South Africa, that it's not just white or First World South Africa — it's non-racial South Africa, which encompasses a broad variety of problems.

In fact, it came at a stage when Black Consciousness was on the way out, from about '77 onwards, with the growth of non-racial movements — in particular with the development of a line of thinking within SASO which was critical of the Biko position. In the early '70s, when white students were attempting to formulate a response to SASO, there were two responses in NUSAS. The one was a liberal response: if people want to set up racially exclusive organizations then we should have nothing to do with them. The other was the dominant response, and I think Rick Turner had a large part to play in that. It was understanding the reasons for a critique of the limitations of white student organizations, and appreciating the need for a period of developing BC militancy and assertiveness.

I think there was a third response, which came later, and it was one which I eventually had some part in. It was to actually say that BC was a very limited philosophy, that its results reflected essentially a philosophy of consciousness of self, that it by and large appeals to the aspirant elites. I felt this was evidenced by the lack of success that SASO had in developing a relationship with workers, and the tremendous success they had amongst journalists and doctors and lawyers.

The success of this campaign was followed by another setback: the revelation that a long-time NUSAS activist, Craig Williamson, was a Security Police spy.[7] What was the ultimate effect of that development on student politics?

There was a lot of cynicism, people saying it was typical of student activists, that the whole thing is rife with informers. It can be self-defeating: it's no use doing anything because there is going to be a spy next to you. I don't know what information spies get, and it may be important and it may not be, but more generally, I think the negative effects of it are more organizational than information loss. What it sets up in the organization is a distressing distrust. It also allows political conflicts and questions to be resolved through personal maligning, and you can see the potential that has to break up groups.

Was the Williamson affair seen as a particularly white phenomenon?

Some people said, 'You can't work with white groups because they have spies in them.' But spies and infiltrators are not confined to the white movement, I don't think. The police spend a lot of money trying to infiltrate the white left, tapping phones and so on. I think there was a time when the unrest wasn't as rooted in the townships as it is now, when they probably wanted to monitor who was who and what was what and the white group would have been an important group to infiltrate.

I don't know how much use it would really be today. Things are not coordinated by the white left. There is that lingering fear of a relationship between white activists and blacks, partly a racist idea that it's whites telling blacks what to do. Also, whites are more identifiable to the police than black people.

The white left has always been perceived as a greater threat than it actually is. At one stage there were conscious decisions not to have non-racial organizations because they were the ones that were most targeted by the police. In other words, BC organizations or all-white organizations could get away with more.

The revitalization of NUSAS was only one of many factors that helped breed a new generation of white political activists. The ANC also played a role.

Unknown at the time to the rest of the 1973 University of the Witwatersrand SRC, the council included three Security Police spies: Craig Williamson (standing, fourth from right), Derek Brune (seated, third from right) and Arthur McGiven (seated, second from left).[8]

Marius Schoon, who was politically active in Johannesburg after his release from prison in September 1976, upon completion of a twelve-year sentence for ANC and Umkhonto we Sizwe activities, until June 1977, when he fled to neighbouring Botswana:

We'd spent a lot of time talking in prison about what I should do when I came out. We'd taken decisions in prison that I should do as much as I could to try and swing a substantial part of the white left behind the ANC.

Then, a few days before I was released from prison I was served with a very stringent banning and house arrest order. I was very fortunate in that I met Jenny Curtis[9] within a couple of weeks of coming out of prison. Jenny was able to introduce me to very wide sections of the white left — people in the trade unions, in the community organizations, students — and Jenny and I did a solid nine months political work at home before we were eventually forced to go. We both deliberately decided that we were basically going to ignore our banning orders. We saw a large number of people. We argued the case for the ANC, we argued the case for the ANC-SACP alliance.

Perhaps I flatter myself, but I feel that the work that Jenny and I did actually made a substantial difference to the white left. I don't think there's anyone on the white left now who can seriously say that the ANC is irrelevant. For the first time, many of these young people were actually being challenged about the incorrect views that they had about the ANC.

The enemy had had a very great propaganda success — and this was not only true of whites, it was true of blacks as well. The enemy deliberately and very consciously denies us our own history. I've spoken to numerous black comrades who left home following '76, and the thing that has impressed them more than anything, once they had made contact with the movement, is that resistance in South Africa did not begin in '76.

Now this was very, very true of whites as well, and I will say whites had less excuse for this, because the bulk of whites on the left are, in fact, intellectuals, and intellectuals always have access to information. In fact, when I came out of prison the white left was all very much into Marxism, but they weren't reading the stuff written by South African Marxists.

Now perhaps I'm being unfair, but I think that at that stage of the struggle a very exciting new generation of radical whites had not yet made the step from intellectual involvement to activism. I think subconsciously people denigrated the ANC because if they actually supported the ANC they would have to be involved in activism, and a lot of the white radical activity was, in fact, intellectual activity.

Then the older people in the white left had experienced the SASO break-away and I think they'd misinterpreted it. I think many of the white intellectuals had been convinced by certain elements in the Black Consciousness Movement that there was, in fact, no role for whites as activists — that the only possible role for whites was to make some form of intellectual input. Then I think a large number of whites made a basic ideological mistake, in that they thought that the only role there was for them was in the trade unions.

Then we spoke to people a lot about commitment — about what does commitment mean? I think it's very interesting that when Ray [Suttner] and Jeremy [Cronin] and Dave Rabkin[10] went to prison, they were regarded by the white left as being aberrant, as though they'd done something slightly ridiculous by actually getting involved with activities of the ANC. When our white comrades go to prison now, I'm sure there are still sections of the white left that think that these people are just wasting their time posturing, but basically the white left is now solidly behind them.

Now one of the reasons for the change of opinion is, of course, that the ANC is palpably there. When I came out of prison we were coming out of a period of quiescence, but now the climate has changed. We continually say the people have legitimized the ANC, and they not only legitimized the ANC for the black people of South Africa, they've specifically legitimized the ANC for the whites.

But I want to make another point here. I was aware all the time that I was at home that whereas we hoped that increasing numbers of whites are going to make a contribution to the liberation of South Africa, we knew we were dealing with very, very small numbers of white democrats. The real political work is going to have to be done with black people, and the real political change is actually going to be brought about by black people. Just because I'm speaking about work done with whites, I don't want you to think that I regard that as by any means the most important work that the movement was doing. It seemed to me as though that was the work I could do at the time.

Notes

1. The commission was convened in September 1972 by A. L. Schlebusch and Deputy Chairman Louis le Grange (later Minister of Law and Order in P. W. Botha's government) to report on 'the objects, organization and financing of NUSAS, SAIRR, the University Christian Movement, the CI and any related organizations, bodies, committees or groups of persons'.

2. Disaffiliation campaigns were mounted by right-wing student groups now seen as the prototype of the more polished and well-funded fronts of the 1980s, e.g., the Student Moderate Alliance and the National Student Federation, immediately identifiable by their glossy and prolific media attacking NUSAS, the ANC, MDM, etc.

3. Workshopped and acted by Patrick Fitzgerald, Ruth Jacobson, William Kentridge, Hannchen Koornhof, Steven Sack, Ari Sitas, Pippa Stein, Anne Stanwix and Astrid von Kotze, under the direction of Malcolm Purkey, this play was the first production of the non-racial company, which went on to produce plays championing progressive political themes from the 1970s to the 1990s.

4. Participants in the workshopping of this play devoted long hours to debate over this final line, and nearly chose another variant: 'The least I can do is be the most obstruction.'

5. Okhela, a Zulu word meaning 'to set alight', has been described as an 'anti-communist faction within the "white" ANC' allegedly encouraged by Tambo as well as the late ANC International Affairs department director, Johnny Makhatini. However there is no evidence to support such claims and it is more accurately viewed as an independent and unmandated initiative. Breytenbach's Okhela disintegrated in 1979, with the return of a key member, Barend Schuitema, to South Africa, and the revelation that he had been a spy for Pretoria.

6. *Work in Progress*, Nos 2 and 3, 1977.

7. Williamson was exposed in 1980 while working for the International University Exchange Fund (IUEF) in Geneva.

8. Derek Brune was unmasked when he appeared as a state witness in the 1976 trial of four students (including two of his former SRC colleagues, Glenn Moss and Cedric de Beer) and a lecturer charged under the Suppression of Communism Act. Despite Lieutenant Brune's testimony, all five were acquitted. McGiven later confessed the rather lacklustre details of his BOSS (Bureau of State Security, now National Intelligence Services, NIS) career to a London newspaper. Note also that Paul Sarbutt (standing, far left) had been a known intelligence agent who continually tabled anti-NUSAS resolutions at conferences and promoted the right-wing media campaign described in note 2 (above).

9. NUSAS Vice-President in 1972, Curtis helped found the Western Province Workers Advice Bureau and the Industrial Aid Society, was detained in 1975 (in the round-up of white activists following the Okhela affair) and banned in 1976. She was working at SAIRR when she met Schoon.

10. White ANC activists who entered Pretoria Central Prison shortly before Schoon was released.

PART FOUR
1976–1989

The desolation of the overcrowded, overgrazed 'homelands' is evident in this photo of KwaZulu; this was the kind of environment into which some political activists were banished.

17 Elders

Many of the political activists of the 1950s and 1960s were jailed, banned and driven out of the country, but there was another method the government used against its opponents, and that was to banish them to obscurity in remote rural areas. Banishment was directed at African political leaders: the 1927 Native Administration Act empowered the authorities, without any prior notice, to order any 'tribe or native to proceed forthwith to any designated place and not to leave it again except by permission'.[1] Dumped in unfamiliar areas where they often could not speak the local language, many banished people were shunned by rural communities who had been warned about trouble-makers from town.

The mutual distrust inevitably melted over time. As popular resistance gained momentum in the late 1970s and early 1980s, it became clear how often this method of eradicating opposition had backfired.

Mongezi Radebe, an activist who grew up in the village of Heilbron in the Orange Free State:

In our township we had a granny called Ma Mokhele, who used to tell us a lot about black history. Later I started understanding that she had been a member of the ANC and she had been sent to Heilbron under banishment. So she used to explain a lot of these things: what they were doing in the Women's League, what ANC was in the initial stages when it became militant, when the young ones like Mandela came into it. She was explaining its historical significance and why we should be proud of it, and why we should take on from where they've left. And that's how we started understanding a lot of things politically. Because of the teachings of that granny in Heilbron, I understood that whites must be regarded as people, irrespective of their colour. She even talked about the problems that were there, and even explained that Mandela himself did have some reservations about whites. But as you grow politically, as you mature, you learn to accept people as they are — not as symbols of colour as such.

When she first spoke to you about non-racialism, did it seem at all strange? Living in the Free State, had you ever met a white who was not racist?

No, not in that little *dorp* [village], but she had talked about comrades such as the late Bram Fisher, Comrade Slovo, and Comrade Goldberg. First I couldn't understand it: how could a white person die for me, for my struggle? What business did he have in my struggle when he was a free man, had his own vote, he had everything? Then she explained that it was because there were freedom-loving democrats who felt that they were not free until you were free, too.

Did your friends also hold such non-racial views?

Generally, people were against whites. They would say, 'Whites are whites, and you can't say that there's a better *umlungu* [white person] and a bad *umlungu* — they're all the same.' But I never gave up, I derived pleasure from explaining, because I was actually proud that I understood it from a person who was much, much experienced and who I regarded as a veteran in politics. And I always felt that I need to sort of give light to the people who haven't yet seen it.

Did you ever meet a PAC elder like that ANC granny?

Yes, I met one old father whom I came to know later on as an old member of PAC before it was banned, and the way he explained PAC principles, one of its many arguments against ANC when they split off was because ANC was dominated by communists. When I asked him about socialism, within the context of Marxism-Leninism, he said to me that those are foreign concepts: in Africa we talk about *ubuntu*, humanism, we talk about communalism, and we lived as not socialists but communalists, and those foreign concepts must not be allowed to adulterate our struggle.

At that stage I had a fair perception of the class struggle, and what he talked didn't make sense to me at all. It was as if he was preaching some form of traditionalism that I was totally opposed to. Because this old lady, again, had explained to me that PAC was led by a hothead who would shout first and think thereafter. She explained them as that part of the ANC that left before it was 'well-cooked' — she meant disciplined — and further explained that one day PAC will only exist in name. And the ANC, she explained, was a government in exile, and after winning our struggle that's the government that will be ruling.

Were you totally uninfluenced by Black Consciousness?

I would say BC, as a philosophy, I was never exposed to, but all that I know was that as blacks we must not feel inferior to whites — and that I got from my parents, I got it from that old lady, I got from some many people in the community. It was not because of BC philosophy. In the Free State particularly, there was no BC at all.

How else did you learn about the ANC, besides from that granny?

In fact, it was just through reading, mostly, that I came to understand a lot of things — through newspapers and books, and even banned literature.

In the Free State there was banned literature?

Yes. I would say, if you go on a farm where people are completely illiterate, it is not impossible that you should come across an old ANC or Communist Party book or some political book that would be regarded as subversive by the system. There are people who may not be very literate, but who'll always be in possession of relevant books, progressive books, and when he trusts you he'll say, 'I want to show you something,' and he'll show you a very good book that you would never have thought that a person of that calibre would be in possession of such material.

I know, for instance, people in Heilbron whom I had never thought were politically aware, and I got friendly with one and he gave me *The Struggle is My Life* by Mandela, and he said it's a good book, it'll make me a man. A man selling coal, who was a delivery boy — I had never thought that he had been to school, and I knew him not to be in a position to read anything or write his name, but he gave me that book. So it was like that in townships all over.

In my opinion, ANC propaganda, it's being read like hotcakes, and even a lazy person who wouldn't read a thing, the minute you show him, this is ANC, this is SACTU, this is the Communist Party, that person will be so keen on reading that, simply because the system denied us to read these things. Anything denied makes people to be as curious as anything.

Even imprisonment on Robben Island failed to achieve the state's goals of quarantining political leaders, for ANC veterans used the opportunity to educate the younger prisoners. Thus the Island came to be known as 'Mandela University'.

Steve Tshwete, who was sentenced to fifteen years imprisonment for Umkhonto we Sizwe sabotage activities in 1964:

I was 25 when I got to Robben Island, so I was quite keen, together with a lot of other young people, to equip ourselves as much as we could. We read

A graphic from the Medu collective of exiled South African artists in Botswana.

Dorothy Nyembe is enthusiastically greeted by supporters on her release from eighteen years in prison for ANC and MK activities. One of the placards reads, 'Jail shall not bend our leaders'.

about all the struggles, you know, and it improved my understanding – and contact, of course, with the leadership itself. We studied the revolution in Indonesia, the Chinese revolution, the Russian revolution, the struggle in India, the struggle in Ireland, the struggle in Latin America, the Cuban revolution, the Algerian revolution, reconstruction after decolonization in Africa – you know, all those things. What parallels are there between those struggles and our struggles here? What lessons can we draw? There's no section of political theory that we never touched on the Island.

I had only matric [secondary school] when I went to the Island, but I graduated from there. I got my degree on the Island. I majored in philosophy and English through the University of South Africa,[2] so some of the material I was prescribed. And we got hold of Marxist literature, we were conducting lectures.

In all your political debates on the Island, did the issue of non-racialism ever come up?

It was an important issue, much as it is still an important issue today. I think it's one of the pillars that the ANC structure could be said to have been built on. You take, for instance, the 1976 uprising: it was quite clear that it was the white policeman and the white soldier who was butchering the kids in Soweto. And there were those who would say the struggle was between black and white and point out these glaring examples. You know, it could have gone the other way, had it not been for our insistence on non-racialism as a realistic, historical approach to the resolution of the South African situation.

The ANC addressed all that, you know. We were not tempted to water it down, even in the era of Black Consciousness. We believed that it's quite good poetry to say, 'Black man, you're on your own', but on the ground the situation is quite different. On the Island, the responsibility of the movement was to equip all members of the organization so that we were not wanting more information on any single aspect of the policies of our movement, particularly non-racialism and the alliance between the SACP and the ANC. As a national liberation movement we are a coalition of various classes and social groups, and it becomes important, therefore, that the cadreship of the movement understands how to harmonize the relations, and not to play one class interest against another.

So we had to do a lot of politicization around this concept and emphasize that non-racialism is entrenched in the Freedom Charter. You know, the word 'people', it pervades the whole Charter: 'The people shall govern' and 'land to the people'. We had to engage in intensive politicization, because 'people', as far as we were concerned, are all those classes, those social groups, irrespective of race, colour, or creed, who rallied around the banner of the ANC for a non-racial, united, democratic South Africa. So once you are discussing the Freedom Charter, you invariably cannot avoid talking about non-racialism.

Now was all this debate purely amongst fellow ANC prisoners, or did you try to move those who held another point of view?

We talked to the [white] warders, we did convert some of them to accept our positions. We preached to them that we are brothers, this is our country and we have to fight for a non-racial democracy. I remember a warder who used to come and eat with us from the same piece of iron zinc when we cooked *imbazas*, oysters that we pulled from the sea. One day I asked him, 'Look here, there is a civil war going on in South Africa. On which side are you?' He said, 'I am standing on the fence.'

And then I said to him, 'But we are going to shake that fence, we are going to shake it very hard, and in all probability you must fall — but make sure that you fall on the right side.' And then he said, '*Ek is 'n Mandela*' — that is, he supports Mandela. And he says, 'When I go to the ANC I will not be going to you, I'm going to my own brothers there: Bram Fischer *is daar* [is there], Slovo *is daar* — they're white men, they're in the ANC. I'll go to them.'

That's why we believed on the Island when things really come to the push, the Afrikaner will turn out to be the most patriotic of all racial groups. After all, they were peasants only in the last century and they don't have a long history of involvement in capitalist morality and whatnot.

Were you similarly confident about those who opposed ANC policies from a Black Consciousness point of view?

We knew that it was the responsibility of the revolutionary movement to direct the Black Consciousness Movement into more progressive positions. I mean, we certainly knew that BC could give problems in the long run, by reason of it being colour politics. Colour politics are dangerous. They are just as bad as tribal politics, you know. That's why we know that the imperialist countries were very much interested in boosting Black Consciousness, knowing that politics of the skin are going to blunt the revolutionary drive of the working class, and in particular, the anti-imperialist nature of the struggle.

Toward the end of your prison sentence did you have a sense of what you wanted to accomplish politically upon your return to society?

When you are just about to leave the Island there's a lot of anxiety, particularly for long-term prisoners. I did not know how the country looked like — the currency, the highways and whatnot, all those things were completely strange to me. You get people like Nelson Mandela who'd sort of arm you, in terms of what you are likely to confront and what the expectations of the movement are about you, and you feel very much inspired and encouraged.

The priority was getting people rallying behind the genuine liberation movement in the country, getting people accepting the policies of the ANC.

Murphy Morobe, SSRC vice-chairman who was detained for two years following the 1976–77 uprisings, then tried for sedition, and was on Robben Island from 1979 to 1982:

Prison, for me, became the most dramatic period for my conception of our struggle, and lots of my views were changed by the experience of being exposed to other people who had been involved in struggle for a long time. It was a combination of both reading from books and being in contact with people who have been in the struggle even before the days of BC. They brought us the tradition of struggle we had been missing in the '70s. And then the realization dawned amongst lots of us that the gap that had been created with the banning of people's organizations in the '60s and the apparent demise of the Congress movement created that vacuum whereby certain ideas that came up as a result of the '60s student movement in America, the Black Power Movement, came to have an effect on the South African scene. Those became the ideas of the day that caught on like wildfire, with us little realizing that as history develops those ideas would run their course and become obsolete.

My previous position as regards the position of whites in the struggle in the '70s was the result of what I would consider a myopic outlook. The historical state in which we were at that time was one where, in fact, we were cut off from our history, the history of struggle, as to what went on before us. When I got involved in politics, it was at the level of the South African Students Movement (SASM),[3] which was essentially Black Consciousness, and growing up in that tradition we had that original aversion for any contact with white people. I think that was a result of that historical gap that was created. But as I developed and got more curious and began to read more, my perception began to change. Then there was a rediscovery of where we stood in history, and lots of us took our ideas from that Congress tradition.

ANC political prisoners released from Robben Island — both the veterans and the ex-Black Consciousness activists — were like yeast in the townships. They spread their non-racial views amongst younger people looking for political guidance and provided a link to the much-mystified movement.

Nise Malange, who was expelled from secondary schools in Transkei and Ciskei in the late 1970s and then sent back home to Cape Town, where she got reacquainted with an elderly relative after he was released from Robben Island:

I heard about the ANC from my mother's uncle. He was one of the guys who was in Robben Island, so when he came out in 1976 he was the one who enlightened me, telling me about his involvements in those days and how he was detained, and telling us about Mandela, Sisulu, Sobukwe. So I have become more and more interested. So he's the person that guided me up to this stage, 'Rev' Marawu. He was an organizer for General Workers Union in Cape Town.

He didn't say that he was fighting whites. He used to tell me, 'Look, baby' — because he used to call me 'baby' — 'I'm sure you don't have the right direction, and I feel from the songs that you sing here that you are really anti-white. You know, we've got our brothers in Robben Island, but we've white brothers, too.' He used to tell me of the white ladies and the men who were involved in the ANC. So he's the one who enlightened me about the

ANC and about the white man in South Africa, because he said not all of them are the same.

You know, there's this freedom song which said, 'The Afrikaners are dogs — *Amabhulu Izinja*'. That was the song we used to sing in 1976, and he said, 'You must stop singing this because not all of them are dogs.' So I used to listen to him. I used to ask my mother and my father, 'What were you doing in that time — were you involved in these things like Rev?' They said, 'Each and everyone, if you are an African, you are involved.' I took all that as history.

Whites who had been banned in the 1950s and '60s also began returning to the political fray to play a kind of elder statesman role.

Amy Thornton, a Cape Town Congress of Democrats activist banned from 1959 to 1973 and then exhorted to return to the political scene by a former SACTU leader who had also been de-activated for more than a decade by successive bans and detentions:

Then I was completely involved in my domestic life. I mean, I was interested but I had four small children. Until one day in 1977 there was a knock at the door and there was Oscar Mpetha, who I hadn't seen for years and years. And he said, 'Won't you come and help with some typing at the Food and Canning Workers Union[4] office?' So I went along to the office, and that is how I came to work at Food and Canning. And then in about 1979, '80, Oscar came one day and said, 'Listen, we're going to start a women's organization again — come.' And we started the United Women's Organization (UWO) with Dorothy Tamana and Mildred Lesia.[5] We got this thing off the ground and it grew to quite a big women's organization.

I was just about the only white person I knew left in Cape Town who hadn't opted out or left the country or something. So to find these young people who were active — and so many young whites — it was amazing to me. There was a whole new generation of people who weren't scared, who could handle banning orders. The new generation had grown up knowing nothing of anything being legal, accepting torture and solitary confinement — I was amazed by these people. And I found myself being drawn back into things. I've never been a kind of high-profile person, I've always been a kind of backroom girl, but I found myself being placed in this situation of chairing things.

My other role was like a sort of living historical monument. I then discovered there was a generation of students doing research who know more about anything than I ever did. I mean, they were researching the women in the '50s, the Congress of the People, the Congress of Democrats — you know, the whole political spectrum. So every now and then students would pitch up and say, 'Can we come and talk to you about this? And do you remember anything about that?' I still get called on in my historical monument act — like, 'We're having a thing on the Treason Trial, will you come and talk about what happened in the trial?' It's been very nice being in contact with young people.

I think I'm reaching the age where I'm becoming an elder, in that I find that, in terms of people having disputes — sometimes personality, sometimes ideological — I have been asked to sit in on a discussion to resolve disputes, along with Liz Abrahams.[6] Why? Because we're both old, we've been involved in the '50s, and they want us to talk about comradeship and discipline.

How would you compare the position of whites, then and now?

I always had this total conviction that there is a place for the whites, never doubted the fact. Speaking to other whites who would say, 'Denis Goldberg was a fool, he stuck his neck out and look what happened to him, he's wasted his life,' I would say, 'Denis Goldberg is a reason that you have a claim to live in South Africa — it's because of Goldberg that you'll be able to say there is a place for whites in South Africa, because he's been willing to be in that position.'

The white population in South Africa is not going to disappear. A lot of racial feeling exists. And I think that the fact that there are whites who have played a minor role in the struggle means that it's not just a straight black-white issue, and I think that's very important. In the same way, I'm always telling my children that 650,000 non-Jewish Germans resisted the Nazis and died in Nazi concentration camps, and I think that is important. All kinds of human resistance to tyranny is important.

Ex-political prisoners plunged straight into sensitive ideological and political debates, offering their political experience as well as theoretical knowledge gleaned from discussions in prison. They included not only ex-Robben Islanders, but also veterans of the white maximum security prison, Pretoria Central.

Raymond Suttner, who served seven years in Pretoria Central for ANC activities, and upon his release in 1983 played a leading role in popularizing the Freedom Charter:

When I was arrested there was not this sort of open debate at all. If you advocated the Freedom Charter in the '70s you would have been banned, and most of those people who advocated it were in jail. So it is a completely different situation now. There is a religious attitude to the Charter — anyone who attacks it is an enemy, that sort of thing. People treat it as an article of faith to support the Charter, and it had never really been debated. I wanted to open it, because I felt you can't defend it in that sort of arrogant way. We have got to engage people, we have got to discuss it. Even in our own ranks people have different views. You can't mount a successful challenge to a state unless you have political cohesion.

Do you see parallels between the mass-based movement then and now?

I don't see us as reproducing the '50s. I think there was a baton that was dropped temporarily, and we picked it up again under different conditions —

a baton, in the sense of cross-class alliances, the broadest-based national alliance against apartheid oppression and exploitation. Like the Congress Alliance, we are trying to isolate the racist regime and to draw in all anti-apartheid forces to oppose them, and that has shown that, in a sense, we believe that the approach adopted then is valid today. I believe that the only way to free South Africa is to consolidate an alliance of all people opposed to apartheid.

Compared with their black comrades, the white political prisoners segregated in Pretoria Central have had less to share in terms of breadth of experience, different points of view, etc. What was it that helped you get through your time in prison?[7]

Prison is not so difficult if you are a political prisoner. Because in the first place, you go in there with your head held high — you're completely proud of what you've done. And if you remember that all along, psychologically, you start off very well. Secondly, your job in prison is to come out a better person, better able to play a role in the struggle, and I think it's important not to waste your time in prison, but to come out feeling that you've grown. I feel I grew, morally and intellectually, and my political understanding is better. It wasn't very difficult because I used every moment — there was too little time in prison, as far as I'm concerned. I worked hard, there was a lot of discussion, I understand a lot of things much better now. Morale-wise, it's very difficult, but out of difficult situations you can either collapse or grow, and I think that most people grow in them.

Notes

1. In her autobiography (*Side by Side*, Zed Books, 1986), Helen Joseph describes the two-month, 8,000-mile-long 'Journey to the Banished' she undertook in 1962, when her own ban lapsed. In response to an ANC call for the 116 banished people to be located and assisted, she and fellow FedSAW member Lilian Ngoyi formed the Human Rights Welfare Committee.
2. Commonly referred to as UNISA and located in Pretoria, Africa's largest correspondence university serves students of all races.
3. The secondary schools organization instigated by SASO, which played a role in the 1976 uprisings.
4. This union was founded in 1941 by Ray Alexander, and Mpetha became its general-secretary in 1951. It fell victim to the government offensive against SACTU and its affiliated unions and was revived again in 1977 by Mpetha and a young white just out of university, Jan Theron.
5. Tamana was a FedSAW founder member who came to the Cape shanties from the Transkei. Lesia had been a trade unionist and ANC activist in the 1950s.
6. A former Food and Canning Workers general-secretary who helped refound the union from her base in Paarl.
7. There is also a separate top security section of the prison for female white political prisoners; whereas Robben Island only accommodated males, and black women political prisoners were usually kept at a prison in Kroonstad in the Free State.

18 We Are Convinced Now

New organizational foundations were laid in the late 1970s and early 1980s, rooted in the segregated communities but committed to a non-racial future. Students once again took the lead, as veterans of the 1976 uprising now armed with both concrete experience of struggle and counsel from the elders.

Wantu Zenzile, a secondary school student from Port Elizabeth, member of the Congress of South African Students since its formation in 1979, and COSAS president 1980—82:

We were planning to form a new student body, you see, and questions were coming up as to how are we going to avoid the problems we experienced in June 1976: firstly, the relationship of the students to the society as a whole, and secondly, the shortcomings of the tactics and strategies which were involved. There had been no change, really, since 1976, in the attitude of the people. They were still anti-white, you see.

Now it was felt that this new organization which is going to be launched should not appear to be racist. In actual fact, it was not going to include whites at that particular stage, but in terms of policy, we had to make it clear that we are non-racial.

But it was not as easy as that to introduce non-racialism — it now meant that COSAS had to start moving people away from Black Consciousness and start showing them the non-racial way. Our argument was that it is not all the whites who enjoy privileges — there are whites who don't enjoy privileges. And secondly, we cannot deny that there are those whites who are well off but who are sympathetic to our struggle. We used to put forward such arguments to try and show them that, in actual fact, the problem is between the rich and the poor, because you actually find even blacks who sell us out. And now the whole class question would come in.

One of the other problems was that in 1976 and '77, very few so-called coloureds and Indians were involved, so our first aim of COSAS was to go to those areas and draw them in. And that's exactly what we did.

What led to the decision that COSAS should formally adopt a non-racial policy?

You see, initially what had happened is that since we were planning to launch a new organization, we had to consult elderly people and experienced people. And in actual fact it was them who showed us our shortcomings in 1976 and 1977. They were trying to show us that we are going to find ourselves in a racist problem if we are going to pursue BC.

COSAS saw countless leaders and members detained and killed. Here, a COSAS banner flies over a funeral, featuring the COSAS slogan, 'Each One Teach One', and its demands for 'dynamic, free and compulsory education for all'.

In 1979 already there was ANC literature coming up, you know, there was an ANC vibe growing inside the country. ANC started intensifying 'armed propaganda'.[1] Now this was helping to sort of change the mood.

The more the struggle was becoming popular, the more this non-racial thing was becoming popular. By the end of 1980, I can say those students who were active, they had accepted it and they made those who later on joined the struggle to accept it. What has happened of late is that some students know nothing about BC — students who can actually speak of BC, it's those who were involved prior to 1980. Earlier on we had to sort of transform these people from this BC mentality to non-racialism, but now we don't actually even go through BC.

'Apartheid Education: The Challenge Facing Students', a retrospective overview of COSAS policy issued by its National Executive Committee, 1984:[2]

It is clearly stated in the COSAS constitution that we are striving towards a non-racial and democratic education, first as oppressed, then as students. COSAS also realizes that for there to be a non-racial democratic education there must be a democratic society truly reflective of the will of all the people.

The preamble of our constitution clearly states that 'students have a responsibility toward ensuring the welfare of society'. Here the organization has isolated a particular and fundamental responsibility: the economic responsibility. Students realize that the clothes we wear, the food we eat, the pens and books we use are produced by the working class of our country — the working class is therefore responsible for the wealth of the country. Yet we find that those who produce the food have no food, those who produce the clothes have no clothes, those who build the houses have no houses. The working class, as the oppressed and most exploited class in society, therefore must first emancipate themselves, since the emancipation of the working class will ensure the emancipation of society as a whole. That is why we are saying that the working class is the vanguard of our struggle. We, as students, through having our site of struggle on our schools and campuses, can only play a supportive role to our parents, the workers.

Jackie Jolobe, a member of the first COSAS executive:[3]

I've been non-racial ever since my involvement in COSAS, since its inception. The COSAS constitution was drawn up in my presence, and I fully participated in its formation. I never had problems with whites because we were a non-racial organization from the outset.

It was in 1976 when I really got involved. I was very young then, but all schools were demonstrating so there was no way in which I couldn't join in. I remember in one of the demonstrations when we were marching to John Vorster Square,[4] I thought that the whites in South Africa are the enemy and as a result I said to one of the SSRC chaps, 'Why don't we give our parents who are working as domestic workers some poison to kill all the whites?' Fortunately I said that to a very progressive and clear person, because he said to me, 'But not all whites are enemies, you know — we have democratic whites.'

He then tried to explain the policies of the ANC to me, and he trained me politically. The type of training I got from this comrade was so clear that I immediately understood that not every white is an enemy, especially when he explained to me about the two opposed classes, the working class and the bourgeois class, and how whites are being given privileges to divide the working class, and as a result, weaken it. What also convinced me was that if we say we are going to drive the whites to the sea, I mean, why should we do that, because South Africa is what it is today because of our joint effort.

Was it common to talk so freely about the ANC in the late 1970s?

I think from 1979, people were very free inside the country to talk about the ANC. I was arrested because I was on the national executive of COSAS and it was believed that COSAS was a front of the ANC — which was not true. COSAS was a student movement and happened to be having very clear political directives, aspiring to a new, democratic South Africa, and it so happened that its constitution, its beliefs, its aspirations are that of the ANC.

Did COSAS have to try not to appear to be linked with the ANC?

You know, COSAS was formed under very difficult conditions. It was after two years of the system having banned all organizations, schools not operating very properly. The enemy immediately felt that this is the ANC in the students' heads.[5] With the armed activities of the ANC immediately after the 1976 uprisings, the students themselves felt that there is no other alternative to this apartheid government but the ANC.

In fact, there was another alternative: a Black Consciousness group called the Azanian People's Organization. AZAPO's leaders were arrested soon after its inception in 1978,[6] and when they regrouped a year later, suspicions were aroused about the minimal state interference in their activities — in stark contrast to the relentless harassment of the newly elected COSAS leaders.[7]

'On Policy', AZAPO, 1980:

The philosophy and policies of the organization will be based on the broad provisions of the philosophy of Black Consciousness. We recognize the fact that in our country, race is a class determinant. Thus the concentration of economic and political power in the hands of the white race enables it to promote a rigid class structure. The black people, on the other hand, constitute a people racially discriminated against and economically exploited. This gives rise to the ever-increasing conflict between the white and black races. The white race accumulates capital by exploiting the black labour, and by virtue of their possession of political power they maintain themselves in a position of privilege. We envisage a state where all persons shall have the right to ownership of property and complete participation in the political machinery of the country, where capital and profits accruing from labour shall be equitably distributed. We believe that the entire country of Azania belongs to the black people, hence our vehement rejection of the bantustan policy.

Mkhuseli Jack, an Eastern Cape Black Consciousness activist who subsequently adopted a non-racial position:

One thing that changed me was at the time when we were going to introduce AZAPO here, we realized that the police were strongly supporting our slogans. And we started to doubt now: why should the state be so arrogant against the ANC and show us how effective PAC could be, with its hostility against whites and so on? You see, in 1980 I was arrested together with executive members of AZAPO from the Transvaal, and we saw this was a calculated plot to try and tell us how good Black Consciousness is. These AZAPO fellows denounced the ANC so much, and the non-racial principle.

When I came back from detention I realized firmly that no, we are being trapped here. Fortunately, elderly people here in PE [Port Elizabeth] stood up against this now, the old people who were in the ANC. There were these fellows who had just recently been released from prison, Robben Island, and they were instrumental in explaining this non-racialism to us. And then we started to realize, hey, but these people are talking sense now. There was that general lull amongst these fellows who were arrested and imprisoned – before they were silent when they came back, but now their goal is to give direction to the youth.

From that time, really, things changed dramatically. All the organizations immediately developed here in the Eastern Cape. They just worked for this non-racial business, and everybody started to understand. And then immediately we embarked on a campaign to expose this, and to learn a lot about non-racialism. And we understood then. As from 1981, I am telling you, we were very clear. And we are convinced now.

What would be the motive for the government to support AZAPO and oppose the non-racial organizations?

One of the reasons is that it will deepen the racial tensions. And this is, of course, a basic pillar of apartheid: racial conflict. The day we do away with that, definitely the state will be in trouble. Why are they afraid of the non-racial group? It is because of the white people who are allowing themselves to be part of us, and they see that really these people are comfortable within our ranks. And now they want to create problems so that these people can be pushed away and go back to support the government and have that stand of white versus black. Now that whole thing is being frustrated by our strategy of non-racialism.

By the end of 1979, another student group had been formed, this one aimed at black university students.[8] While many of its members had 'grown out of' Black Consciousness, the Azanian Students Organization's name reflected the continued need for a degree of caution in moving towards explicit non-racialism.

Simpiwe Mgoduso, a member of the Azanian Students Organization (AZASO) Natal branch since 1980 and national president 1984–85:

The formation of AZASO was not at all representative of the student fraternity in South Africa. Only one campus was represented: Turfloop. The whole idea was originally proposed at an AZAPO meeting, so as such there was an AZAPO influence. We did discuss this at Fort Hare and other areas, but we felt that since a student organization has been formed we mustn't debate and indulge unnecessary issues. We felt that we all had to support it and give it a thorough and a proper direction.

Do you think that when South Africa's free it will be called 'Azania'?

Personally, I feel it would be wrong for South Africa to be called Azania. Historically, politically and topologically, South Africa is not Azania.

Resolution taken on AZASO policy at its first conference, July 1981:

We at the AZASO conference, learning from the struggles of oppressed people in the world against oppression, pertinently in Angola, Mozambique and Zimbabwe, and realizing that they have fought against the system and not against individual Portuguese colonialists and white Rhodesians, note [Mozambican President] Samora Machel's statement on racism and capitalist exploitation: 'There are nationalists who think that the purpose of our struggle should be a struggle between black power and white power, whereas for us the struggle is between the power of exploiters and people's power. A black state of rich and powerful men in which the minority decides and imposes its will would be the continuation in a new form of the situation against which we are struggling.'

We wish to dispel the myth that all blacks are workers, whilst we confirm that black workers in South Africa are the most exploited and therefore the vanguard in the national struggle for democracy. We therefore resolve that:

1. AZASO urges the oppressed community to take cognizance of the above and support those who have already taken this position to confirm that we are struggling against the system and not individual whites;

2. We must seek a working policy relating directly to the struggle of the workers as conducted by the progressive trade union movement;

3. Since the success of our struggle depends upon effective mobilization of all people committed to democracy, we call for genuine unity of the oppressed against the oppressive system.

It took a year of what AZASO members later described as 'serious debate, informed by our experiences in the field of struggle' and 'signifying the maturation of our theoretical position' for the organization to totally discard Black Consciousness, adopt the principle of non-racialism and endorse the Freedom Charter.[9] AZASO's leaders then boldly initiated the first public black-white student cooperation since the walk-out from NUSAS that had sparked the Black Consciousness Movement a decade before.

Media urging students, the community and workers to unite; produced in 1980 by the Wilson-Rowntree Support Committee and printed on the UCT SRC press.

Andrew Boraine, NUSAS President, 1980–81:

A number of campaigns were very important for that process of starting to cement alliances between black and white students: firstly, the Freedom Charter Campaign of 1980, which we ran in conjunction with COSAS. We had the resources and we had access to money, and they would approach us and say, 'We need 10,000 pamphlets for tomorrow,' and we would print them and see that as our role, as a support for student struggles.

Another area of struggle, particularly in Cape Town, was the support for labour struggles, particularly the Fattis and Monis [food workers] strike which was taking place at the time, then later on the meat strike with the General Workers Union, and then later on still, the SAAWU [South African Allied Workers Union] strike and the Wilson-Rowntree sweet boycott which we organized on campus. We printed posters, pamphlets, we had demonstrations.

But I think our biggest achievement during 1980 was bringing the University of Cape Town out for a whole week of boycotts in solidarity with the black school boycotts. A lot of black students would come onto campus, both at UCT and at Wits [University of the Witwatersrand], and inject a spirit of militancy into the white students. We would do this deliberately, to try and start non-racial alliances going, and try and break down this notion amongst white students that their only role was in the white community.

I think that whites, at that stage, were playing a disproportionately important role, in terms of national politics. Like the Freedom Charter campaign — the fact that NUSAS ran that nationwide meant that Freedom Charters got not only onto the campuses, but into all the schools and the communities, often for the first time since the 1950s. A lot of the black leadership was still banned at that stage and I could travel around. I'm not saying this to exaggerate our importance — because that's a very dangerous thing — but I think NUSAS at that stage, together with COSAS, played quite an important part in reviving the non-racial tradition from '79 onwards.

Look at the Free Mandela campaign of 1980, and the following year the Anti-Republic Day campaign[10] — which was the first of the series of broad front coalitions against the government — where we had the emerging trade unions, COSAS and AZASO, we had the Natal Indian Congress, we had the Black Sash. NUSAS printed over a million Anti-Republic Day pamphlets, flags were burned at our meetings, and I was then detained, having done a nationwide tour with Wantu Zenzile, the COSAS President, and speaking on the same platforms. I think I was the first NUSAS President to speak on a black campus since the 1960s, when I spoke at Durban-Westville [Indians-only university][11] at the beginning of 1981. The black comrades that I was working with were very apprehensive that this would be rejected. They thought maybe they were in the minority, that BC was still going to say, 'Ag, we don't want this NUSAS president on our campus,' but the meeting was packed out. It was the first time that I gave an *Amandla* salute — I mean, in those days you just didn't do those sort of things. I remember the Security Police later interrogating me for two days about why had I given a 'black power salute' since I was a white person.

I remember seeing Wantu argue with other black students and saying, 'I'm going to resign before I let non-racialism be challenged.' I remember people in NIC defending publicly their working relationship with NUSAS.

They were very, very, very strong on that. Those were the sort of influences I remember at that time, of people actually specifically stating that non-racialism is the tradition of the Congress movement. I think I never would have had the confidence to speak on a black campus if they hadn't given me that support – I would have been terrified.

'The Charter Leads Us', leaflet announcing AZASO-NUSAS-COSAS Resistance Rally, 22 August 1985:

A resistance rally has been organized by the three major student groupings in South Africa – COSAS, NUSAS and AZASO. Together they form the non-racial student movement in this country. While it has been necessary to organize separately because of the practical and ideological effects of apartheid, we are all striving for a South Africa based on a single, united and democratic future.

Our vision is encapsulated in the Freedom Charter. As the government cracks down on all resistance, it is more important than ever that we stand together and show our opposition to apartheid. We call on all students to attend the rally so that we can build non-racialism in the process of our struggle.

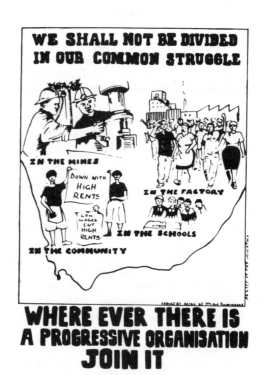

A poster produced by a Cape Town community organization.

Another student organization in the vanguard of non-racialism was the Young Christian Students, the South African affiliate of an international youth movement. YCS had included both blacks and whites in its membership and leadership since reaching out to black high schools in 1979.

Father Albert Nolan, a Jesuit priest who helped introduce YCS to South Africa after visiting Latin America and served as its national chaplain from 1977 to 1984: [12]

One of the things about religion is that we don't have a political policy in any way or a blueprint for the future, but we do have a vision of a just society. And in a South African context, there's no doubt about it, our vision would have to be a democratic society, one person, one vote. It has to be a non-racial society, and not a multi-racial society where you've still got groups where their interests balance out against one another in some formula or other that's not going to bring peace. Non-racialism means that race is as irrelevant as creed or gender or anything else.

It has to include a redistribution of wealth in some form or another, and obviously, common citizenship. How do you build a new South African culture? It's in how you sustain the system — now we're assuming it's changed — which is the area where I think religion has a role to play.

Mike Mailula, YCS member since 1979, when he was in high school in Pretoria's Mamelodi township, and YCS national organizer 1985—87:

I used to subscribe to the BC ideology very strongly, but the change came in when I joined YCS. It was exciting to hear priests speaking a different language, interpreting the gospel differently. Before I was a staunch Catholic, I used to go to Mass every Sunday and I was in charge of the altar boys in the church, but I wasn't seeing that the struggle needs to be brought into the church.

I was starting to understand the system much more because of the type of publications I used to get from YCS. I started to understand the problem is to fight the system that makes white people hate us, and have a new system that will bring about human values, like non-racialism and so on. So one started to realize that we can kill as many whites as possible, but you are not changing the system. You can have actually the same system, but not run by white people, run by black people. Like in other countries like Kenya, for instance: the system hasn't changed that much, people are still poor, opportunities for education are still restricted to very few people, the middle class and the rich people.

And also my participation in YCS exposed me to white people who were involved in the struggle, and that was quite a surprise, you know. I remember one day a white comrade came to my place and he talked to my mother about Mandela, and she said it's the first time she hears a white person wanting change in the country. Realizing that there are whites who support the struggle, that actually reassured me that we are not fighting white people as white people, but we are fighting the system in which white people participate and are being used against us.

What we do in YCS is we have personal testimonies of a white person, to come and talk and tell how he got involved. Blacks normally ask those questions when we have inter-regional meetings: how does the white community regard you, being involved in the struggle? And what is interesting is that black people will say, 'Ag, they can reject you — we'll stand with you.'

Were there any problematic issues?

It wasn't easy. We had differences, because of different backgrounds, you know, and sometimes we'd debate issues and really clash. Some white comrades would start saying the problem is not colour, but the problem is capitalism. We didn't want to accept that. I mean, we are kicked around by white people, and they don't kick other white people like they kick us, so why do you say colour is not important? It is important!

The non-racialism now entrenched among the students spread into the community, as civic, youth, women's and popular media structures evolved around struggles over issues like jobs and rents.

Cheryl Carolus, an activist at the coloureds-only University of the Western Cape who got involved with community issues upon leaving campus:

By the late '70s it was quite clear to us that you couldn't go back to Afros and wearing *dashikis* [African shirts] and saying — in a very sexist way — 'Black man, you're on your own.' I personally decided that I should now get into class. And I started reading Marx's *Capital* and waded through two volumes before I realized that I was not going to understand class struggle by reading *Capital.*

Then we started seriously looking into our past, approaching questions of how we view the participation of the different racial groups in a racially divided society like South Africa. We started reading the Freedom Charter. Now the Charter before had always been a fairly symbolic document to us: now we started analyzing it.

I think the next point was 1980, with the Western Cape student boycotts, when we had a far more systematic approach going into the community. We started building links with the trade union movement, through things like the red meat boycott. There was the Fattis and Monis boycott as well, where the student movement worked directly under the supervision of the trade union movement. Then we started building civic organizations and we saw emerging, for the first time, really solid youth structures. It was in that context that the Freedom Charter started to acquire a new sort of meaning for us.

Saleem Badat, a member of the AZASO national executive from Natal who became national organizer for Grassroots *community newspaper in Cape Town:*

In early 1983 I was detained and the issue that they were trying to pin on me was that AZASO is a front for the ANC, and so is COSAS and so on. That interrogation, in some sense, confirmed the correctness of the policies we had adopted, because one could get a feeling that they weren't afraid of exclusive BC politics — what they were afraid of was non-racial politics, or a politics that was starting to be based much more on class analysis.

The Security Police were starting to become very aware of the links that were being formed between NUSAS and AZASO and COSAS and the United Women's Organization (UWO). They would ask: how can you work with whites? Aren't whites the problem in this country? I got the impression that it was not just a case of an ascendant ANC that they were having to deal with, but they were also having great problems with the new non-racial politics.

I don't know if it was fear in terms of us making cracks in the ruling class, or whether it was just an inability to cope with the fact that blacks and whites were mixing on equal terms and working and living together. We didn't call ourselves 'Charterists' ever — that's what we were called by BC people. We would say we are non-racial, and non-racial meant Congress movement, ultimately. So it was more that resurge in non-racialism, a resurgence of Congress politics. I think the authorities had a notion that if you were BC you were PAC, and if you were non-racial you were ANC.[13]

The main emphasis during interrogation was: 'You've got a good career in front of you, why don't you stick to that? Do you know what the ANC's all about, really? I mean, do you know what Tambo and them say about you Indian people?' They went on, saying, 'Saleem, you come from a civilization — we can get on. And you know changes are coming. We can come together — you as Indians, and maybe the coloureds as well. We whites can come together, but these blacks will never be able to come together — never, never. And if you think the ANC's going to be able to bring everyone together, forget it, because the ANC is just Xhosas.' I mean, that's always in their arsenal, to play out that sort of theme.

Non-racialism opens up a whole new sort of dimension, in terms of how you need to mobilize and organize. You come to a greater understanding of the state — that it exists at the level of the education system, the health system, the administration in the townships, and those are the levels at which you need to start focussing, on a day-to-day basis, in terms of building unity of the people, around bus fare increases, around rent increases, around gutter education. And in doing that you start to dent the structures wherever they exist.

That sort of perspective isn't there at the level of BC — it flows out of a class analysis, a greater understanding of capitalism and state power. And I think above all, it's not simply the state as a monolithic structure which can repress you and control every aspect of your life. There are areas that you can challenge, and areas that you can roll back in some sense and make gains.

In the past I operated very much at an intellectual level. It was like pure Marxism with no grey areas — you're either for socialism or against. The petty bourgeoisie was the enemy, there was no notion of winning them over, of contesting their terrain — despite the fact that I came from that sort of background. In that sense, the Cape was very important for me, in terms of understanding the necessity of alliances, of understanding adherence to principles, but also displaying a creativity and a flexibility of tactics. Because the moment you get involved in mass struggle it means dirtying your hands at some times. At the end of a struggle people want to see some benefits, some gains that they have made, and in that sense, again getting involved in concrete politics, getting involved in the community, is important in reformulating a lot of your intellectualism.

Lechesa Tsenoli, who grew up in a village in the Orange Free State and first became politically active there, before moving to Durban, where he helped found the Joint Rent Action Committee (JORAC) in 1982:

For people in an area like the Free State, what is important is the alleviation of the problems they are confronting. The very question of non-racialism, the way it comes into the picture is: what is the root cause of the problem? If in the struggles that people have gone through they have come to understand the root problem not as being the white person or the person's race, it is going to be difficult for that person to accept anybody who comes and tells them, no, the problem is the white person.

Throughout a worker's trade union activity, the lesson that he came to learn was that the root problem is the question of distributing the resources of the country unfairly. This is experience. It becomes intellectual if it does not reflect itself in practice. If in practice, however, people begin to come to grips with the root cause of the problem, that is what literally removes the rug from under BC perceptions.

When you are young boys and you are fighting, if a guy beats you, you want to go and organize more people to come on your side, and that's the kind of logic that would be there. In the same sort of spirit, we are all human beings and we've got one problem we are facing here. What is the bloody problem with us coming together and sorting it out all together? Non-racialism is not a denial of African leadership. What you need to do away with is this system. You maximize support and cooperation among all those who agree on the need to do that.

Nosizwe Madlala, a founder member of the Natal Organization of Women (NOW), which includes women of all races in its membership and leadership:

From the experience that I have had in our organization, I think the most unifying fact is that we are women, and that comes before the fact that we belong to different race groupings. The Natal Organization of Women is one of the few organizations that are completely mixed. Most organizations are not mixed, even though they believe in a non-racial democratic South Africa, because of the nature of their formation. Take, for instance, JORAC. JORAC is a residents association and it is based in the townships, so it is all black. Take, for instance, the Natal Indian Congress: it is all Indian.

What that actually means is that our belief in NOW is that we are working towards a non-racial society and we feel that we need to have participation of all the people in the process of change, because we feel that inasmuch as black people have been affected by the racial situation, some white people also have been affected because of the fact that we are made to live separately. So we feel that it is an important process for us to start to know each other better. And if we are working towards a non-racial society, I think we can start living it now — wherever it is possible, we are encouraging it. So that is why in our organization we have got white people, Indian people, and so-called coloureds and Africans.

For the government, the revival of mass political organization was a worrying sign, especially as it resulted in growing community support for labour issues. Even more alarming was the resurgence of a tradition of alliance politics, coupled with sporadic yet ever-increasing ANC guerilla activity. In 1983, the state responded to these mounting pressures with a constitution aimed at reforming, but not abolishing apartheid. Coloureds and Indians were to be represented in two new chambers of parliament, with whites continuing to dominate and Africans still locked out. This attempt to thwart the budding non-racial alliances by co-opting coloureds and Indians into the ruling bloc failed. Instead it prompted the formation of the most powerful legal anti-apartheid body since the ANC in the 1950s: the United Democratic Front (UDF).

Statement by the Commission on the Feasibility of a United Front against the Constitutional Proposals, 23 January 1983:[14]

Whereas the constitutional reform proposals devised by the minority white government for South Africa avoid recognition of these fundamental needs of democracy, now therefore we democrats do hereby unanimously form ourselves into a united democratic front to oppose the implementation of this devious scheme disguised to divide the people.

We declare that the broad principles on which this UDF is constituted are:
- a belief in the tenets of democracy;
- an unshakeable conviction in the creation of a non-racial, unitary state in South Africa undiluted by racial or ethnic considerations as formulated in the bantustan policy;
- an adherence to the need for unity in struggle through which all democrats, regardless of race, religion or colour, shall take part together;
- a recognition of the necessity to work in consultation with and reflect accurately the demands of democratic people wherever they may be in progressive worker, community and student organizations.

The participation of a tiny minority of coloureds and Indians in the 1984 elections for the tricameral parliament pointed up the critical function of black collaborators in making the system work. The UDF's successful election boycott demonstrated how building anti-apartheid alliances could ensure that the system broke down. Developing the theory and practice of 'broad front' politics was the UDF's main preoccupation in its five years of existence, until the government banned its key affiliates in 1988.

'Build the Front', Isizwe: Journal of the UDF, September 1987:

'Building the front' is more than building the UDF itself, and more than working closely, if not merging in some cases, with our natural allies. The UDF must seek to extend its political and moral influence far beyond these limits to include the widest possible range of South Africans. This means developing the capacity to intervene politically on the smallest localized instances of oppression and exploitation, up to the broad national issues.

In the first place, this broadening of our influence must be directed to the people's camp — to the ranks of all oppressed South Africans. To carry out this task successfully, we must ensure that we work much more consistently with groups that are not immediately drawn into our mainline sectors: trade unions, youth, women, civics and students. Our relationship with taxi-owners, traders, sports bodies and religious and cultural groups has often been very unsystematic. We must conduct work on this front in a much more coordinated, principled and strategic manner.

To give an example, we tend to approach traders each year early in June. We ask them to observe June 16th and June 26th by closing their businesses. And then we don't speak to them again until just before December 16th![15] When there is going to be a large political funeral in a distant township, at the last moment we suddenly ask cooperation from taxi-owners for transport. This cooperation must be deepened into a purposeful, structured, political relationship.

Of course, we shall continue to affirm the need for working class leadership on all fronts of the struggle. To call for progressive initiative from traders is not a call for them to lead our struggle. But nor do we think it healthy if traders, taxi-owners, black business people, sports clubs, etc. are treated in an unstructured, or even opportunistic way. All these groups must be won over politically — otherwise some may even become a recruiting base for the vigilante death squads,[16] or for apartheid's local authority structures.

But broadening our political and moral influence must go beyond the people's camp. We must increase our influence over sectors within the ruling bloc. At the national level, our call before the whites-only election was a good example of what is meant by seeking to broaden our political and moral influence within the ruling bloc. This call endeavoured to address a wide range of whites, but perhaps even here we were not comprehensive enough. We failed to address white workers in Afrikaans —

the language they mostly speak — around the issues, grudges and grievances that concern them. We failed, therefore, to snap the connection between legitimate grievances — to which we alone have the solution — and the racism within which the ultra-right wing parties opportunistically embedded these problems.

By its very nature, this very widest level of broadening the front will produce uneven results. Many of the sectors to be addressed within the ruling bloc may well join us on one specific issue and betray us on the next. But this does not mean that work on this, the broadest front, is pointless. Our duty is always to deprive the enemy of every support base and of every potential ally. To the extent that we render some of the regime's natural allies wavering and untrustworthy for it, that in itself is a gain for our national liberation struggle.

Discussion Questions
1. What have the democratic organizations in your area done to extend their influence to this broad range of organizations?
2. Discuss what is meant by the paper when it says these groups must be won over politically, rather than in an opportunistic way.
3. The paper also says our political approach should 'deprive the enemy of every support base, and of every potential ally'. Have you done this in your area?

The UDF launch in Mitchell's Plain, Cape Town in 1983, with veteran activist Helen Joseph.

Notes

1. The Umkhonto we Sizwe campaign against symbolic government targets — e.g., police stations, power installations — which became a focus of media coverage from 1979.
2. Although much lobbying for the non-racial policy took place on an inter-personal level, non-racialism was not strongly emphasized in early COSAS media. This tactic was motivated by a concern to avoid alienating former SASM members still loyal to the BC tradition. Note that while the organization's non-racial policy dates back to its founding document in 1979, the constitution referred to here was adopted in 1983.
3. Jolobe was one of a small but growing number of female leaders in black political organizations in this period.
4. Central Police headquarters in Johannesburg, infamous for Security Police detentions, interrogations, torture and deaths.
5. In its first year, COSAS took up two commemorative campaigns that the authorities saw as ANC-supporting: the 1978 hanging of MK guerilla Solomon Mahlangu, and the centenary of the Zulu victory over British troops at Isandhlwana.
6. Those arrested included Lybon Mabaso, Ishmael Mkhabela and Sammy Tloubatha.
7. The first COSAS president, Ephraim Mogale, was arrested, tried and convicted of furthering the aims of the ANC in the Northern Transvaal. So many COSAS leaders and members were detained over the following years that often the entire COSAS executive would be in jail, underground or out of South Africa, having fled the country.
8. AZASO was active in both the whites-only and blacks-only universities (the homeland universities, as well as the coloured and Indian campuses). By the late 1980s, the proportion of blacks studying at the nominally whites-only universities was nearing twenty per cent at many campuses, but by law blacks still had to apply to the government for permission to study subjects not offered on the black campuses.
9. This historical perspective on the organization is contained in the *South African National Students Congress (SANSCO) National Newsletter*, First Quarter, 1988. The newsletter goes on to explain that, 'The final break with our BC origins came at the 1986 Annual Congress, where the name of the organization was changed from AZASO to SANSCO.' SANSCO and NUSAS began working towards a merger of the two organizations following a decision taken by both at their annual meetings in late 1989.
10. A nation-wide protest against the government's celebration of the twentieth anniversary of the transformation of the Union of South Africa into a republic.
11. In this chapter the University of Durban-Westville is described as an 'Indians-only' institution, and the University of the Western Cape as 'coloureds-only'. This was certainly the intention of apartheid higher education, and the overwhelming number of students at these universities still fall into the designated racial category despite a trend towards non-racial admissions policies.
12. The development of YCS in South Africa was spurred by the Young Christian Workers (YCW), a movement started in Belgium in 1923 and introduced to South Africa in 1959, as well as the National Catholic Federation of Students (NCFS). By 1980 YCS was mainly active in black high schools, and in 1981 its organizing extended to black universities. Its three 'options' or principles are: the option for the poor, the option for liberation and the option for non-racialism.
13. Western countries also seemed to favour Black Consciousness over non-racialism. An article entitled, 'US Quietly Aids South African Black Activists',

Los Angeles Times, 11 November 1986, concludes that, 'Much U.S. money is going to Black Consciousness groups, many of them small, rather than the larger organizations that look for political leadership to the exiled ANC and the UDF inside the country.' Journalist Michael Parks quoted a US official visiting South Africa from Washington DC as saying, 'After liberation, we want to see a politically pluralist society in South Africa. Frankly, we don't want apartheid replaced with some system modelled on East Germany or Bulgaria. Naturally, we try to help those whose interests coincide with ours.' According to Parks, the key figure in an unpublicized US-sponsored $1.1-million leadership development programme was a former president of AZAPO.

14. This motion was mooted at the Transvaal Anti-SAIC (South African Indian Council) Conference, spurred by a speech by Revd Allan Boesak urging the formation of a body to fight the government's constitutional reforms. The UDF was launched in Cape Town on 20 August 1983.

15. The anniversary of the Soweto student uprisings (16 June) has come to be commemorated as 'South African Youth Day'. The adoption of the Freedom Charter at the Congress of the People on 26 June 1955 is celebrated as 'South African Freedom Day'. And the launch of Umkhonto we Sizwe on 16 December 1961 (also the Day of the Covenant commemorated by Afrikaners to mark their ancestors' military victory at Blood River) is celebrated as 'Heroes Day'.

16. 1985–89 saw an escalation of right-wing vigilante attacks, sanctioned or even led by police, on anti-apartheid activists and opponents of homeland rule.

19 In the Spirit of the Nation in the Making

The development of non-racialism in the coloured community was repeatedly derailed by shifts in government policy: after first alienating coloureds through disenfranchisement and the relentless Group Areas Act removals of the 1950s to mid-1960s, over the next decade the regime renewed its emphasis on the 'coloured preference' policies aimed at undermining coloured-African relations and incorporating coloured 'moderates' into the middle level of the apartheid hierarchy.

Trevor Manuel, UDF Western Cape executive member:

When I was younger there was a kind of striving towards whiteness. Some of my forebears were whites so we tend to look a lot like whites, and there was quite an issue in the family because so many relatives had applied for reclassification. So whiteness was something that was sought after: very basic notions like what your hair looked like and were you fair, etc. being things that actually mattered within the coloured community at that point in time. Some of our relatives succeeded in being reclassified, but it had never been on in our family.

Did you know these whites in your family's background, or was that many generations back?

The strange thing is that when the generation before me related stories about our forebears the whites were remembered, but I haven't been able to trace my black roots as yet. That's the kind of emphasis that's always been there.

How did you first hear about the historical political organizations?

There was somebody in our community, Toufie Bardien, a taxi driver who had been banned for some fifteen years, and he'd been active in the Coloured People's Congress. I tuned me a copy of the Freedom Charter in the early '70s — that was my first kind of exposure.

How did you respond?

I think my first response to the way in which the Congress Alliance had organized was that it made perfect sense, given the extent to which areas had been segregated and that people lead entirely separate lives — the cultural divisions which do obtain and were further entrenched by the pass laws. But I'd say the period between 1970 and 1976 was a very hazy and mixed-up period for me. Given all my early experiences about some members of the family having tried for white and some actually having

Coloured students marching during the 1980 Western Cape school boycott, holding a banner reading 'We want free, equal education for all!'

succeeded, there was that difficulty in trying to define how coloureds relate to a South African context: were we a buffer group? Were we part of the solution? Were we part of the problem?

An important legacy of the Black Consciousness era in the coloured community was the emergence of a qualifier that preceded references to the word 'coloured': 'so-called'. It was enunciated with an inflection of disdain that conveyed the mandatory inverted commas − often people would motion in the air with two fingers of each hand.

Patrick Flusk, Anti-President's Council committee [1] *member from Johannesburg's coloured township of Riverlea:*

I think it was in 1979 when I first heard 'so-called coloured'. To me, it was rather fascinating, because at school quite a number of students used to ask, 'What is a coloured?' You know, 'Explain a coloured.' In my family we have one brother who looks like a Chinese, my one brother looks like a so-called Indian, my one brother looks like a white, and we have one brother who is dark of complexion. So we always used to call one another, 'You, "China", you, "coolie", you "*swartskaap* "' [black sheep] − that's why we say 'so-called' coloureds.

I come from a community which is very stratified, in the sense that there's a line dividing the sub-economical houses from the others, and therefore people used to call each other the 'high bucks' and the 'low bucks'. I realized afterwards that it is a class struggle as well, because some people were living worse off than what other people were living. Like people that's living bad in Riverlea, we have no hot water, no electricity, very small rooms and very crowded places. And that, to me, is just like a link that we are no different − South Africa is our country and we are African people, and the word 'coloured' means nothing to me. It has no meaning at all.

Others, however, refused to negate their 'colouredness' by attaching 'so-called' to the term.

Letter to the editor of Sechaba, *June 1984:*

I have noticed now in speeches, articles, interviews, etc. in *Sechaba* that I am called a 'so-called Coloured' (sometimes with a small 'c'). When did the Congress decide to call me this? In South Africa I was active in the Congress Alliance and was a member of the Coloured People's Congress, not the 'so-called Coloured People's Congress'. When we worked for Congress of the People and the Freedom Charter we sang, 'We the coloured people, we must struggle to exist ...' I remember in those times some people of the so-called Unity Movement referred to so-called Coloured people, but not our Congress.

Comrade Editor, I am confused. I need clarification. It makes me feel like a 'so-called' human, like a humanoid, those things who have all the characteristics of human beings but are really artificial. Other minority people are not called 'so-called'. Why me? It must be the 'curse of Ham'.[2] In the meantime, I remain, respectfully,
Yours,
Capie (Alex La Guma)

Editor's note:
As far as I can remember, there is no decision taken in our movement to change from 'Coloured' to 'so-called coloured'. All I know is that people at home have been increasingly using the term 'so-called coloureds'. I suspect that what you have noticed is a reflection of this development.

Not long ago, *Sechaba* said: 'It is not enough to say the so-called coloureds or to put the word coloureds in inverted commas. A positive approach to this problem needs to be worked out because we are dealing w. h a group of people who are identifiable and distinguishable.' In other words, a discussion on this issue is necessary, and I think your letter may just well be a starting point for such a discussion.

Letter to the editor of Sechaba, *August 1984:*

The mass of young people, after and during the 1976 national youth uprising, more and more questioned apartheid terminology, not as ethnologists or professors of anthropology, but rather as hurt and confused human beings sick to death of manipulation by those who had set themselves up as their white masters. The term 'so-called coloured' was commonly used amongst the youth in popular expression of rejection of apartheid terminology.

I am in full agreement with what was said in *Sechaba*, but would add that it would be equally wrong to accept the term coloured. Coloured is a term which cries of lack of identity. The term was fundamental to the racist myth of the pure white Afrikaner; to accept the term is to allow the myth to carry on. Today people are saying, 'We reject the racists' terminology,' and are beginning to build the new in defiance of the old, right in the midst of the enemy. We should see the prefix 'so-called' as the first step in coming towards a solution of something which has been a scourge for years. We have got to move on from the term 'so-called coloured' in a positive way. People are now saying that we have the choice of what we will be called, and most, in the spirit of the nation in the making, opt for 'South African'. If one really needs a sub-identity to that of being a South African, maybe through popular debate the question could be sorted out.

Yours in the struggle,

Mayibuye i Afrika!

Moulana Farid Esack, founder member of the UDF-affiliated Call of Islam:

This reference to 'so-called' coloured was a contradiction, because you never thought of yourself as a so-called coloured — you thought of yourself as a coloured. The community was completely suspended between the blacks and the whites. My only memories of blacks were of the bogeyman who was going to catch you at night: '*Die boetie kom jou vang kom slaap.*' I had no contact with black people, and what was amazing is that on the other side of the road were the Langa [African workers'] hostels. People ask me what is apartheid all about — this is what apartheid is: to have people living on the other side of the road or the railway line or the hill, and not to have any kind of human contact or recognize the person on the other side as a human being.

I mean, BC had some very primitive and very bare ideas, quite simplistic, about the differences in the levels of oppression: no, coloureds aren't different from blacks — you're either pregnant or you're not pregnant. Whether you're three months pregnant or nine months pregnant is not the point, so whether you're oppressed to this degree or whether you're oppressed to that degree, it's not the point. But the reality of the Indians is also different from the reality of the blacks, and the coloureds are different from the Indians, so why should the coloureds and Indians be a part of the black community? My social experience does not give any kind of credibility to the idea that the coloureds regarded themselves as a part of the black community. It's one of the most bizarre communities in the world, the coloured community — a community in limbo.

Of course, now people don't have any qualms about using the term 'coloured'. I think that the last few years have really brought the coloured community a very, very long way in moving towards a recognition that our destiny is tied up with the rest of the people of South Africa. The fact that the coloureds see Nelson Mandela as a leader, this would have been unbelievable ten years ago — certainly for the Muslim community. You see, Muslims' sense of race has been tainted by a religious arrogance, which is also characteristic of a minority ethos. It is Congress that has moved people.

When you refer to 'Congress', you mean the ANC now, not the Coloured People's Congress of the 1950s?

The Coloured People's Congress is never mentioned: now that's very significant. We have a sense of embarrassment about it. We really feel uncomfortable about the fact that there was actually a time when the coloured people called themselves 'coloured', and we're ashamed of it. Politically, ideologically, we ought to be supporting that idea for that time, but no, we gloss over the idea that our people did actually organize as a separate community. The Indian Congress is legitimately a part of the tradition of the Indian people, but the Coloured People's Congress is not a part of the tradition of the coloured people. You didn't have a Gandhi in the coloured community. It's a tragedy that you actually have a whole community without any traditions, without any folk heroes.

In the coloured community the tradition of non-racialism had thrived among organized workers,[3] but the vacuum left by SACTU's demise was not filled for another decade. By then the conservative unions had so successfully depoliticized their coloured members[4] that even the independent non-racial trade unions of the late 1970s were daunted by the challenge of organizing coloured and African workers together. Thus it was not workers but the coloured youth that led a political reawakening of their community, first joining in the 1976 Soweto-inspired student uprisings, then taking the lead in a wave of school boycotts that emanated from the Western Cape in 1980. These coloured students cemented the most enduring alliance to date with their African peers.

Report of the State Commission of Inquiry into the Riots at Soweto and Elsewhere from 16 June 1976 to 20 February 1977:

Witnesses who had given a great deal of thought to the matter gave the sense of solidarity with Soweto as the main cause of the riots, and explained why the Coloured, who used to be closer to the White man than the Black man, had changed to the extent that he was prepared to regard the Black man as his comrade in distress and to continue the struggle for improvement with him.

The Coloured community has been caused pain and suffering by institutions such as race classification, group areas and even separate universities. This classification is humiliating; they reject not only the word 'coloured', but also the idea of a separate Coloured identity, and 'Non-White' is unacceptable because it is a negative definition in the language of a dominant White group.

As a result of the unnatural separation of population groups forced upon them by the White Government, the view gained ground that the White man had rejected the Coloured as a friend and fellow citizen. The attraction felt earlier gave way to resentment, frustration and aversion. The Coloured then turned anti-White and took a closer look at the various facets of the Black man's struggle. He joined up with the Black community so as to remove his grievances and obtain his rights through concerted action.

Other witnesses traced a shorter course. According to them, dissatisfied Coloureds had sensed an uneasiness among Whites about the rise of the Black man and had found a new comrade-in-arms in the Black man. To this may be added that the Coloured might well have thought that the Black man was gaining the upper hand and would rule the White man; for this reason, he had joined up with the Black man.

'Manifesto of the Committee of 81', 14 May 1980 (statement of the students who coordinated the school boycotts):

The boycott has deliberately been made a coloured issue by the ruling class newspapers and television. To attempt to solve the problem of coloured education is not enough. From Mamelodi to Manenberg, from Rylands to Riviersonderend,[5] students taught under Coloured Affairs, Bantu Affairs and Indian Affairs have come out together in the boycott. In spite of the deliberate tribalism fed into our brains, we realize that our inequalities spring from the same root causes and that we are not Bantus, Coloureds or Indians, we are human beings. Power to the People! *Amandla Ngawethu! Alle Mag Aan Die Mense!*[6]

Preston Geswint, a secondary school student in Port Elizabeth during the 1980 school boycotts:

The interesting thing is that at first I didn't understand why the coloured students were also boycotting. I was a prefect at school at that time, and one day I was walking in town and I met this African fellow, you see, and he called me. That was the time when these type of questions came up − the role of the prefects at school and the way they are seen as being superior to other students, doing the dirty work of the principals and the authorities, maintaining discipline − questions that I couldn't give answers to. Because that was the first time I was actually made to think about these things. The boycott made me see that the whole education system was unequal.

All those questions were thrown at me and that made me realize that I mustn't just see this thing in terms of a coloured issue, but that it affects us all in the country, with these divisions that's been created between the coloureds and the African people and the Indians and the whites. I think the coloured community has been very affected. They've developed that consciousness of being separate, because you find that the coloured people are more privileged than the African people. And then again the Indians were a little bit more privileged than the coloureds. There's that whole point of co-opting the people in that way, having more privileges, somehow a sense that you've got more to lose.

Peter Williams, a Cape Town student who was still in primary school during the 1976 and 1980 student uprisings:

I think the coloured community is a really racist community, so I had a sort of fear for the African people. But also, although I had that fear for the Africans, in a way I sympathized with their oppression, and somehow I just knew that what was happening to them was wrong. Because I came from a poor community I could always sympathize with poor people, and the Africans being the poorest people, I could, in a way, associate with them.

How did you move from that fear and sympathy to feeling equal?

My idea of my fellow South Africans changed from 1983. I attended the COSAS Annual General Meeting in Durban in 1983, and I came into contact with various African people and I spoke to them and I learned about them as people — not as politicals or revolutionaries or whatever, but I learned to know them as people who perhaps had the same longings that I had. And I think that contributed to the acceptance of the Africans as my brothers.

What was it like, those first conversations with African people at the conference?

To tell the truth, I was actually afraid, because at the COSAS conference

Candidates in the 1984 elections to the coloured chamber of the tricameral parliament were so fiercely heckled that they found it difficult to hold campaign meetings in their communities.

we sang political songs. In fact, that was the first time when I heard such militant songs being sung, and I was actually afraid. Because in the history books they've always taught us that the Africans, they invited Piet Retief there and they sang and danced with him and afterwards they murdered him.[7] So that image drew up in me of how you think they are friendly and all of a sudden they would murder you. So when we had that intense atmosphere in that hall I was getting afraid of it, but as the days passed I learnt to fit myself into that atmosphere.

This newly fortified solidarity across racial lines prepared the ground for the campaign against government efforts to woo coloureds and Indians with its reforms. Opposition coalesced around censure of the Labour Party's decision to participate in the 1984 tricameral elections, and was mobilized by UDF affiliates like the Cape Areas Housing Action Committee (CAHAC) and the UWO.

Zelda Holtzman, who canvassed for the anti-election campaign not only in the coloured community, but in African, white and Indian areas of the Western Cape as well:

People were initially saying, 'Now, let's see what the coloureds are going to do.' On a large scale, under the banner of the UDF, people mobilized around that, and it gave us an opportunity to speak to different kinds of people. And I think it wasn't strange for an African woman to go into Bonteheuwel [coloured area] and knock on the door and speak to the person about the anti-election campaign and ask her to sign the UDF declaration. And in the same way, lots of coloured people went into Crossroads [African shanty-town].

I think that struggle proved our principled position on non-racialism. The oppressed — the black oppressed, including the Africans, coloureds and Indians — had a chance to show that they are united. I think that struggle in itself was a breakthrough. I mean, the African comrades were there at the polling station — everybody was excited to see whether our work in the anti-election campaign bore fruits. And it wasn't a coloured struggle — we tried throughout to project it as a non-racial struggle. One demand was clear in the anti-election campaign: what we are fighting for is a non-racial South Africa. We are being offered the vote, but what about the majority of the people who are denied the vote? And that was the theme that ran throughout.

Noma-India Mfeketo, a UWO founder member:

Do you think that non-racialism is now widely accepted in the African areas of the Western Cape?

I think so, because of the experience. Like from '76, when coloured schools went out in support of the African schools, that started to educate people from the African townships that we are all black. Even now, the government announced that it is going to move all African townships into

Khayalitsha, and then put coloureds in all these established townships like Langa, Nyanga, Gugulethu. The government wanted a fight between so-called coloureds and the Africans, but the coloured people were saying, 'We're not moving, we're not moving to Gugulethu, Nyanga and Langa — black people stay there. Build more houses for us — and for Africans!' That helped in educating the people.

While the national media focus tended to be on Western Cape politics, coloureds all over the country spurned the government's 'reforms' and demanded non-racial democracy — in ways as diverse as their differing regional experiences.

Cliffie Collings, founder member of the United Committee of Concern (UCC), a UDF affiliate in Natal's coloured community:

It was only after the tricameral elections that we started getting involved in political education and began to find out why we needed a coloured organization. We thought that it's important that we take people from where they are to a stage of understanding of why we need to practise non-racialism. I think that if the UDF wasn't there we'd have problems in defending our stand, because we always argue that we are all UDF — it's non-racial, it's Charterist, and we support that. In fact, most people don't see us as the United Committee of Concern — they see us straight as UDF.

With the difference in conditions between the Indians and coloureds, the types of struggles we get involved in is very different, how we organize them is quite different, and people's reactions in the two different communities is quite different also. African people are almost naturally conscientized by virtue of their repression — it's not the same with coloureds and Indians, definitely not.

People in the Cape would disagree very seriously with how we operate. I meet with them and I always argue it: I say you can never relate the conditions from the Western Cape to Natal or the Transvaal. Cape Town is largely coloured, they've got over two million coloureds there. The Indians are in the minority there, and even Africans are in the minority to the coloured people.

Western Cape has years and years of political experience, but we don't have it in Natal. Our people are very conservative. The only type of Africans that coloured people meet are the ones who pick pockets and fight, so they [coloureds] can be quite racist as a result. The difference between coloured and Indian has been very sharp in the Durban area. If you saw an Indian guy with a coloured girl, or vice versa, there would be lots of fights taking place.

It's the system that exploits the differences between people. They spend more on Indians than they do on coloureds, and Natal being more Indian-orientated as such — only about two or three per cent of the coloureds of South Africa are in Natal[8] — the coloureds see themselves being exploited by Indian people.

Now the problem would be that the coloureds are exposed only to the Indian who owns the businesses in Grey Street, or Indians who come to their discos all flashy. They're not exposed to people deep within, say, Phoenix or Chatsworth, to some of the Indians who are suffering. They pick up anti-Indian vibes, you can see it all the time, and you actually have to explain to people how apartheid is ensuring that these differences exist.

One is always conscious of race in South Africa, because of the Group Areas Act. It's essential to the government's policy that that is the case. I think that people might begin to realize that we can actually live together, and once the people can see that, they will see less differences between each other and will begin to stand more united. And when people stand united, the government's got problems.

In the towns of South Africa the segregation of the different race groups into discrete Group Areas was largely successful,[9] but in the rural areas it has proved more difficult to effect such rigid separation.

Reggie Oliphant, community activist in Oudtshoorn, in the Southern Cape:

There was no real contact at certain stages between the coloured people and the African people. But as time went on, because the African people had to come through to Bridgton [coloured township] to go to town, we restored the old type of relationship that existed, and so we were not fighting any more. I think they were more the better-off type of African people that lived there, and our families would share, and I think that that broke the type of thing that was created through our separate schools. Our parents, I think, played a very important role in relating to us also that these are not our enemies, these people are undergoing the same thing that we are undergoing, and that's why I think that we came together again. Gradually the bonds were restored.

We have been able to form youth congresses with people from both areas, coloured and African. Every organization in Oudtshoorn is non-racial. African and coloured people have been working together, hand in hand. The youth basically broke down that fear, through their interaction all the time in community organizations.

Do people in the Oudtshoorn coloured community ever ask you what it will be like in the future under a non-racial government?

People ask me that regularly. People ask me, 'Don't you think that because we are treated as a buffer group by the system now that the African communities would do the same thing in the future?' My response to that is that we are talking about liberating ourselves from those evils that have been practised by the system. This system has used every possible means to dominate, whereas in our organizations today, in everything that we do, we don't have any colour bar. Let's take the UDF: we have a lot of coloured people on the national executive committee, we even have white people. On the ANC executive there are people of all kinds of groupings.

Do you do all your politicizing in Afrikaans?

Basically, and the Charter has also been translated into very beautiful Afrikaans because particularly the older people is not that good in English. They speak either Afrikaans or Xhosa. Most of the youth, they speak English, except for the youth that have not been to school.

Did you ever go through a stage where you felt that Afrikaans was 'the language of the oppressor'?

I think that many people went through that stage, but I'm only basing my politics on realities, and it is the reality that a lot of people, particularly coloured people, do speak Afrikaans. I think that it'd be totally unfair of anybody to come afterwards and say that Afrikaans has to be ruled out because of the fact that it was the medium through which our people were dominated and oppressed. I feel that Afrikaans is a beautiful language, and I feel that, particularly in the Cape Province, there is certain words, there is certain phrases in Afrikaans that cannot be said in English. It's beautiful, it's the language of the *klonkies*, the coons, the carnivals.[10]

Do you call yourself a 'so-called coloured'?

That's a difficult one. I don't have any problems about whatever people call me. It's no big deal.

Youths wearing masks to conceal their identities unfurled the flag of the banned ANC before a crowd of several thousand at a May Day meeting at the University of the Western Cape in 1988. The T-shirt reads (in Xhosa): 'Go well Comrade Ashley Kriel', a reference to a popular coloured MK cadre who was killed by police.

Notes

1. None of the UDF-affiliated groupings in the coloured communities use the term 'coloured' in their names; thus the Transvaal's 'Anti-PC' refers to the refusal of the coloured (and Indian) community to be co-opted onto the President's Council. Established in 1980 in an effort to simulate 'power-sharing' while perpetuating white domination, the council consisted of government-appointed whites, coloureds and Indians – but no Africans.
2. A Biblical reference from the Book of Genesis to the curse Noah put on his son, Ham, for mocking his drunken father: that Ham and his descendants were to be enslaved, thus condemned to serve as 'hewers of wood and drawers of water'. In one of the crudest forms of racist reinterpretation of the Scriptures, South African Dutch Reformed Church theologians argued that the 'Hamitic curse' had predestined black people to a lowly status, while Afrikaners were likened to the 'Chosen People' of Israel.
3. Non-racialism has also thrived among a certain politicized sector of sports enthusiasts. The South African Council on Sport (SACOS) claimed a commitment to non-racialism from its inception in 1973, and made an important contribution to the popularization of its Unity Movement-inspired understanding of non-racialism. The fact that its membership remained largely confined to the coloured and Indian community, together with its steadfast adherence to the principles of non-alignment and non-collaboration, led to its threatened marginalization and ultimate eclipse by a new pressure group formed in 1989, the UDF-aligned National Sports Congress.
4. Since the Coloured Labour Preference Policy had mainly benefited skilled and educated coloureds, the management-aligned garment workers and public service unions were able to capitalize on exacerbated class divisions, resulting in a decline in progressive trade unionism and the further estrangement of coloured and African workers.
5. Respectively, African, coloured, Indian and coloured living areas of Cape Town.
6. Translation of the popular slogan into Zulu and Afrikaans. It should be noted that Afrikaans is spoken by more blacks than whites, for in the coloured community English is largely confined to the middle class and educated elites.
7. A reference to the encounter between the Natal Boer leader and the Zulu King in 1838, in which Dingane ordered the Zulu armies to execute the Boers (see Chapter 8, note 2). The incident gained mythic proportions in the work of Afrikaner nationalist historians who ignored the violent Boer invasion that provoked Dingane's response and the countless other amicable encounters between Africans and frontier whites.
8. Lineage in Natal's small coloured community is sometimes directly traceable to prominent English settlers. The 'Dunn's Descendants Association' of nineteenth-century trader John Dunn's progeny numbers some 5,000 in the Mangete area of Zululand.
9. However, by the late 1980s even segregation in the urban areas was breaking down. Johannesburg's Hillbrow, for example, had become a 'grey area' housing blacks as well as whites.
10. References to the coloured working-class culture of the Western Cape 'Coon Carnival', an annual post-New Year celebration featuring crazily costumed revellers parading through the streets.

20 Isn't That What We're Fighting For?

Like the coloured community, Indians also gained a new level of political credibility through their overwhelming rejection of 'reformed' apartheid. Even before the tricameral parliament was mooted, the Indian community had begun mobilizing opposition to the 1981 elections for another government-controlled ethnic body, the South African Indian Council (SAIC). The Anti-SAIC Campaign had its roots in a critique of an organizing style that denies race-determined realities.

Mohammed Valli Moosa, a former SASO executive member active in the Anti-SAIC Campaign:

The one major weakness that we had recognized in the past was that the Black Consciousness movement was based amongst the students, amongst certain sections of the youth and other educated or professional people, and that we had very little contact with the masses of our people as such. The fact that our organizations didn't actively involve our people, that was the one major criticism we had made of ourselves, and we needed to look at how to overcome that.

The UDF picketed outside Durban City Hall in 1983 to protest the Prime Minister P. W. Botha's appeal for Indians to support his 'reforms'.

A second point is that there were two trends within the BC movement: there were those who believed that BC emerged out of nothing, that it stood on its own, that it was not part of historical developments, and rejected — even scorned — the traditional movements of our people and our history. Whereas the other trend said that we need to see ourselves as part of a struggle which has been going on for many centuries now, we need to see ourselves as part of what was happening in the 1950s, part of the Congress Alliance, all of those kinds of things.

We found that without that kind of historical analysis we would be unable to move forward, because we would be unable to communicate with our people. The people did not know us, they knew Nelson Mandela. In the community which I come from, the so-called Indian community, people did not know SASO, BPC, they knew the Transvaal Indian Congress (TIC). If we were to organize effectively the masses of our people, we needed to understand their own culture of resistance, we needed to understand who the leaders were, what their background was.

TIC poster advocating a boycott of the 1984 elections for the Indian and coloured houses of the new tricameral parliament.

Natal Indian Congress (NIC) vice-president Jerry Coovadia, speaking in Durban on the 112th anniversary of Gandhi's birth, 11 October 1981:

Mahatma Gandhi, the father of the Congress of Indian South Africans, was a leader who was alert to the problems of the people and also an advocate of socialism. And the source of Natal Indian Congress philosophy is rooted in an era and in this man of achievements and ideals. You and I are the custodians of a great and noble tradition which we should nurture, enhance and defend against the dangers of dilution. For these dangers, from the little men in our midst who wish to betray this trust by participation in the President's Council and the South African Indian Council, are indeed serious today.

It requires little imagination to guess what Gandhi would have done if he were alive today and surveyed the sorrowful spectacle of our public life. His code of social freedom which rejects distinctions on the basis of birth, sex, caste, creed or colour would have, as it did during his stay in South Africa, made him lead the fight against apartheid. Gandhi believed in allowing people to decide for themselves. They are the final arbiters of independence and democracy. This is the single most important lesson we have to learn from Gandhi's experience: the absolute necessity for working with the people and articulating their demands. This is, therefore, the quintessential legacy of Gandhi for you and me.

Appeals to the Gandhian tradition had more resonance for the older generation than for the youth.[1] The politicization of many Indian students stemmed from the more immediate experience of the nationwide school boycotts of 1980.

Alf Karrim, chairperson of the committee coordinating the boycott in Natal, who was detained in Modder Bee Prison in the Transvaal:

Student leaders from all over the country actually converged in four big cells, and in fact, all those people who went into that particular experience came out ten times stronger. I think we [Indians from Natal] learned some fairly serious things in the couple of months that we were in detention. We learned that unless the African people are liberated in South Africa, there can be no liberation for any other community. And that although we went in idealistically, believed in non-racialism and all that, we hadn't, up to that point, understood it: that non-racialism actually means the liberation of the African people in the first instance. What we learned from those experiences was basically that one needs a national democratic approach, where any single person interested in challenging apartheid is welcome into that broad struggle.

You have that kind of ethnic division between Indians, Africans, coloureds and whites, with Indians having it, not the worst in terms of oppression, but the worst in terms of the minority syndrome. They are the smallest percentage of people. They always fear that, 'We can't challenge the white government because they'll trample all over us, we can't actually challenge the Africans because they are far superior in numbers, and they will wipe us out and send us to the Indian Ocean,' as the saying goes. And then there is a lot of fear attaching to that, together with apartheid propaganda, which consistently attempted to keep the Indian community as the sort of jam between two slices of bread.

The boycott campaigns against elections to the SAIC and the tricameral parliament were led by the Indian Congresses of Natal and the Transvaal, the two provinces with the greatest concentration of Indians. The NIC had been revived back in 1971, when it weathered attacks from Black Consciousness supporters chanting, 'Think Black, not Indian'. The revival of the TIC in 1983 sparked a hot debate within anti-apartheid circles over the issue of ethnically-based organization.

Work in Progress *editorial, February 1983:*

The re-formation of the old Transvaal Indian Congress has created something of a stir. One of the oldest political organizations in South Africa, the TIC was an integral part of the ANC-led Congress Alliance. Now the reconstitution of the TIC has again raised questions about a racially-specific organization adopting a non-racial position. AZAPO publicity secretary Ishmael Mkhabela has stated that the formation of TIC will strengthen the forces of ethnicity. 'From our point of view, any ethnically-based organization by Indians, coloureds or Zulus is directly in line with Pretoria's policy of apartheid,' said Mkhabela.

Others disagree with AZAPO. General and Allied Workers Union (GAWU) president Samson Ndou sees the TIC as a people's, not an ethnic organization. Transvaal Anti-SAIC chairperson Essop Jassat points out that South African laws have forced different people to live in separate ghettos. 'It is easier for them to organize and mobilize politically from their respective areas,' says Jassat. And GAWU's Sydney Mafumadi suggests that, 'How the TIC is structured is not fundamental: the fundamental issue is that its aims and objectives are non-racial.'

AZAPO's categorization of the TIC as 'ethnic' needs to be assessed in the light of three factors: the TIC's adherence to non-racialism, whether it manipulates ethnicity and racial symbols in its activities, and the interests which it represents. The Congress Alliance comprised racially- or nationally-specific organizations, linked through organizational structures and joint campaigns. Non-racialism involves a statement about a future society in which racism will be eradicated; it also implies that race is not the most important social category in society. This suggests that the class structure of South Africa is a more fundamental force than racial factors.

Ethnic organizations mobilize on the basis of a set of perceived ethnic interests and symbols. This, for example, is a component of Inkatha's Zulu nationalism.[2] But there is no indication that the TIC, or any of the other racially-specific Congress organizations, operated on that basis.

Finally, there is the question of the interests which an organization represents. This involves the relative weight that working class, petty bourgeois, peasant or other interests enjoy within an organization or alliance. An attempt to establish the primacy of working class or popular interests is unlikely to merit the ethnic tag. These are some of the issues which need to be raised in assessing AZAPO's attack on the TIC.

Kumi Naidoo, NIC member and an SRC leader at the University of Durban-Westville:

Occasionally when you do field work and you go to people's houses, they ask you, 'What guarantee do we Indians have that when the blacks take over we won't get booted out?' Then when you're talking to them, you can't talk as a black person — you have to then sort of connect with people at the level at which they are thinking. When relating to ordinary working class people, you have to talk in terms of Indian and coloured. That is why it's necessary to have an Indian Congress: because that's how people perceive themselves.

The sophistication of the ideological state apparatus,[3] the fact that people live in separate areas, the fact that in your documents, in any application, when there's 'race' you have to write 'Indian', the school that you go to is Indian — it just has such an impact on people's way of thinking. It would almost be inhuman for people not to have that initial kind of Indian, African, coloured or white consciousness.

They've got a special radio programme for Indian people, something called Radio Lotus. It's such an important thing, in terms of this whole move by the state of using Indian people to develop this kind of Indian consciousness. Because it has a certain kind of appeal, through the songs and stuff like that — especially older people would listen to the radio station. All those things, collectively, have a tremendous impact in shaping the way people think of themselves and the way they think of others as well.

I look forward to the day when there won't be a need for an NIC, and I hope that it's around the corner. I think it would be a good thing for the cause of non-racialism when eventually we are in a position to do away with the Indian tag, but I think in this period, so long as the majority of the people still see themselves as being Indian, it is necessary to retain the label.[4]

There is one exceptional circumstance in which the apartheid system groups Indians together with Africans and coloureds: in jail. For many, the prison experience marks the first time they have ever lived in close contact with people of other races. Yet even political prisoners feel the tensions arising from divergent ethnic identities, with the smallest minority group finding it most trying — though often also most rewarding.

Devan Pillay, a university student who served a year in prison for ANC activities in 1981:

First I was kept in Port Elizabeth prison. That was a really weird experience, because there were murderers and robbers and what-have-you, and they really looked up to me as a political prisoner. In Port Elizabeth — everywhere out of Durban — Indians are well-off, by and large, because the professionals moved out of Durban. And so that's their experience of Indians: professionals, doctors, lawyers, businessmen. Here was an Indian who was fighting for black people, and it was quite something, you know. You just felt these positive vibrations, and you said, 'This is worthwhile, it's a contribution to non-racialism.'

Prison was the first time I'd actually lived with African people in very, very close daily contact, and I was very conscious of being an Indian, of being different. And wanting to be accepted — ja, I was very conscious of that. The other political prisoners were very accommodating. Of course, the problem that crept in was the language — especially when a lot of youngsters came in from Port Elizabeth who couldn't speak English very well. The others were forced to speak Xhosa most of the time to them, and I would feel a bit alienated. Later on other political prisoners came, who weren't so sensitive to my being Indian. I remember when we were discussing a hunger strike and them deciding a course of action, and I asked, 'What have you decided?' and they interpreted my questioning as not wanting to be part of the action. So all those tensions were there.

I was very conscious of it, though at the time I tried not to admit it. Because you wanted to feel that you were a black person and you were part of the struggle. But right throughout I was conscious of being Indian, and trying to prove myself.

It was this palpable reality of ethnic identification that sustained the argument favouring constituency-based politics. Judgment of the Indian Congresses was ultimately based more on their achievements — most notably, the overwhelming boycott of the tricameral elections — than on the structures used to realize these results. Debate continued, however, on how best to bridge the gap between the theory of transcending ethnicity and the on-the-ground experience.

Jessie Duarte, organizer for the Federation of Transvaal Women (FedTraw) from Johannesburg's coloured township of Riverlea:

When I look at how people organize today I'm very concerned. Although people don't directly say that they are organizing on a racial basis, the reality is that they are. I understand the value of that kind of strategy, but at the same time you're actually pandering to a very backward mentality by assuming that a coloured person won't relate to, say, an Indian person in Lenasia, or that a comrade from Soweto couldn't come and organize in a coloured area or vice versa. I've often heard activists say, 'If we have African comrades coming to Riverlea, maybe they'll have problems.' My feeling about that is perhaps they will have problems, but isn't that what we're fighting for?

I remember quite well during the anti-election campaign, going door to door people would say, 'How come you people are talking about black majority rule but there are no African people here with you?' There's a need for people to see this non-racialism that we talk about in practice. You can't say, okay, for now we're going to work like this as ethnic groupings, and then in the next five years we're going to double our efforts so that people will accept one another as different races.

The Federation of Transvaal Women, for instance, organizes on a non-racial basis. We have women's groups in communities all over the Transvaal, and some of those groups are mixed groups — it depends on who comes together in a certain geographical area. In my particular area, the women that have come together are only coloured women, and for me, that's problematic. And yet on a pragmatic level, I can understand that we have to organize those women into projects within their areas.

I believe we're going to have a hell of a problem after liberation. Because it doesn't mean that we are suddenly going to have non-racial living areas, you know. I think for a long time after liberation there will still be Soweto and there'll still be Newclare, and there will still be Riverlea and Bosmont and Fordsburg,[5] and the people who live there now will live there then.

This is something which one raises in the UDF, and I think that many people share the concerns I have, but have the same problem as I do as to exactly how do we get to the point where our strategies can also include non-racial campaigns that everyone can become involved in. We mustn't just speak about non-racialism — we must work in a non-racial way.

The perennial debate over the nature of white involvement in mass-based organization also resurfaced, this time without the racial overtones of the Black Consciousness era, but linked instead to an attack on the class base of organizations that included whites and liberals.

Rehana Rossouw, Cape Youth Congress (CAYCO)[6] activist:

In 1983 CAYCO was formed, and I remember there was this message of support from NUSAS. A lot of people felt that there was no ways that whites could be involved in the struggle, and there was no way that they would allow white people into CAYCO — which caused lots of big differences. I lost lots of good friends during that argument, who felt that white students who were involved in political organizations were sons and daughters of the ruling class, and we can't trust them all the way in the struggle.

I knew that there were a lot of white people who were just as committed as I was. I was sure that a lot of coloured or African people who were involved in student politics, once they got their degrees, there were chances that they'd also become managers or doctors or lawyers and forget about the struggle.

Strangely enough, most of the people who were anti-white in the debate were from middle-class areas. For myself, coming from a middle-class family, I could understand and sympathize with that kind of argument that they [whites] weren't going to go all the way, but my feeling was that it's a broad struggle and we need to fight apartheid on all fronts, and therefore we should include all those who purport to be part of the mass movement and are willing to work, and whether they dropped out along the way had nothing to do with whether we were going to work with them now.

That was the basis of the argument — but then we were out-voted and NUSAS wasn't allowed observer status in CAYCO. It was a very dirty fight. In our branch of CAYCO in Lansdowne [middle-class coloured area] we had the person who led the argument that we shouldn't have NUSAS involved in any way. She tried to present it as a class thing, that you don't want the bourgeoisie to lead the struggle, that if the working class aren't leading the struggle we're going to be deflected from our socialist path. Then this very person, two weeks after this whole debate, went to NUSAS and expected them to print pamphlets for her.

How did NUSAS respond?

They said that they weren't prepared to be used any longer, that people

Non-racial women's organizations were formed all over the country in the 1980s; the Natal Organization of Women (NOW), United Women's Congress (UWCO) in Cape Town, and the Federation of Transvaal Women (FedTRAW) all supported the revival of the Federation of South African Women (FedSAW).

should accept that they were just as committed as anyone else was — which they were.

Do you support the tactic of 'ethnic' organizing, in which the different race groups work in their own group areas?

Let me put it this way. Since the launch of the UDF in 1983, we needed everyone who could work to give all their free time to organizing. We had students from NUSAS, we had the white members of the United Women's Organization coming with us into areas like Mitchell's Plain, into Gugulethu, into Langa. And this was the first time that something like that had ever happened in Cape Town, that you had white people going into black areas to politicize people.

And that hasn't stopped since then. With the Million Signatures Campaign of the UDF[7] we had white comrades who went with us, who went into areas that I'm too scared to go into, where gangsterism is rife and where young ladies don't walk around late at night, and since then it's never been a problem or a question of: you're a white person and therefore must only organize in your own area. So that whole non-racial way of organizing has been ingrained since the launch of the UDF.

It's the whole question of attacking and destroying apartheid on all fronts. We're fighting for a non-racial South Africa — we don't want the problem of having to build non-racialism after the revolution or after negotiations or after whatever's going to happen. And it's important for us to show people that our organizations are non-racial, to show that we aren't going to do to white people what they do to us, that we're just as prepared to work with them now as we will be in a new society.

Are you critical of groups like the Transvaal or Natal Indian Congresses that organize mainly in their own communities?

No, I'm not. For me, it's the same principle that I'm a member of a women's organization. Why do we have women's organizations and we don't have men's organizations? There are certain sectors of the community that need to be organized as a sector, in order to ensure that when freedom comes we'll be able to have as many people supportive of us as possible.

The strongest criticism of mobilization on ethnic lines came from a new alignment of political groups that jelled shortly before the UDF was launched. A wide range of organizations and political tendencies came together in the National Forum Committee (NFC), from the BC-oriented AZAPO to the fringe-left Cape Action League.[8] What united them was a rejection of the 'national democratic struggle' endorsed by the UDF and the ANC, which aimed to build the broadest front of opposition to apartheid, led by workers but supported by all sections of the oppressed, as well as progressive members of the white minority.

The NFC stood for the eradication of 'racial capitalism' and its replacement by an 'anti-racist' socialism. This transformation was to be brought about by the black working class; the NFC rejected any 'un-principled' alliances that might dilute the revolutionary content of the struggle.

The Azanian People's Organization (AZAPO), Azanian Students Movement (AZASM) and Azanian Youth Organization (AZAYO) were among the smaller Black Consciousness-aligned groupings that supported the NFC.

'Manifesto of the Azanian People', adopted at the National Forum Committee launch, Hammanskraal, 12 June 1983:

Our struggle for national liberation is directed against the system of racial capitalism which holds the people of Azania in bondage for the benefit of the small minority of white capitalists and their allies, the white workers and the reactionary sections of the middle classes. The struggle against apartheid is no more than a point of departure for our liberatory efforts. Apartheid will be eradicated with the system of racial capitalism.

The black working class, inspired by revolutionary consciousness, is the driving force of our struggle. They alone can end the system as it stands today because they alone have nothing at all to lose. They have a world to gain in a democratic, anti-racist and socialist Azania. It is the historic task of the black working class and its organizations to mobilize the urban and rural poor, together with the radical sections of the middle classes, in order to put an end to the system of oppression and exploitation by the white ruling class. Successful conduct of the national liberation struggle depends on the firm basis of principle whereby we will ensure that the liberation struggle will not be turned against our people by treacherous and opportunistic 'leaders'. Of these principles, the most important are:

I. Anti-racism and anti-imperialism;

II. Anti-collaboration with the oppressor and its political instruments;

III. Independent working class organization.

Adherents to the Azanian Manifesto represented a small minority, with a perspective that tended to alienate potential allies. UDF activists argued that the struggle for non-racial democracy required the widest possible anti-apartheid base — in which workers and their allies are strong enough to support the building of socialism. Furthermore, the UDF suspected that behind the NFC's slogans and semantics lay an intellectual elite's fear of the cut and thrust of mass-based politics.

'Nation and Ethnicity in South Africa', address by Cape Action League executive member and NFC founder member Neville Alexander, delivered at the NFC launch:

The word 'non-racial' can be accepted by a racially oppressed people if it means that we reject the concept of race, that we deny the existence of races and thus oppose all actions, practices, beliefs and policies based on the concept of race. If in practice — and in theory — we continue to use the word non-racial as though we believe that South Africa is inhabited by four so-called races, we are still trapped in multi-racialism, and thus in racialism. Non-racialism, meaning the denial of the existence of races, leads on to 'anti-racism', which goes beyond it, because the term not only involves the denial of race, but also opposition to the capitalist structures for the perpetuation of which the ideology and theory of race exist. We need, therefore, at all times to find out whether our non-racialists are multi-racialists or anti-racialists. Only the latter variety can belong in the national liberation movement.

The fact remains that 'ethnic' or 'national group'[9] approaches are the thin end of the wedge for separatist movements and civil wars fanned by great-power interests and suppliers of arms to opportunist 'ethnic leaders'. Does not Inkatha in some ways represent a warning to all of us? Who decides what are the 'positive features' of a national group?

Only the black working class can take the task of completing the democratization of the country on its shoulders. It alone can unite all the oppressed and exploited classes. It has become the leading class in the building of the nation. It has to redefine the nation and abolish the reactionary definitions of the bourgeoisie and of the reactionary petty bourgeoisie.

A non-racial capitalism is impossible in South Africa. The class struggle against capitalist exploitation and the national struggle against racial oppression become one struggle under the general command of the black working class and its organizations. Class, colour and nation converge in the national liberation movement. Cultural organizations that are not locally or geographically limited for valid community reasons should be open to all oppressed and exploited people. In this way the cultural achievements of the people will be woven together into one Azanian fabric. In this way we shall eliminate divisive ethnic consciousness and separatist lines of division without eliminating our cultural achievements and cultural variety.

In this struggle, the idea of a single nation is vital because it represents the real interest of the working class and therefore of the future socialist Azania. 'Ethnic', national group or racial group ideas of nationhood in the final analysis strengthen the position of the middle-class or even the capitalist oppressors themselves. I believe that if we view the question of the nation and ethnicity in this framework, we will understand how vital it is that our slogans are heard throughout the length and breadth of our country. One People, One Azania! One Azania, One Nation!

By the mid-1980s, there was no doubt that the concept of non-racialism held far more sway than 'anti-racism'. The NFC's racial capitalism had been eclipsed by the broad front politics now enthusiastically embraced by UDF supporters.[10] This period also saw a revival of the theory of 'colonialism of a special type',[11] which compared the conflicting forces in South Africa to a colonial ruling bloc and a colonized majority contained within the same territory, with both camps comprising all races and classes. In many ways, these theoretical debates echoed those between the ANC and the Africanists of 25 years before, for the NFC accommodated individuals and organizations whose rhetoric recalled that of the PAC.

Joe Thloloe, jailed for PAC activities in 1960, but released on paying a fine, arrested again in 1982 but acquitted on appeal, and a founder member of the BC-oriented Union of Black Journalists and its successor, the NFC-supporting Media Workers of South Africa (MWASA):

Only after we have got our land back can we then talk of reconciliation, can we then talk of a non-racial society, can we talk of complete democracy. But before the contradictions are resolved, we are just dreaming that we are free already, and we aren't.

It is the Africans themselves who have to take political decisions about the struggle — any white who comes in can come in only to assist. What we've had up to this point is we've had whites who are sympathetic to the struggle, who come essentially to try and give advice. They, in fact, take over the struggle. I've never ever met a white who will just accept a place and say, 'Okay, I'm just a member.' I believe that we need to work out our own solutions ourselves, and in the process of struggling, we will be able to get the confidence we need.

When you said, 'We Africans have to do it ourselves', did you mean to exclude coloureds and Indians?

I have found that very many coloureds don't accept themselves as African – but there are coloureds who accept themselves as African. There are some Indians who do not identify with the Africans, but there are some who have thrown in their lot entirely with the indigenous Africans. But to be very frank, very few of them do realize that they are, in fact, in exactly the same position as the indigenous Africans.

And what about African people who ally themselves with the state: the homeland leaders, the informers, the police?

By the way, we shouldn't look at this as a racial sort of division. It's essentially those who are oppressing as against those who are oppressed, so that the Africans, the coloureds, the Indians who choose to align themselves with the oppressor have no place in this struggle.

Would you accept that there are whites who align themselves with the oppressed?

The problem we have found with the whites who align themselves with the Africans is that they are beneficiaries of this whole system of oppression. When they come in and say we want to be on your side, they try to improve our conditions rather than to break down the entire structure. There might be one or two who are committed to a complete breakdown of the structure, but when you organize a political party, you don't organize in terms of the exceptions to the rule. Ultimately, we have to carry the burden of the oppression and we are the people who have to break it.

'We' means ...?

The indigenous Africans, and those coloureds and Indians who call themselves Africans.

But couldn't you also say that there are Indians and coloureds who are beneficiaries of the system of oppression just as whites are?

I think the essential difference is that the Indian's historical experiences are the same as that of the indigenous African: he was robbed of his land, carried by force and brought here. So that even in South Africa he enjoys second-class citizenship. The Indian might get a little more pay at work, he might be a little more educated, but he has been through exactly the same experiences as the indigenous African, so that at the emotional level it is much easier for him to identify with the African. That is why it's much easier for us to accept him as an African.

Do you recall engaging in arguments and discussions about non-racialism back in the 1950s and 1960s?

Our major problem then, as it still is today, was that people try to project the PAC and the BC as being anti-white, and that is not true. So you had to try and explain the difference between being anti-white and between wanting Africans to take their own political decisions. We would, in fact, be accused of being racist, but our documents stated very clearly that we believe in only one race, the human race. We believe that once we liberate Azania, we'll have a non-racial society, because we don't believe in any specific race.

The parallels between the historic ANC-PAC debate over non-racialism and the current controversy were not lost on the South African government. The widespread dissemination of anti-UDF pamphlets, purporting to be issued by the NFC but clearly aimed at provoking divisions, immediately raised suspicions that they were smear pamphlets produced by a Security Police 'dirty tricks' unit.

Pamphlet distributed in Johannesburg in late 1983:

National Forum Committee rejects the so-called 'United Democratic Front' for the following reasons:
1. Any black person genuinely committed to liberation from white oppression will reject participation by members of the white oppressor class in the liberation struggle.
2. The UDF is the old white-dominated South African Communist Party/ ANC alliance dressed up in a new disguise. Admission of 'sympathetic' white organizations such as NUSAS and the 'Black Sash' is merely the pretext for continued white minority control under a different ideology.
3. The UDF is an obstacle in the path of the total liberation of Azania by blacks for blacks.

Issued by: National Forum Committee, AZAPO, SACOS.

The debate over 'ethnic' mobilization for non-racial ends was reopened five years after the 1983 TIC controversy, this time with regard to the NIC. Critics charged that it was being manipulated by a 'cabal' that was exercising undue influence over Natal political affairs. Underneath the accusation lay the African majority's recurrent fear of potential domination by a more privileged minority. In Natal, these fears were compounded by the fact that Africans were actually outnumbered by Indians in the major city of Durban.[12] Mistrust between Africans and Indians had been further exacerbated by the 1985 Inanda violence, an upheaval which tore apart an African-Indian community that had been invoked as a model of non-racial co-existence for the past century.[13]

Yunus Carrim, NIC executive member:[14]

Criticisms of the NIC often confuse arguments about ethnicity with the failure of the NIC to develop a sufficiently strong mass base (particularly among workers), the class basis of its leadership, the lack of a deeply-rooted enough democratic practice, and a certain monopoly of resources and skills. Although some of these problems are to an extent related to the constituency the NIC organizes, they do not automatically flow from the fact that the NIC organizes the Indian community. It is possible to address these difficulties without the NIC having to abandon its organization of the Indian community.

Many of these difficulties are not peculiar to the NIC. In different forms, most political organizations, in this country and elsewhere, have had to deal with similar problems. To the extent that the NIC deepens its democratic practice, the question of monopoly of skills and resources can be addressed. This is mainly a problem at the subjective level. But it also reflects the objective situation: NIC activists often have more formal education, more developed skills in certain respects, and greater freedom to operate politically, compared to people in the townships. The more democratic structures are entrenched in the townships, the easier it will become to attend to these problems.

The issues surrounding skills and resources apply to many organizations in this country and elsewhere in the world. In the South African context they take a racial form and are therefore more sensitive. But they must be addressed in their wider general context as well. Many of the questions raised about the NIC reflect the complexity of the South African struggle, and point to the difficulties in creating true non-racialism and democracy. They have lessons to offer the entire democratic movement. And the challenges they pose will ultimately have to be addressed by the democratic movement as a whole.

African and Indian activists joined together to protest the hanging of three ANC cadres.

Notes

1. Many Indian activists identified more closely with radical Indian leaders like Yusuf Dadoo, the former Indian Congress leader who became SACP chairman after leaving the country. His death in 1983 was commemorated with a publication that was so enthusiastically received by the Transvaal Indian community that it was said that the Security Police had tried to ban it and, failing that, had restricted access to 'one copy per family' (*Congress Resister: Newsletter of the Transvaal Indian Congress*, September 1983).

2. The movement led by KwaZulu's Chief Gatsha Buthelezi, who initially won popular support for refusing to accept 'independence' for the homeland, but is now widely criticized for building a personal and regional power base rooted in Zulu chauvinism, in (often violent) opposition to mass-based movements like the UDF and ANC.

3. This articulation of the concept of the material basis of ideology, as contained in institutions such as family and school, is drawn from the French philosopher Louis Althusser (see Chapter 15, note 8).

4. The unbanning of the ANC, SACP and other organizations in February 1990 sparked a debate over whether 'ethnic' organizations like the TIC, NIC and JODAC (see Chapter 21) should disband and dissolve into the ranks of their ally, the ANC. A discussion paper for a Johannesburg activist forum, 17 March 1990, 'The Road Ahead', argued: 'What we must avoid at all costs is sidestepping the problems that led us to establish organizations catering for the distinct character of specific communities. We must organize in such a way that these people trust us and feel that their security is best achieved through the ANC.'

5. Coloured and Indian areas of Johannesburg.

6. A UDF-aligned coordinating body for youth in the Western Cape.

7. A petition against the new constitution in 1983-84.

8. Launched in 1982 as the Disorderly Bills Action Commitee (DBAC), a loose association of Western Cape organizations opposed to the President's Council and the so-called Koornhof Bills. By 1983, the larger groupings that went on to form the Western Cape UDF (e.g., CAHAC) had dropped out of DBAC, and it was renamed CAL. Various incarnations of the Unity Movement represented the dominant political tendency in CAL.

9. This term is taken from the Freedom Charter (second clause): 'All National Groups Shall Have Equal Rights'.

10. The concept of racial capitalism was prevalent in South African left political circles in the late 1970s and early 1980s, but the fact that anti-UDF and anti-ANC forces embraced (their version of) racial capitalism as a means of negating the theory of national democratic struggle contributed to a discrediting of the term and a decline in its currency.

11. Initially articulated by and associated with the SACP.

12. Durban's racial balance began shifting during the 1970s, the result of a tremendous influx of Africans caused by factors ranging from deteriorating rural conditions to Inkatha-related violence. Quantifying the African-Indian ratio of the Durban population is complicated, however, by the fact that a number of African areas traditionally considered part of Durban have been incorporated into the KwaZulu homeland.

13. Studies of this unrest have debunked the facile comparison with the 1949 African-Indian violence, highlighting the historical framework and political context of the 1985 conflict, and specifically exploring the role of Inkatha vigilantes in attacking UDF supporters. See Heather Hughes, 'Violence in Inanda, August 1985', *Journal of Southern African Studies*, Vol. 13, No. 3, April 1987 and the numerous studies she cites.

14. Excerpted from 'The Natal Indian Congress: Deciding on a New Thrust Forward', *Work in Progress*, No. 52, 1988.

21 Straddling Both Camps, the People's and the Enemy's

In early 1982 a trade unionist and medical doctor named Neil Aggett became the first white political prisoner to die in Security Police custody.[1] At the end of the year, a part-time student and community worker, Barbara Hogan, was sentenced to an unprecedented ten years in prison for gathering information about trade unions and community groups for the ANC.[2] The effect of these events on the 'white left' was profound.

David Webster, a social anthropology lecturer at the University of the Witwatersrand:

A group of us sat down and tried to plot out what role there was for progressive whites in South Africa. We never got terribly far — the wave of detentions[3] took out half the people in one swoop. What that group said is that whites are doubly disadvantaged: mainly they are intellectuals, so they are not actually going to play a major role in working-class struggles. Secondly, progressive whites are a very small minority and we have no chance of forming a mass-based party, so any role we have to play is in conjunction with other progressive forces in the country, whether they be democratic trade unions, community organizations or political organizations. Our finding was also that in order to offer our support to progressive black organizations we had to do so from a position of strength, and you could only do that from being organized at a certain level.[4]

When Barbara Hogan was detained that changed my life totally. She was someone I knew really well: she was my student and friend. Then came Neil Aggett's death, and suddenly I realized that the police were serious about what they were doing. We all developed politically at that time, because up until then it had been a rather abstract kind of game, and then suddenly it was the real thing: torture and life and death. I helped form the Detainees' Parents Support Committee (DPSC) and Detainees' Support Committee (Descom). By working in the detention field, one learned in a very empirical way what you were up against: the ruthlessness of the state and what it is capable of, in terms of raw power. It was an alarming thing — I was quite naive until then.

We started to broaden out, to monitor the police, to make their life as difficult as possible, to make each new detention a high political price to pay. And then taking on the state itself — because it becomes clear that apartheid is undemocratic and that the only way you can maintain such an illegitimate structure is by repression, so if you really want to end detentions you have to end apartheid.

Tens of thousands of black workers attended Neil Aggett's funeral and took part in job actions to protest his death in detention.

I think also, by the way, you can't underestimate the influence of Helen Joseph. She was unbanned in 1982 and she went straight onto the campuses and started talking and reviving. With this lack of knowledge about the ANC and its policies, broadly, whites hadn't heard of the Freedom Charter until about 1981 — it was a forbidden topic. So Helen being unbanned was quite an influential thing, because she immediately hit all the campuses and started talking about this glorious non-racial past. She was a point of entry, because she looks like a granny and she is so reasonable and so sweet. She was critical in raising a whole white generation's consciousness about the non-racialism of the struggle in the old days.

A lot of people just grew up with the idea that there is no role for us to play, because Black Consciousness has been with us for quite a long time and it has more or less always been like that. Then people started reading *Time Longer than Rope*[5] — that was a really important kind of buzz book to read — and began to realize that there is a whole tradition of non-racialism around. You began to realize that, in fact, there was a longer tradition than Black Consciousness, a tradition which was more respectable in many ways. And then structures emerged which actually proved the idea: the emergence of progressive community organizations, student organizations that you could work hand in glove with as whites. So that you knew you were actually playing some kind of role, in a very personal, experiential way.

One of the most pressing political issues for whites is military conscription, for every white South African man is compelled to serve in the South African Defence Force (SADF). The experience of educating whites about conscription and militarization offered important insights into how this community is most effectively organized.

Janet Cherry, 1982 NUSAS Secretary-General during the build-up to the launch of the End Conscription Campaign (ECC) in 1983: [6]

At the University of Cape Town we took up a big campaign around the issue of the extension of conscription. It was extended in 1982 to two full years, plus annual camps, and we had a lot of debate around that issue. I think it was then that I started developing an idea about the importance of organizing in the white community, and the importance of whites' resistance to the military and to the government. We realized that national service was an issue that white students were really concerned about – because it affected them personally, it disrupted their lives, and they were very unhappy about it.

There was the argument that whites have to actually make a choice: either they support the ruling class or they support the people. We all go through a process, to some extent, of breaking away from our backgrounds and our parents and from our very sheltered upbringing, and we felt that it was incredibly important that people make that break. So that was the argument that we used: it was like dividing the ruling class.

You know, there is an incredible difference between South Africa and Rhodesia before independence. There you had an almost homogeneous white population, with very few voices of dissent. The whites were prepared to just fight unquestioningly until the end, not actually knowing at any stage what was really happening and what the black community thought. Here it is different because we have got that room to move and to change white people's attitudes.

Why did the conscription issue only emerge in the early 1980s?

There had been a very small group called Milcom[7] which was taking up this issue, and it came to be seen as something which was actually jeopardizing the building of a legitimate student movement on campus. And in addition, you had a situation where your progressive or left leadership of the white student movement at that stage was very small and it was quite elitist in its approach. They were working from an understanding that committed white democrats should stay and work in the country and build up organization, and that led to a line that student leadership should actually participate in the army – 'strategically' participate.

ECC media reflected an alternative white youth culture.

During 1982 the national student movement started discussing this issue, saying obviously we can't say to people, we mustn't go into the army — but we can expose exactly what the SADF is doing and the role that the system of conscription is playing.

'Stop the Call-Up', ECC pamphlet, April 1986:

The SADF claims to be defending all South Africans. The End Conscription Campaign and a growing number of young people who object to service in the SADF refute this claim — and so do millions of South Africans living in the townships. The fact is, the SADF is being used more and more to suppress opposition to apartheid, not only on the borders of the country, but in the townships and homes of ordinary South Africans. In anyone's language, this is civil war. And many patriotic young men are deciding that they cannot be part of this war. They are refusing to be conscripted to fight against unarmed citizens, their fellow South Africans. The numbers refusing to fight apartheid's war grow annually — so much so that the Minister of Defence, Magnus Malan, has refused to release the figures of those who have failed to report for duty.

ECC calls for an end to conscription because we feel that these young men should have the right to choose not to fight in a civil war on the side of apartheid. It is the right of all people to refuse to take up arms when their conscience dictates otherwise. The overwhelming majority of South Africans support us in our defence of this right.

Relentless media attacks attempting to link ECC with every 'communist-inspired' body from the ANC to the KGB revealed the extent of state alarm at ECC's popularity. In fact, the ECC had decided to operate as a 'single issue front' — a strategy based on the assumption that the number of whites who opposed conscription far exceeded those who would actively campaign against the government.

Laurie Nathan, ECC national organizer 1985—86:

Initially I had quite a strong liberal position, often attacking the left, NUSAS, mainly because I didn't like their style, rather than their content. I thought they were arrogant and cliquish — which we are in the left, often. They were not open, not welcoming. I think we have shifted a lot in NUSAS since then, but I think we have still got a long way to go before we appreciate the importance of working with liberals — not in an expedient way, but in a genuine and sincere way.

ECC is as broad a front as one can imagine. We have Black Sash, the South African Institute of Race Relations, Women for Peace, and some church groupings which are relatively conservative. The broader our support, the greater the threat that we pose to the state, the more legitimacy we have within the white community, and the more protection we have. I also believe that we have the ability to move people, so when we have PFP Youth coming into ECC, I don't believe that that is going to cause us to move backwards and to compromise our position.

The same scepticism of the liberals now would have been applied to the Christian left within NUSAS in the old days. That has had a really powerful influence on my work, meeting the Cathsoc [Catholic Students Society] and YCS people and coming to understand that their commitment and the energy that they put into their work is no different from ours. And I think I would go further: that we can learn a lot from them, that there is a sense of compassion and humility that the left often lacks. I think that all of us come into the left from a moral position — then we develop a scientific analysis and that moral position is repressed.

I think what is happening as the course of struggle intensifies is that the white community becomes increasingly polarized — which means that a greater number of people will be hostile to what we are doing, but a greater number of people will take a step of supporting us. Because I think it is becoming increasingly intolerable for the white community to be sitting on the fence. We are never going to mobilize the entire English-speaking community, or a significant section of the Afrikaans sector, but we are mobilizing a significant sector of the white community — significant in terms of its quality, rather than its quantity.

Paddy Kearney, director of the Diakonia ecumenical centre in Durban since 1976:

I think I have learnt something of democracy from being involved with non-racial groups. I have found that very impressive, the degree to which people are consulted, and the need to have mandates to act. I think the kind of tradition out of which I came was very much the white liberal tradition, where everything is on a kind of individualistic basis. Here, for the first time, I was really confronted day to day by people who were not so concerned about individuals, but were concerned about communities and organizations, and finding out what those groups' opinions were before acting, and referring back issues to get a wider support for them. All this was very new to me and quite startling, and it affected me.

Often it was contact with blacks — or more importantly, an insight into their experience of repression — that whites found most educative.

Molly Blackburn, Port Elizabeth Black Sash leader and PFP Member of the Provincial Council[8] active in support of Eastern Cape community organizations from the early to mid-1980s:

When we were having our Black Sash conference I got a telephone call from the chairman of the parents' committee in Uitenhage township, and he said to me, 'Molly, please come quickly, they're killing our children.'

Well, I didn't know what to expect, so I said to the girls I was going to leave the conference and go out, and did any of them want to come? When we arrived in Uitenhage we found a little cluster of distracted people, and they were terribly worried — their children had been taken that morning by the police and they felt they were being assaulted.

By some strange quirk we got to the police station and the policeman said, 'Oh, you can go down to the cells.' Well, we took a wrong turning and we walked in on a torture scene there. A young man was handcuffed to the leg of a table and there was a man whipping him. The point that I am trying to make is that that story actually hit the headlines — because Sash gave a very, very clear statement to the press of exactly what we had seen — and still people said, 'Oh, he must have deserved it.' That's the average white reaction. I mean, the fact was that a young man was handcuffed to the leg of a table and there was a man whipping him — he was lying on the floor with blood coming out of his mouth and terrible scars on his head — and people still say, 'He must have done something wrong.'

Which do you see as more important: going to the black areas and standing up for rights there, or making changes amongst your own community of whites?

I don't think it's possible to make changes amongst the white community without black involvement, and by that I mean not only taking terrified whites over to the other side to go and look at the community problems and showing them that really they don't need to be so fearful, but I also mean that it's important to bring articulate, sensitive, clear-thinking black leadership over to this side to talk to the whites, and let them question and cross-question. Those sort of meetings which we've had with them have been very, very productive and useful.

Black leaders attached great importance to involving whites in non-racial politics, though they often found the outreach effort taxing.

Revd Frank Chikane, General-Secretary of the Institute for Contextual Theology (ICT) 1983–87 and Transvaal UDF executive member:

It is painful to speak to white audiences, to help them out of the heavy propaganda they have been subjected to, but I feel I have to do it, even if it is only a few who become committed. They may disagree with you, but at least when the consequences and the result of their activity come, they will remember you have spoken to them. These people are also victims of apartheid as I am a victim of apartheid, and all of us are battling to come out of that apartheid system.

My understanding is that in any struggle there is an option for dissent from the ruling group, and therefore my theory makes allowance that there would be a few people — I'm not expecting a lot of whites to come on our side, but a few — who become committed and give their lives to be part of that struggle. It is a matter of them participating and proving their genuineness in action more than trying to theorize about the possibility of their participation.

What would you advise a white person who wanted to become politically involved?

I would make him aware of the situation that apartheid has created — the tensions that are there, the fact that he is privileged, the fact that he has more education. And therefore the white person has to be humble enough to also accept and understand the positions of the others, that they will be suspicious and might not trust him. A white person must also be conscious that he can easily dominate and irritate people because of his privileges. It will demand a lot of commitment over a long period. You must be prepared for hard words against you.

The UDF launched a 'Call to Whites' campaign, aiming to counter the emigration of liberal whites with the slogan, 'Stay and Contribute'. Whites were being offered a political home, but at the same time being told that they would have to build it themselves. Many activists argued that it was time for whites committed to the UDF's non-racialism to construct an organizational base from which to affiliate to the front. The Johannesburg Democratic Action Committee (JODAC) was one of the first attempts at building such a base.

Tom Waspe, former YCS national coordinator and first chairperson of JODAC:

The general thrust of the UDF is not to start with a model of a non-racial organization, but to start with consciousness and with the conditions that operate on the ground and build towards a non-racial organization. There are a lot of whites who feel that they simply want to work with blacks, and sometimes JODAC is not able to fulfil those expectations. The fact is that one has got to operate in the conditions that are created by apartheid so as to transform those conditions.

How did you derive the name of the organization? Why the word 'democratic'?

Because we are trying to put on the agenda, as openly as we can, the central political problem, which is the question of democracy. Now in itself democracy is open for debate: one can stop at one person, one vote or one can deepen it into the economy. So it's a dynamic concept. We would never use the word 'white' in the name of an organization because we see ourselves as being part of the non-racial movement, first and foremost. We happen to be the organization that is addressing people who live in the white group areas and our membership is predominantly white, but that is because of the conditions that we have to deal with.

Has JODAC been successful in reaching out to whites, or does it just preach to the converted?

Well, first of all there's nothing wrong with organizing the converted, because you can never operate effectively as an individual — you've always got to operate through some form of organization. But more and more people are joining our structures because of the way the struggle has gained momentum and created confusion and division within that white ruling group — and then we move in and provide alternative political perspectives.

We work very closely with the people in the townships. For instance, JODAC went into Alexandra township [after a 1986 massacre of protesters by police] and laid flowers at the cemetery. The whole thing was planned with the people in Alexandra and they came out in full force to support and protect the whites from the army — a very strong expression of non-racial solidarity. It's not only whites that are organizing whites — more and more blacks are seeing the need for themselves to start organizing whites. There's a growing realization that the white community is the responsibility of the democratic movement as a whole.

The enemy's camp is never a static camp — it's always in a state of fluctuation and change. And the interesting thing about JODAC is that it straddles both the people's camp and the enemy's camp, and that's what gives us our unique position. See, JODAC doesn't see itself as a leadership organization — we see ourselves as playing a leading role in facilitating a process. The leaders are the people in the townships.

Do you see any parallels between efforts to organize whites in the 1980s and the efforts of the Congress of Democrats to organize whites in the '50s?

We formed in a very different historical context. COD had a very elevated position in the Congress Alliance: each had an equal number of representatives, so COD had as many representatives as the ANC, for instance. So

As part of the UDF's 'Call to Whites' campaign, JODAC organized a visit to Johannesburg's Alexandra township to join with the Alexandra Civic Association in laying wreaths at the graves of youths slain by police in 1986. Some 300 whites went into the black township for the service in defiance of police orders.

in a sense it had a position out of proportion to its membership. One difference that exists now is that white structures have no elevated place at all. We operate as equal partners completely, so there's no possibility at all of talking about white domination or control.[9]

As in earlier periods, organizing whites in the 1980s reflected differing political approaches and regional contexts. For example, the strong Congress tradition of mobilizing in the Eastern Cape contrasted markedly with the historical resistance to organization on ethnic lines in the Western Cape. Thus whites in Grahamstown joined together as a UDF affiliate in 1984, while whites in Cape Town debated for years before finally forming the Cape Democrats in 1987.

Roland White, a Grahamstown Committee of Democrats (GCD) founder member who served on the Eastern Cape UDF executive:

In the Eastern Cape there is a lot of non-racial contact between white activists and progressive organizations, and black people and black organizations. Grahamstown is a small community; the process of organizing in townships is quite new. Township people would need resources, so they would approach white people who they had begun to meet. I think Congress ideology has always had far more of an influence in the Eastern Cape than BC ever did. So I found when I first started making contact with the comrades in the townships that they were always very accepting of whites.

That has all been affected by the State of Emergency. I don't often go into a township these days, because if I get bust there by the police or military I am going to get hammered for it. Also, because clearly the kind of relationships I had established were with leadership activists and not the mass of youths in the townships, they are going to see me as any whitey going in there. I was stoned once in the township by some militant.

Is that a serious obstacle to building non-racialism?

Look, it is a difficulty. However that is not to say that simply by having contact with black people you are actually furthering non-racial struggle. Black-white contact represents one understanding of non-racialism, but non-racialism as an abstract goal can be anything. It can be that you are going to have a coloured kind of people running around in a couple of hundred years' time, or it can be simply that no racial differences are acknowledged.

So one concrete question posed on the ground is: what are all these white people going to do that are becoming increasingly active? They can't all be involved in resource work — the days of whites playing an important role in trade union formation are largely over — so you need to develop appropriate structures and organizations which will give those people a role to play which is productive to the goals and aims of the struggle.

Our usefulness to the democratic movement is basically to the extent that we are successful in disorganizing the white bloc through actually organizing a part of it, through driving into it. There is no way that we are trying to organize to the extent which the civics and trade unions do. Your class context is totally different. We are organizing members of the ruling class – to put it quite crudely – against their interests, and the civics and the trade unions are organizing members of the oppressed classes in their interests.

Cheryl Carolus, UDF Western Cape executive member, in a keynote speech at the GCD launch, May 1985:

I think that the meeting we are at tonight bears living testimony to the fact that we are in the process of building a cohesive nation, a non-racial, democratic South Africa. For the first time in many years, we see that white democrats are confident about the fact that they can actually play a role in the changing South Africa, that they can struggle side by side with the oppressed and exploited. In fact, they are as much victims of an oppressive, vicious system of apartheid as blacks are.

South Africa is at present a country at war with its own people. That is why we in the UDF are grateful for opportunities like this, where we are afforded the opportunity to put forward our case. We feel that white South Africans are being cushioned from the realities out there. And that is why we want to urge everybody present here tonight in all communities to throw their lot in with the extra-parliamentary organizations.

It is important that you become part of this big wheel that's turning inevitably towards our freedom, because the fact of the matter is that the tide is unstoppable. Our people will get freedom. It may not be in five years, ten, twenty years time, but it's certainly going to be helped along if there are a lot more people joining in, particularly in the white areas, where the Nationalist Party seem to claim that they have a base in people like you.

The State of Emergency, first declared in 1985, then reimposed in 1986, hit hard at all resistance. 'White democrats' were among those detained and forced into hiding. Yet in the face of this crackdown, groups of whites flouted the laws restricting contact with banned organizations and flew to Lusaka to meet with the ANC – first businessmen, then liberal parliamentarians – blazing a trail that hundreds of concerned white South Africans were to follow over the next few years.[10]

The quest for political alternatives was motivated by a deteriorating economic and social climate, buffeted by international sanctions and escalating militarization. The white initiatives that arose next were more broadly based, extending to a range of less politically experienced sectors, from professionals feeling the economic squeeze to mothers worried about their sons' army service, in new organizations ranging from Jews for Justice to Afrikaanse Demokrate [Afrikaans Democrats].

Outreach to the white community spawned a number of institutional bases: the Institute for a Democratic Alternative for South Africa (IDASA), founded in 1986 by PFP members who responded to the UDF's call for whites to pull out of the sterile environment of parliament;[11] the Five Freedoms Forum, which gained prominence in the debate over white participation in the 1987 parliamentary elections;[12] and the Consultative Business Movement, an outgrowth of a 1988 meeting between representatives of industry and the UDF.

In 1989 the Five Freedoms Forum led the largest group of whites ever to meet with the ANC, representing businessmen and trade unionists, academics and activists, city councillors and students, as well as members of the newest parliamentary grouping, the Democratic Party, an amalgamation of the PFP and two smaller liberal parties.[13] The ANC, in turn, put forth a high-powered delegation that included more than half its NEC members and President Tambo himself, for the meeting was seen as a forerunner to the kind of negotiations that might eventually take place between the ANC and the white power bloc.

Revd Beyers Naude, General-Secretary of the South African Council of Churches (SACC) 1985—87 and UDF patron:

To what extent do you think it is possible to make inroads into the white community?
You mean in sufficient numbers for them to be able to change, and thereby positively to make a contribution? I can't see that happening. There is too much fear. There is too much self-interest. There is too much ignorance of what is happening in black society.

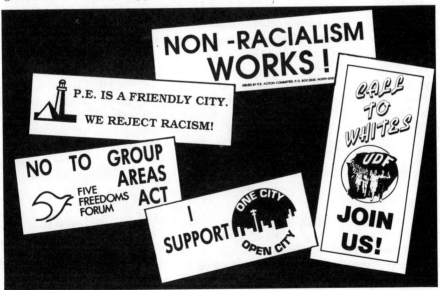

Media campaigns of the white extra-parliamentary initiatives of the late 1980s.

I think whites will only discover the truth from the one shock after the other. It could have been avoided if we had had the foresight and the understanding to work this through in a much more open association with the black community. But I am afraid that we simply have to accept the fact that the white community will experience the one reaction of anger and bitterness after the other. And therefore there will be increasing fear. We see this now: for the first time the white community is experiencing, materially, the cost of apartheid. Before, the price — I mean financially and otherwise — was always paid by blacks.

Do you feel that when South Africa changes, you yourself will benefit?

I personally don't think I will benefit. I'm convinced if, by benefit you mean materially or financially, it is going to be a period of very deep and serious sacrifice. But that is the price that we have to pay for this longstanding system of injustice and oppression that we have devised and imposed. It is going to be painful, stormy and difficult. But I believe that, in human terms of building, eventually, a society where people of different cultures and different backgrounds will learn to live together, in that respect South Africa could make a contribution to the challenge which is being presented to the whole world. Because in the real sense of the words, South Africa is a microcosm of some of the major problems and issues facing the whole world.

So where does that leave whites? Is there anything positive at the end of that long road?

Oh yes, certainly. Eventually, with the tremendous economic richness and potential of the country, I think there is a possibility of a much higher standard of living for everyone. There will certainly be a lower standard of living for the whites, but I don't think their standard of living was a good one: I think it was detrimental to the white community in many respects. Secondly, I think they will rediscover their humanity which, to a large degree, the white community of South Africa have lost, or are in the process of losing.

Thirdly, they will discover that, if they know how to handle it, they will be rid of many of the fears and anxieties which simply kill whites in their responses. It certainly won't be easy, but I am convinced that in the long run we will have a society which will be therefore more human and more warm and more open than the one that we have built up on the basis of apartheid.

Notes

1. An inquest into Aggett's death acquitted the Security Police of his murder, despite testimony from a fellow detainee who had witnessed Aggett being beaten shortly before he was found hanged in his cell. Aggett was the 54th political prisoner to die in detention.

2. Hogan was the first person in South Africa to be prosecuted for treason in a case that had involved no violence against the state, and upon sentencing became the first white female political prisoner since the 1960s. She served seven years of her ten-year sentence before being released in February 1990 in the amnesty announced with the freeing of Nelson Mandela.

3. The detentions of some 15 white activists in 1981 marked the most extensive clampdown on whites since the 1960s. Though many were held for up to a year in solitary confinement, the state failed to mount a threatened security trial aimed at proving a white-run conspiracy, and the only white detainees convicted of major ANC activities were Hogan and Robert Adam (who was sentenced to ten years in prison, with his co-defendant, Mandla Mthembu, sentenced to five years).

4. In an effort to put across this kind of analysis to a wider audience, NUSAS produced a booklet in 1981, *Dissension in the Ranks: White Opposition in South Africa.*

5. An overview of South African history analyzed in terms of class and nationalism, by Edward Roux (University of Wisconsin, 1948, 1964).

6. While South African women have generally tended to be under-represented in political organizations, women have attained some prominence in NUSAS, which elected its first female national president in 1951 (Pat Arnett from the University of Natal, Pietermaritzburg). Women became particularly active in NUSAS from the mid-1970s, partially as a result of the trend of young male war resisters taking lower political profiles in order to dodge military service, with many ultimately forced to leave the country.

7. The other precursor to ECC was the Conscientious Objectors Support Group (COSG). Note also that as early as 1979, the ANC's NEC issued a statement saluting white war resisters.

8. Blackburn was open to criticism of her participation in this government body. She defended it on grounds that the council was due to be phased out and was not a creation of the new 'constitutional dispensation', also hinting at her possible resignation from the PFP.

9. JODAC disbanded in response to the 1990 unbannings and encouraged its members to join the ANC.

10. The first delegation of whites to meet the ANC at its Lusaka headquarters was led by Anglo American chairman Gavin Relly in September 1985; the second, later that year, by the PFP's Frederik van Zyl Slabbert; and by 1990 more than thirty meetings had occurred, involving clerics, students, academics, Nationalist Party members and even former SADF officers. Most of the meetings were convened in Zambia, but a crucial summit, including Afrikaans establishment figures, took place in Dakar, Senegal in July 1987, and top business leaders discussed future economic policy with the ANC in Harare in March 1990. Similar meetings have been organized by other minority groups: in October 1988 more than 50 Indian South Africans – businessmen and religious leaders, as well as NIC and TIC members – travelled to Lusaka to meet the ANC.

11. Frederik van Zyl Slabbert and Alex Boraine, in early 1986.

12. The Five Freedoms Forum was founded in late 1986, in reply to a call from the black community for whites to respond to the State of Emergency. It was among a variety of groups that came together to consider putting up a left-of-the-PFP candidate for the 1987 white elections, but dropped the idea in favour of a campaign to publicize the five basic freedoms against which the policies of the parties could be measured: freedom from want, from fear, of speech and association, of conscience, and from discrimination.

13. The National Democratic Movement, formed in 1988 by a breakaway PFP parliamentarian, Wynand Malan, and the Independent Party, led by a former South African ambassador to the UK who resigned from the National Party, Dennis Worrall.

PART FIVE
Present and Future

The COSATU national executive and delegates to the 1986 congress in front of a banner listing COSATU's five founding principles: non-racialism; one industry, one union; worker control; representation on the basis of paid-up membership; and cooperation between affiliates at national level.

22 The Whole Pyramid is Shaking

The end of 1985 saw the formation of the largest labour federation in the country's history, the Congress of South African Trade Unions.[1] Non-racialism was one of its founding principles and at its first annual conference COSATU formally adopted the Freedom Charter as its lodestar.

Billy Nair, a former SACTU organizer who spent twenty years on Robben Island for Umkhonto we Sizwe activities, and upon his release was elected to the Natal UDF executive, working closely with COSATU:

If we pursue a racially exclusivist philosophy it will mean that we are not recognizing reality. What we say is workers require allies. If you look at it purely from a worker's point of view, from a purely tactical point of view, the idea is to strip the ruling class of all props that it has. Take the churches, for instance. The churches are a formidable force, having approximately sixteen million members. The vast majority are workers, peasants and so on, and therefore to exclude the church would be suicidal for the working class.

As a parallel, take the patriotic movement that developed during the last world war against Hitler and Mussolini — the forces were wide-ranging. The church played a very important role in those popular fronts. Monasteries, for instance, were used to store arms. And in Nicaragua the clergy actually sat in the cabinet, for you had a popular front government in power. So for the working class at this stage to suggest that they want to be exclusivist and espouse a pure workerist[2] line, it would be just simply not addressing themselves to reality.

The ruling class actually wants allies desperately — hence the tricameral parliament and so on — and they succeeded in getting only a small segment of that middle class. Our approach is more scientific. The very shifts that are taking place in ruling class circles are indicative of the correctness of our line, the non-racial policies we are espousing.

Do you believe that non-racialism can best be achieved at the workplace?

No. You may have a tentative non-racial thing for eight hours a day, but this is mitigated by the fact that you are in a wider racial set-up, so unless you actually smash the wider prison in which the workers are engulfed, you are not going to have real non-racialism. Unless there's an across-the-board solution to our problems, any piecemeal solutions at the factory floor are not really going to answer the problem. Those concessions that the ruling class makes simply evaporate unless you have a broader democracy to protect those hard-won rights of the workers.

Now this is the challenge that the workers face, and this was the problem that SACTU faced in the '50s and '60s: do they, in the face of repression, say, 'Look, we have to preserve our hard-won rights and not engage the enemy until we are ready for it?' The question then arises: when would you be ready, if you're not prepared to engage them on a day-to-day basis? The workers cannot extricate themselves from the community, because they are part of it.

Shasha Mereyotlhe, an organizer for the South African Domestic Workers Union (SADWU), a COSATU affiliate:

Do the domestic workers you deal with really care about non-racialism?

I'll tell you something: our people never have any hatred. That should be understood clearly. The only thing they've got is a problem that the whites don't pay them well. But we also come out clearly on the fact that the Africans who employ domestic workers also don't pay them well. Now we discuss along those lines: those Africans, are they not exploiting us too? The workers' understanding of non-racialism is that we cannot do away with whites simply because they've got more experience on jobs than we Africans. Even if there are whites who maybe refuse to agree with us now, it's a reality of our country that we cannot afford to lose them.

Cyril Ramaphosa, General-Secretary of the National Union of Mineworkers (NUM), South Africa's biggest and potentially most powerful union:

At the first NUM congress we debated the question of a clause in the constitution — whether we would like to say 'black workers' or 'all workers' — and there was an overwhelming rejection of 'black workers'. The feeling was that if a white worker who renounced the apartheid system wanted to be a member, his application could be considered.

What do you think is the source of that commitment to non-racialism on the part of black workers?

It's very difficult to answer the question: where did they get that from when they are working in such an oppressive and racialistic environment? What came out from our congress was that the nature of the mines is such that the white person is only seen as an enemy because he's oppressing them and exploiting them. I remember at congress one man stood up and said that, 'We are going to re-educate those whites because they are workers like us. They are just being used and they need to come to a realization that they are being used.'

NUM's support for non-racialism was such that it pulled out of the Council of Unions of South Africa (CUSA), a Black Consciousness-oriented federation, and joined COSATU. CUSA and another small BC grouping, the Azanian Council of Trade Unions (AZACTU), refused to join COSATU because of its explicit support for non-racialism. The National Council of Trade Unions (NACTU), the labour federation formed through a merger of CUSA and AZACTU, pledged its support instead to the principles of 'anti-racism' and 'black working class leadership'.[3]

Pule Thate, who served five years in prison for ANC activities, and after his release in 1981 became a factory shop steward:

In my first union, the Food and Beverage Workers Union affiliated to CUSA, I was trying to push for a direction that will be pro the national liberation movement, especially the ANC. But when COSATU was formed and CUSA did not agree to be part of that, I had no choice but to move towards COSATU.

Non-racialism is a very important issue, one of the basic issues. You can't talk of class consciousness if you don't have a base for it, which will be a non-racial society. It's a non-issue if you already have class consciousness. That's why the ANC is talking about African leadership — it's not in a narrow sense, but we need to see our black people, who are the majority, coming up. And only then, when they are actually holding the bull by the horn, then one will know that one will be going somewhere. We mean that they are the lower stratum of the oppressed, so if they shake, the whole pyramid is shaking.

Was COSATU wise to refuse to compromise its non-racial stance at the time of its formation? Would it not have been more expedient to concede on non-racialism and accept other ideologies as well, thereby gaining COSATU greater membership?

Look, after discussing the difference between 'non-racialism' and 'anti-racism', finally it was agreed that okay, let's embrace them both — we will say one of our objectives is 'non-racialism/anti-racism'. So there was a compromise. But still CUSA and AZACTU pulled out. So it means they were not sincere. When unity was achievable they wanted a pretext of running away, because they realized that its achievement will mean losing some of their personal gains. So it's not really a question of a compromise — it's a question of dedication, commitment and honesty.

James Mndaweni, a former CUSA leader who was elected NACTU president:

In NACTU we believe in a non-racial future, but first we accept the status quo. The land belongs to the indigenous masses — that must be accepted. Secondly, we believe that the colour of a person should not be the issue. Look at the Pan-Africanist Congress approach of saying that you recognize the human race, irrespective of the colour of the person. If you accept that you pay allegiance to Azania, then you'll be part and parcel of that country. The Africanist approach is that first they are looking at themselves as the African people who belong to the African continent, without saying are you black, white, whatever.

The Freedom Charter says the land belongs to everybody — I mean, that's totally wrong because the land should belong to the people of the country, the indigenous masses. I can't go to America today and claim part of the land. Now if you take the arrival of the settlers — that is, the white people in South Africa — to say that those people actually now are part and parcel of our country, it's a distortion of history. The black people are the owners of the land.

By black people, do you mean only Africans, and not Indians or coloured people?
I would say it's people who are black like myself, and coloured people. The coloured people are the people of Africa because they emanate from Africa.

Where do Indians fit in?
I'm not leaving them out altogether — if an Indian accepts that he should not be called an Indian, he should be called an African.

And if a white person says, 'I see myself as an African'?
I think it's a question of a person himself accepting where does he belong. Maybe on the political scene I might not be able to give a clarity, because I'm not a politician, I'm a worker.

If you take a black personnel manager and a black worker, would you say both of them are Africans so they're both with you in the struggle?
Yes, they will be together, there's no difference. The division that will come in, it's purely in terms of practicalities, because one has got certain privileges. But it doesn't necessarily mean that he's totally being dissociated from the masses.

What is your view of white involvement in the trade union movement?
We don't recognize a question of colour within our federation. We are saying that every person who accepts that he's a worker is welcome. But for us to go out and appoint or employ a white and say he's a general-secretary, that will not do because it's something that has been imposed by the leadership.

White manipulation has its history in our struggle and I reject that hidden agenda: it's the control of the black people's struggle. In actual fact those people are neutralizing the militancy of the people. The SACP, it is there within the ANC with its own purpose. It's a question of trying to implement Russian policies in our country — which we will not accept. Because immediately we involve a superpower, then the other superpower will try and come in and destabilize, and that's exactly what is happening in countries like Ethiopia, Angola, and Mozambique.

So what is your advice to whites who want to fight apartheid?
I think they should mobilize their own white community, whilst the blacks are mobilizing themselves. They've got leverage because they've got voting power — they can change the status quo within that. Basically there would be no development on the part of a black man if there is a white man in our organizations — so it is to safeguard, and to try and promote that development, self-confidence, self-determination, that we promote black organizations.

This 1940s-style Africanist position eclipsed 1970s-style Black Consciousness as the dominant tendency within NACTU. In 1987, NACTU's leadership met with the PAC in Dar es Salaam and emerged with a joint statement of mutual support, giving rise to claims of a revival of Africanism in the trade unions. These were soon discredited, however, by evidence that NACTU's strength had been greatly exaggerated. With the disclosure that COSATU's members outnumbered NACTU's by more than five to one,[4] it became apparent that the critics of non-racialism represented a minority view. In 1988, NACTU met in Harare with SACTU[5] and the ANC, concluding in a joint communique that 'unity in action is a prerequisite for the quick defeat of apartheid'. Soon thereafter COSATU launched a policy of conciliation, stressing the need for cooperation between the two labour federations.

'United Front: Fight vs. Common Enemy', Solidarity: Voice of the Cape Action League, *June 1988:*

The ugly head of disunity, a cancerous leadership disease of the '80s, has received another death blow in the last six weeks. NACTU, after a historic meeting with the PAC in Tanzania in October 1987, took the next step on the road to worker unity by talking to the ANC in Zimbabwe. The main issue was the need for unity in action within the labour movement. In explaining the basis of unity, it was agreed that the Freedom Charter was not a prerequisite for unity. Further, that all legitimate organizations of whatever persuasion have a meaningful role to play in the national liberation struggle.

To support this, ANC National Executive member and SACTU General-Secretary John Nkadimeng said, 'Certain people think it is a prerequisite that anyone who wants to join the new united front must support the Freedom Charter. We say this is incorrect.' Asked if this meant that the ANC believed groups like AZAPO and NACTU, who counterpose the Freedom Charter with the Azanian Manifesto, should cooperate with COSATU and UDF, who have adopted the Charter, Nkadimeng said, 'Yes, that is exactly what the united front stands for.' Nkadimeng claimed that the front is something that brings people together to fight a common enemy. This does not mean that they agree one hundred per cent with each other. These developments have no doubt been welcomed by all serious and mature militants in the liberation movement.

COSATU could afford to make concessions over non-racialism in theory because of its substantial gains when it came to non-racialism in practice. An important index of COSATU's non-racialism was the unwavering support of its predominantly African membership for an Indian as its general-secretary.

Jay Naidoo, COSATU General-Secretary since the founding of the federation:

It is very important that non-racialism, as a concept, was built up by SACTU and by the other Congress parties. It was an important principle really defended by workers — even though that principle is constantly being broken by whites, even though other race groups are treating African workers like pieces of garbage. But workers still defend non-racialism.

But I don't think we can disguise the fact that there are tensions between Indian and African, African and coloured, Indian and coloured, between the different groupings within the African community itself. On the factory floor there are differences between Indian and African workers. There's a lot of suspicions as well, and it's a long struggle to overcome that.

There was very strong solidarity in the '50s between Indian and African workers. In the '60s, through the manoeuvring of the state and capital, divisions started to appear: one, by separation of the communities by the Group Areas Act, secondly, by promoting Indians to more skilled positions. And that created tensions. So overcoming those tensions at one level, and overcoming the fact that people are staying in separate areas, has been a long and difficult struggle, and is still a big problem for us, even today.

In the garment and clothing factories,[6] where it's the most substantial concentration of Indian workers, though they were very, very militant in the '40s and the '50s, in the '60s and '70s the unions catering broadly for Indian workers became very bureaucratic, very much benefit societies, and the perception of Indian workers started to change. So that if you talk to Indian workers who are in these unions you have an enormous problem, because their first question is, 'What benefits do you have?'

With African workers it's a question of an organization that is militant, that is able to mobilize workers, that's able to win things in the factory — not a question of benefits. With Indian workers, it's whether you have a doctor, do you have funeral benefits? Because this is what they've become accustomed to. And it's a big battle to break through those barriers.

WE BUY IN INDIAN SHOPS

- SIYATHENGA
  KWIIVENKILE
  ZAMA-NDIYA
- REYAREKA
  HO MABENKELE
  AMA-INDIA

COSATU issued this sticker to encourage township residents to exclude Indian shopkeepers from their boycott of white-owned shops in the East Rand town of Boksburg. The UDF and COSATU called the boycott to protest the newly-elected Conservative Party council's attempts to re-establish segregation of public facilities in 1988.

In strike situations you would have Indian workers coming under very much more pressure than African workers from management to scab. Like what happened with the tricameral parliament: even though the majority of Indian and coloured people boycotted, the manipulation of those collaborators was played up very much by the press and the TV and so forth. So for African people, they don't look at the fact that eighty per cent of the community boycotted, they look at the fact that there's people there who are selling us out. Although the majority of the Indian community are workers, the problem that we have now is that the exposure of African people to Indian people is through the traders, so their perception is of a group where every Indian person is a trader — which is a misunderstanding.

Divide and Profit: Indian Workers in Natal, *Worker Resistance and Culture Publications booklet, Shamim Marie, 1986:*

At present, Indian workers are employed increasingly in skilled, supervisory and clerical jobs. But in many industries and many factories there are large enough numbers of Indian workers in production to prevent unity when they don't join up with African workers. Management tries to win over Indian workers through offering promotions, perks like loans, and through trying to keep a friendly, patronizing relationship. The bosses' actions encourage workers to see each other in racial terms. When Indian workers don't join unions or become involved in strikes, African workers see Indian workers as a problem. This increases the distance already existing between Indian and African workers.

But in many cases where Indian workers have joined, they are strong union members and have helped to organize other Indian workers. What these workers have come to see is that Indian workers can't get any improvements for themselves using the old ways of keeping in the bosses' good books, taking samoosas and biryani for the boss and so on. The Indian workers are in the minority and the only way they can win any real improvements for themselves is by joining with the African workers in the strong, fighting unions.

COSATU sees that the struggle of workers can be won only through unity among all workers, and by linking up factory struggles with community and political struggles. One of the main tasks of this new federation is to fight the divisions that exist amongst workers of South Africa and to unite them into a strong and confident working class. In the words of an organizer: 'For Indian workers the choice is clear. A handful have the option of standing with the bosses as managers and foreman against the workers and their unions. But for the majority, a better life can be won only through strong organizations in the factory and in the community.'

Another indication of workers' support for non-racialism is their acceptance of white union officials. Whites had focussed on shop-floor struggles in resuscitating the dormant labour movement in the 1970s; by the 1980s, some whites found another role, in building a community support base for a new brand of militant mass-based trade unionism. 'Community unions' like the embattled South African Allied Workers Union (SAAWU) in the Eastern Cape encouraged their members to support township political structures, thus linking up community and workplace issues.

Mike Roussos, who worked in SAAWU and other community unions from the early 1980s, and in 1987 became national organizer and then education secretary for a revived SACTU affiliate, the South African Railways and Harbour Union (SARWHU), as well as a member of the COSATU Central Executive Committee:

Although academically I'd done a lot of work on industrial relations, it was very, very different going into a union office. I remember one of the first meetings I attended, a lot of the workers were a bit surprised to see a white guy there — it was quite clear from the way in which they looked at me as they walked into the room and kind of gave me a sideways glance. Later on when we sang the songs and shouted *amandlas*, there was a different kind of response: you know, 'You're really welcome amongst us!' In a way, it's as much of a problem, because until people start treating you normally, you can't actually properly do work with people.

Another problem was that management, in negotiations, they'd address a lot of what they say to me. I suppose they find it easier to talk to a white person than they do to a black person. You have to do things actively to break that down: I'd have to just keep quiet and not say anything, and they would just have to talk to the other union officials.

Why do you think it is that most whites who joined the trade unions first got involved with FOSATU, and not the community unions which later aligned with the UDF?

Well, let me go back a bit. In the early '70s, a lot of white students and university lecturers were involved in helping to set up trade unions, people who came from a background which intellectually stressed the fact that it was really important to organize workers. The broader political climate in the early '70s was also slightly different: there wasn't the kind of contact between civic groups, youth groups and trade unions that emerged in the '80s.

At the same time, a lot of those white people had just walked from a fairly academic environment straight into setting up trade unions, and they didn't want to mix political issues with trade union issues — basically because they felt the union movement couldn't survive if it got involved in political issues. Whereas in what eventually became the UDF-aligned unions, there was a much greater focus on linking up to the broader struggle.

Sometimes our people made a lot of mistakes on a basic sort of trade union level, because people were so involved in a whole range of political commitments it was difficult to spend the amount of time that was necessary to just build up the union side. On the FOSATU side it was quite clear that you had a very strong base, a fairly large number of ordinary workers taking charge of things in their own workplace, who were being influenced to remain distant from the broader political struggle. The politically active trade unionists' perception of whites in the FOSATU unions was that they were pushing for a direction that was anti the ANC and the tradition that that represented, and anti-SACTU.

Now I happened to be one of the few whites who went into the non-FOSATU unions. There was always the problem that you had to be very careful of the type of role you played, as one, an intellectual, but two, just a white person who comes out of an environment where you have a lot more skills and education — which would enable me to do things, like hire a car or find a venue in town. Now I saw that happening in the FOSATU unions. Whites were elected general-secretaries, and the reason was basically because it's easier to just put somebody in who's got those skills than to try and train somebody else who hasn't. There was a big stress on non-racialism, so it seemed to be quite a progressive thing, but I think in the long run it's a problem to just absorb whites in and to dump them in those kinds of positions, because it actually blocks the growth of other people, it divides the organization. And that meant we would fall back into exactly the same kinds of tensions that had emerged within NUSAS at the time when SASO broke away.

So I didn't think that non-racialism was a kind of unproblematic, treat-everybody-as-equals business — it wasn't that at all. We were working in a situation where there were big inequalities, where there was a developing political struggle, which quite clearly had to ensure that ordinary grassroots people were actually being trained to take on the whole range of tasks. So I think it's going to remain a big problem because, despite the fact that whites are and should be accepted as full citizens of a liberated South Africa, the reality is that we've got to overcome a whole process in which whites still are dominant, in terms of the kinds of skills that they have, the sort of background, the educational opportunities.

By the 1990s, there were far fewer white officials in the progressive unions than there had been in the 1970s: the intervening decade had produced more black worker leaders. As for white union members, their numbers were tiny, but the fact that there were any at all represented a significant gain for non-racialism.

'Can We Win Over White Workers?', Umsebenzi: Voice of the SACP, *Fourth Quarter, 1988:*

We speak about our commitment to non-racial, working class unity. But can we honestly make any progress among white workers? Consider recent developments. In militant struggles black workers make gains despite the difficult times, while collaborating white unions lose ground. True, white workers still earn far more than blacks. But the wage gap is narrowing. It is no longer just black workers but whites, too, who increasingly feel the effects of the economic crisis.

A white Chemical Workers Industrial Union (CWIU) member makes a point at a strike meeting in Durban in 1989.

White workers are a fairly small and decreasing section of the working class. But they have a strategic importance because of their economic position and place within the white bloc. In earlier periods, some white workers developed traditions of non-racial class struggle. Today they have generally been corrupted and confused by racial privileges over many decades. But the situation is beginning to change again. White workers now realize the regime is more concerned to please big capital than them.[7] This sense of betrayal is used by the ultra-right to make gains at the expense of the NP [National Party]. But is this recruitment of white workers by the ultra-right inevitable?

The contact of growing numbers of white workers with COSATU unions shows it is not. In fact, we ourselves can begin to win over sections of white workers to more progressive positions. But this requires a clear strategy. Any significant headway will be made in the first place by appealing to white workers' growing sense of economic hardship. Moral appeals to non-racial justice or equality will almost certainly fail at this point.

Existing progressive organizations in the white sector are not well equipped to address white workers. The progressive trade union movement is better equipped for beginning to approach white workers. This in turn means addressing the understandable doubts of black workers who daily confront white workers as supervisors, racist bullies and strike-breakers.

Above all, we must remember the strategic possibilities in winning over white workers. One example: imagine the confusion of Afrikaans-speaking riot police, themselves from working class backgrounds, finding not just blacks, but their own brothers and sisters on a picket line or in a factory sit-in!

It was the government's escalating attacks on unions toward the end of the decade that deepened the spirit of cooperation in the labour movement. In 1989 COSATU called a Workers' Summit where all workers — and no union officials — were invited to speak. Members of eleven NACTU unions defied their executive's decision not to attend and sent representatives to meet with their counterparts in COSATU[8] — a rebellion in the ranks that took the NACTU leadership by surprise. The message from NACTU's workers was clear: opposition to non-racialism was not seen as an uncompromising point of principle, even by those with a Black Consciousness or Africanist background. In the drive toward worker unity, support for non-racialism was accepted as the dominant trend.

COSATU and NACTU campaigned together against the Labour Relations Act, which sanctioned a rigid code of what were widely viewed as unfair labour practices: limiting the recognition of majority unions, the right to strike, and negotiations over retrenchments.

COSATU President Elijah Barayi, convening the first Workers' Summit in Johannesburg to protest against new labour legislation, 4 March 1989:

There are many things which have kept us apart, but our very coming together is a powerful statement that our differences are nothing compared to our commitment to the principle of working class unity. As unions, we cannot deny the fact that the actions by management affect all workers. Issues facing all sectors demonstrate clearly the need for workers to act jointly to defend and advance our interests. It is this drive for unity among rank-and-file workers everywhere that has brought us to the summit, which represents an important consolidation of the labour movement.[9]

This transcendence of ideological differences extended beyond the trade unions. COSATU and the UDF joined with church leaders and Black Consciousness supporters in convening an historic 'all-in' conference to round off the decade. Invitations were extended to all groups that endorsed the 'Unifying Perspective'.[10]

Call by the convening committee of the Conference for a Democratic Future, November 1989:

All organizations committed to the reunification of our country and a democratically constituted government and adhering to the unifying perspective are invited to the conference.
Unifying Perspective:
- One person, one vote in a democratic country
- The lifting of the State of Emergency
- Unconditional release of all political prisoners
- Unbanning of all political organizations
- Freedom of association and expression
- Press freedom
- Living wage for all

Notes

1. At its foundation COSATU comprised 33 affiliates, including the eight affiliates of FOSATU (which dissolved) and the other independent unions, with 500,000 signed-up members and 450,000 paid-up members. By the end of the decade its strength had more than doubled.
2. An approach that argues for exclusive working-class organization and political mobilization, i.e. that workers should give priority to building a solely worker-controlled trade union movement, which when strong enough should assume an independent, leading and directing role in the struggle against apartheid. This philosophy is generally opposed to broad alliances, and to workers taking up community and political issues.

3. While the merger was effected in late 1986, CUSA-AZACTU was not renamed NACTU until the next year.
4. At its 1988 conference NACTU conceded that the membership figures routinely quoted by the International Confederation of Free Trade Unions (ICFTU) were greatly overstated, and released a new national paid-up membership total of less than 150,000 (as opposed to COSATU's more than 750,000). The lower figure also reflected a decline in support for NACTU's BC-oriented affiliates.
5. SACTU had operated from exile since the 1960s.
6. The South African Clothing and Textile Workers Union (SACTWU), formed in 1989, was the first COSATU affiliate to unite large numbers of coloured, Indian and African workers.
7. The crisis in profit rates due to black labour militancy motivated big capital to push the state for concessions to reform apartheid — at the expense of white workers. The waning influence of the white working class also stemmed from demographic factors: lower white birth rates, emigration of white professionals, and decreasing European immigration.
8. The NACTU leadership had responded similarly to the October 1988 all-in Anti-Apartheid Conference, which was banned by the government. In interviews with *South African Review: 5* (Ravan Press/South African Research Service, 1989), Africanist leaders conceded 'a reluctance to risk diluting this one source of strength (NACTU) — which would certainly occur if unity developed with the far more powerful COSATU'. By the time of the August 1989 Workers' Summit, held to map a response to the white, coloured and Indian parliamentary elections, NACTU was working closely with COSATU.
9. A smear pamphlet allegedly issued by the (non-existent) 'Concerned Workers Association of South Africa' in the Western Cape in early 1989 bemoaned the union unity moves: 'We have no room for leaders like Mndaweni who changes like a chameleon overnight and listens to the ANC.' Another apparent indication of the government's antagonism towards NACTU's rapprochement with COSATU came with another fake document: a letter claiming to be from the PAC (though the PAC Harare office denied any knowledge of it) posted to NACTU shortly before the first Workers' Summit, urging its affiliates to resist attempts by the ANC to co-opt them.
10. The conference traced its origins back to a resolution taken by delegates at a UDF National Working Committee conference in May 1987, leading to a planned Anti-Apartheid Conference in September 1988 which the government banned.

23 The Movement is Very Big Now

In 1985 the ANC formally adopted non-racialism at all levels: from the grassroots to its top policy-making body. At its National Consultative Conference held in Kabwe, Zambia, the decision was taken to open the National Executive Committee to people of all races. After new elections, the NEC consisted of 25 Africans, two coloureds, two Indians and one white.[1]

James Stuart, a veteran of Umkhonto we Sizwe's Wankie Campaign, one of the first coloureds elected to the NEC:

With the rapid growth of the struggle in the country and with the discussion taking place round about '84, '85, I personally was of the view that we should begin to have members of all communities in the NEC of the ANC, and this was a view which was supported by the overwhelming majority of members of the ANC. Because it does say something if you have one or two representatives from the coloured community on the NEC. Coloured people would then feel that they have a home in the movement, they are not just stepchildren or second-class members, but they are full participants and full members.

Aziz Pahad, a senior member of the ANC's London office and one of the first Indians elected to the NEC:

The important thing was that these were open elections and nobody was elected on group tickets. It was secret ballots and people were voted on in terms of how the delegates saw their contribution. There was nobody there who was voted on the basis of, 'Ah, this one must be put on because he represents this sector, this one must be put on because he represents this section.'

The Kabwe conference also reaffirmed the enduring relationship between the ANC and the SACP, with the seminal role of communists in non-racial organization cited as a cornerstone of the alliance. A few weeks after the conference, the state-run South African Broadcasting Corporation televised the most flagrant public defiance to date of the ban on the SACP: the unfurling of the Party flag at a mass funeral of four assassinated UDF leaders in the Eastern Cape village of Cradock.[2] Another milestone for the SACP came in 1987, when the government released imprisoned ANC and CP veteran Govan Mbeki: he immediately pledged his continued dedication to the communist ideals for which he was imprisoned. When seven top political prisoners of the ANC and SACP were released in 1989,[3] their Soweto welcome rally was a living embodiment of the alliance,[4] in terms of the flags, chants and speeches in support of both organizations.

Such daring public promotion of the SACP symbolized the ultimate challenge to the state more than it reflected the degree of popular support[5] for the party. Even non-CP members backed this assertion of the democratic right of all political organizations to exist and to campaign openly. For the SACP itself, it was a demonstration of the party's concerted effort to raise its own profile — a departure from the past emphasis on its partnership with the ANC.

Mzala, a SASO leader at the University of Zululand who joined the ANC underground, then left South Africa in 1976 and became active in both the ANC and the SACP:

I never knew what communism was, but I can tell you, I was fifteen years old when I was first detained by the Security Police and I was already being accused of being a communist. That naturally triggered an interest in me, an interest to find out, first of all, what a communist was, and secondly, what

One of the large SACP flags boldly displayed in Cradock in 1985.

communism had to offer us. I'd never read a single work of Marx, Engels or Lenin. The regime said I was a communist at a time when I only rebelled morally — I did not even belong to an organization at that stage.

What I believe is that a truly just society is one where people have a common share in the social means that is producing wealth, and in the distribution of that wealth it is the actual producers — the workers — who take the lion's share. The reality of capitalism, however, is that that share goes to the private owners, even though they do not themselves participate directly in the production process. This is the logic of communists all over the world when we challenge the inherent injustice of the capitalist system.

Would you use the term 'racial capitalism'?

It's an ambiguous and awkward formulation. My objection arises from its inability to make an historically informed characterization of the South African problem. The term 'racial capitalism' creates the impression that South Africa's political problem emanates from the development of capitalism after the minerals' discovery. But what of the period before then, when South Africa's mode of production was pre-capitalist, and the indigenous peoples were opposing only colonial domination?

We need a more objective, historic and scientific assessment of the problem. It is this which led to the Communist Party's conclusion that, although South Africa is a capitalist society, it retains for blacks the features of a colonial society. This division of the population into a large and colonized people, robbed of their right to political and economic independence, and a minority of colonial settlers who possess the country's wealth and control its political institutions and the armed forces, is the major source of conflict. Since South Africa has not resolved this principal political contradiction by way of the liberation of the oppressed, for blacks the country remains in the pre-independence era historically.

In today's capitalist South Africa black workers experience racially defined problems of exploitation. Although they constitute the same class as white workers, they are not treated equally by the capitalist class which takes advantage of their colonial status. Black workers therefore are not sensitive to anything as much as the feeling of national inequality and the violation of their right to self-determination. The identity of their class interest, therefore, is overlaid by national differentiation. The concept of 'racial capitalism' does not even make the first step towards the articulation of this complexity. It is an ignorant formulation.

Do you see class as a greater factor than race?

The SACP avoids ranking these concepts in any order of importance. Rather we see their relationship as being expressed in the reality of the black workers' position — exploited as a class, oppressed as a race. Where our party makes a distinction in regard to this relationship is to assert that, because South Africa's mode of production is essentially capitalist, institutionalized racism serves the interests of class exploitation and not the other way around.

It is actually outside the ANC-SACP alliance that there is an over-emphasis of class over race. In regard to the alliance we should never lose sight of the extent to which the ANC has influenced the Communist Party in the acceptance of a programme of national liberation. So there is a healthy political climate in the relationship of the ANC and the SACP. They have a common understanding that the goal is national liberation, the building of a democratic society on the basis of the Freedom Charter. The ANC does not address itself to the question of socialism but the ANC and SACP agree that the political programme, at this stage of the revolution, is the establishment of a non-racial democracy that is anti-monopoly capitalism.

The South African government continually tries to make political capital out of the alleged white domination of the SACP, focussing on its leader, Joe Slovo. How do you see the race factor in the SACP's leadership and membership?

Whites are an almost insignificant minority in the SACP. The predominant force is composed of black people, Africans in particular. For us in the liberation movement there is absolutely no awareness and concern about Joe Slovo's colour. We are instead more aware that his part of the collective leadership comes about solely because of his personal qualities and merits, which can be traced to his record of participation in the liberation struggle. It shouldn't be forgotten incidentally that Slovo became General-Secretary after a line of African holders of that post who were also elected by virtue of their qualities — persons like Moses Kotane and Moses Mabhida.

Joe Slovo is carried aloft by ANC cadres at the funeral of SACP leader Moses Mabhida in Maputo in 1986.

I think we need to ask: who are the people who are worried about Slovo's colour? Is it the black people in South Africa? Is it the people who are singing about Slovo and Tambo? Is it the MK cadres whom Slovo has been commanding at various stages of struggle? No, no, these people are not worried about Slovo's colour — these people are overwhelmed by the fact that Slovo is a committed and sincere freedom fighter.

The people who are worried about Slovo's colour are the very people who posed the colour problem for South Africa: the racist regime and those who support them from outside. They're caught up in their own racist set-up. We are defying that, and then they're worried about why we are not race-conscious in the ANC and SACP.

There has been this image that whites are the ones who are coming into the ANC as communists, when as a matter of fact, if one looks at history properly, as early as 1927 already 70 per cent of the members of the Communist Party were blacks. Incidentally, for some reason there's been the prominence of white leaders — I mean Joe Slovo, Jack Simons and so on — but maybe in a way this also has been useful for us, because it has consolidated our very non-racial approach. It is precisely these white communists who have demonstrated, perhaps more than other political groups among whites, the level to which they are willing to go, not only in defending this non-racial perspective, but also in sacrificing towards the struggle and helping to crystallize and to solidify this non-racial approach.

Freedom song (in Xhosa with English translation) sung by Umkhonto we Sizwe *cadres outside South Africa and at gatherings inside the country:*

Uph' u Tambo	Where is Tambo?
UTamb' usehlathin' bafana	Tambo is in the bush, guys
Wenzenina?	What is he doing?
Uqeqesh' amajoni	He's teaching the young fighters
Fall in —	Fall in —
one line, two lines	One line, two lines
Uph' u Slovo	Where is Slovo?
USlov' usehlathin' bafana	Slovo is in the bush, guys
Wenzenina?	What is he doing?
Uqeqesh' amajoni	He's teaching the young fighters

Joe Slovo, Communist Party member since 1940, a founder member of Umkhonto we Sizwe, SACP General-Secretary since 1987, and a member of the ANC NEC:

How would you compare the role of whites in resistance politics today, inside South Africa and in the ANC and SACP, with that of the Congress Alliance era?

It is fundamentally, absolutely different now. There's been a sort of bridge of a very important psychological barrier: in general, the whites as a community have lost confidence in their capacity to survive within racist structures permanently. And this has triggered off all kinds of defections and demonstrations on the ground — a significant minority of whites have been risking imprisonment, resisting the draft, coming to speak to the ANC, etc. So I think the fundamental difference is that there's a real search by the white community for a way out of a crisis. There was no crisis for the whites in 1953, or even in 1960.

And therefore an appreciable number are moving — not completely to our side, but certainly they are what I would call part of the forces for change. It's not so much what we've done. It's happened because the chemistry of the whole situation has fundamentally altered.

How broad is the broad front going to get?

I think it is going to get as wide as possible, but perhaps at different levels. And what I mean is this: what I would call the sort of national revolutionary forces consist of the ANC-SACP alliance, the trade union movement, those who really sort of have a minimum common liberation programme. Beyond that you get an enormous panorama of different shades of opposition. I think we should certainly do our best to find a common basis for acting on those things on which we agree. As a party, we don't say to people, 'Unless you agree with socialism, we are not going to struggle against the high rents in the townships.' And in turn, the ANC should not say, 'Unless you accept and proclaim the Freedom Charter, we are not going to have a demonstration with you to protest against the Labour Relations Bill.'

I don't think the ANC has moved away from its position — or the Communist Party. We believe that the Freedom Charter is the fundamental objective of the present phase, and we continue, with whoever we collaborate, to get that across. I think even at the early stages, before the Congress of South African Trade Unions was formed, our thinking was that if the Freedom Charter is going to be an obstacle to creating a united federation it's not necessary to, at this point, make it a do-or-die question. But at the COSATU congress, the mood was so overwhelmingly in favour of the Freedom Charter from the bottom up that it swept in.

At the time of its formation, COSATU did not embrace unions that rejected non-racialism; are you saying that now that fundamental difference seems to be bridged?

I think there is a difference, but that difference should not be allowed to be an obstacle to acting together on specific issues. COSATU is not changing its policy: it's still got the Freedom Charter as its fundamental document. But what it is saying — and I think quite correctly, and should have said this from the beginning, actually — is, 'Listen, where we can, let's act together. There's a three-day strike, there's a campaign for a living wage — why don't you join in the campaigns?'

I think you must remember the movement is very big now, very big, and it's not all part of some monolith, where instructions are handed down. There are lots of people who support us who even go further than we go, who are much more hard-line and who refuse to work with people unless they are full members of the church and can recite the catechism, you know, and this is a phenomenon which we've learned to live with. But as a movement, I think we must distinguish between what our policy is and what the basis of our alliances are with other groupings — these are two completely different things.

You see, there's a difference at the formative stage, where you're trying to define your character. It's an understandable process: we stand for this, we oppose what they stand for. In fact, in the early stage, when we used to say to COSATU, 'Why don't you open up?' their answer was, 'We're not strong enough yet, it's going to create all kinds of diversions and in-fighting, internal squabbles.' I think, in a sense, COSATU's new stance is not a change of policy — it's a measure of the fact that they are now strong enough.

Let me give you an example: up to about 1984, '85, I was one of the strongest opponents within the movement of opening up the ranks of the ANC's NEC to minority groups. This wasn't just discussed in 1985 — it's been discussed since 1965. I opposed it then because the ANC was enormously weakened after 1960. It didn't exist inside the country: it was like a tender plant, in a way, that had to take root and grow. And at that stage, had the ANC decided to open up its ranks, it would have faced such a salvo from right and left, from BC, from Africa, that it would have been damaging to the ANC.

One changed one's attitude towards that question when the ANC was transformed from a purely agitational opposition into an alternative power, which it started becoming from about 1984. With the massive sort of welling-up of sympathy and support for the ANC, it then became strong enough to risk the kind of flak which inevitably would be hurled at it. What I'm trying to say is that you've got to analyze policy in relation to a context. Things change.

The mainstream media portrayed the ANC as communist-controlled, and the SACP as white-dominated — with Slovo said to be doing much of the domination.

White hostility to the *rooi gevaar* (red danger) has been orchestrated by the Nationalist Party ever since it outlawed communism in 1950. In the black community militant anti-communism is largely confined to a tiny clique of state-supported politicians and conservative church leaders,[7] but opposition to communism has also been a recurring strand in the ideology of the Pan-Africanist Congress. It was the alleged 'infiltration' of white and Indian communists into the ANC, plus the non-racial preamble and 'leftist' economic clauses of the Freedom Charter, that provoked the PAC breakaway. Three decades later, despite ideological detours that led to its policies being labelled variously, 'Maoist', 'Marxist-Leninist' and 'Africanist-socialist', the PAC's anti-communism remained implacable. Its chief target was the SACP.

Azania News: The Official Organ of the Pan-Africanist Congress of Azania, *Vol. 26, No. 3, 1989:*

The PAC regards the SACP as quacks rather than communists. This position was restated by the PAC Secretary for Economic Affairs, Comrade Mfanasekhaya Pearce Gqobose, in Dar es Salaam recently. Addressing a regular closed meeting of PAC cadres on the topic, 'The PAC position towards the SACP', Comrade Gqobose quoted the founding president of the PAC, Mangaliso Sobukwe, who stated that South Africa was unfortunate in her choice of Christians and communists. They were all quacks.

They are all settlers, at heart and mind. They continue to resist the propagation of or the practical implementation of the idea of working on the basis of one African Nationhood, whereby all that pay their only allegiance to Africa and accept the democratic rule of an African majority shall be regarded as Africans.

The SACP, Comrade Gqobose charged, pandered to white supremacist ideas when in 1922 it marched under the banner proclaiming that position. Similarly, in 1928 it rejected Stalin's 'Black Republic' thesis despite the fact that its membership consisted of 1,600 Africans against only 128 whites, the latter of whom were mainly in the leadership. When in 1950 the South African Parliament was debating the Suppression of Communism Act, the SACP chose to disband rather than organize underground.[8] They then chose to infiltrate the ANC, water down the struggle of the African, thus causing division among the African ranks, Comrade Gqobose continued. Africans must lead. That is their country.

Compelling evidence that non-racialism prevailed even in the most sensitive sectors of the liberation movement emerged from trials of Umkhonto we Sizwe cadres. A daring bomb blast at the infamous John Vorster Square Security Police headquarters turned out to be the work of a white female 'terrorist'.[9] The prosecution of an alleged Western Cape ANC cell was dubbed the 'Rainbow Trial' because its fourteen defendants represented a colour and class spectrum of South African society.[10] An

eminent black priest testifying before the sentencing of three white MK
members told the court that they were seen in Soweto as 'kings and
queens' because 'whites who do not have obvious reasons to cast their lot
with blacks are regarded as more than heroes'.[11]

Another important element of the non-racialism of the ANC is its
internationalism: the theory that the interests of oppressed peoples
transcend national boundaries. Thus the broad front of forces for change
in South Africa welcomes not only non-Africans, but non-South
Africans who share the goal of non-racial democracy. Foreigners have
been involved in South African resistance politics for decades, in unions,
churches and universities. This kind of international solidarity has also
benefited the ANC's underground military operations.[12]

*Pierre-André Albertini, a French citizen who spent a year in a Ciskei jail for his
involvement in Umkhonto we Sizwe, in a statement to the ANC's international
solidarity conference, December 1987, in Arusha, Tanzania:*

At the beginning of 1985, I made the mistake of accepting a post to lecture
at the University of Fort Hare in the bantustan of Ciskei. I know now I should
not have accepted this post. Its creation was the direct result of the
scandalous cooperation between the French government and the apartheid regime.[13] But I am present here today also because of the people of
France, who mobilized against apartheid and against the relationship
between the Botha government and the French government, and finally
forced my government to obtain my release.

When one has, as I have, lived in South Africa and participated in the just
struggle of its people for freedom and rights, one can only be convinced of
the completely non-racial nature of this struggle. It reminds me of the
complete solidarity which linked us together — my comrades of the ANC
and myself — in the Ciskeian jails where I happened to be the only white
man. The struggle for a non-racial, democratic South Africa continues in
the prisons of that country.

Today I am proud to be in a position to continue the struggle against
apartheid in France to obtain comprehensive and mandatory sanctions
against South Africa and to increase the support for the ANC in France.
Amandla!

*Klaas de Jonge, a Dutch citizen who was arrested for Umkhonto we Sizwe
activities in 1985, then escaped from the Security Police and sought refuge in the
Dutch Embassy in Pretoria, where he spent two years holed up until his release in
a prisoner exchange:[14]*

South Africa, it's a racist country, so if you are white you're less suspicious.
Once I was with a load of arms and there was a roadblock and they stopped
me. And then they said wait, because there came a car with black people, a
small bus full of people, and they were searched — everything, body-
searched and under the car and in the car. But they were very friendly to

Anti-apartheid media from European and North American solidarity groups.

me, because I was white. They said, 'So you're lost. That doesn't matter, we'll bring you.' So I was with my load of arms, and with police cars they brought me more or less to the spot where I wanted to be!

Do you think it was important on a political level that you, as a white, a foreigner, were doing underground ANC work?

No, because then you are conscious of the fact. If you believe in democracy, if you believe in non-racialism, if you believe in ending exploitation, then everything in South Africa goes completely against every value that you think is important. And the way the ANC interpreted only attacking economic and military and strategic objectives, I was completely behind that. It's not terrorist attacks.

All these things I thought over before starting, but now I have to discuss these kind of things in Holland because I'm very much attacked by a lot of people who are against apartheid, but who see it often only in terms of a human rights struggle. The moment a Dutchman shows that he took part in the armed struggle, they say you are a terrorist.

And then I have to explain why I think it is a bit like in the Second World War. I compare the situations: the children who are tortured, the exploitation, the destabilization of the frontline states,[15] no political rights, deportations — all the things done by the Nazis are comparable. And then people say, 'Ja, but the South Africans didn't kill six million people.' Well, the Nazis didn't need the Jews, and the South Africans need the black South Africans — they are the cheap labour power. You don't kill the chicken who lays the golden egg.

The fact that I admitted that I had smuggled arms, that gave way to this whole discussion of the use of violence. 'By your actions you could have killed harmless civilians, women and children' — the same thing the South Africans say. I tried to explain the structural violence under apartheid. And I also said, 'Consider me, for example, like a Swede or a Swiss who is during the Second World War in Holland. Switzerland was neutral in the Second World War, isn't it? And Sweden also. So if a Swede or Swiss was living in Holland, would it be so strange if he sees what Nazism means and he would say, 'Okay, I'm going to join the Dutch resistance movement'?

The consolidation of the ANC's own power and the fortification of its alliances contrasted with the faltering confidence of the minority government, which had lost the strategic initiative. The political tide was turning, a point not lost on that important shaper of ruling ideology, the secret Afrikaner Broederbond. Behind the public bravado geared at impressing the domestic right wing and the international community, the Broederbond was constructing a fall-back position. Its new pragmatism precipitated a serious erosion of classic apartheid, but stopped short of conceding the non-racial unitary democracy demanded by the liberation movement.

*'Basic Political Values for the Survival of the Afrikaner',[16] 'strictly confidential'
Afrikaner Broederbond memorandum, 1989:*

The existence of a variety of groups and sub-groups within the geographical area of the Republic of South Africa is recognized by means of freedom of association. Ethnicity is certainly a reality regarding the identification of minority groups and communities, but this does not imply the absoluteness of group rights. Furthermore, the exclusion of effective black sharing in political processes at the highest level is a threat to the survival of the white man, which cannot be countered by maintaining the status quo or by a further consolidation of power in white hands.

This means that everyone must be able to serve on the highest legislative and executive levels, whatever the future political system may be. This can also mean that in some models the head of government does not necessarily have to be white (as is presently not excluded), but the post must be defined and the executive power restricted in such a way that the power that this post entails will not be applied in such a way that one group dominates the others. Power-sharing must be such that there can be no group domination. The rights and aspirations of groups must be protected and satisfied.

This means that there can no longer be a white government. There can, however, not be a black, e.g. Zulu, government, either. The majority of the government members will indeed be black, but the system and procedure will be operated in such a way that all the groups can participate effectively and not be dominated by one group. The status quo can, therefore, not continue to exist, but can also not be simply reversed so that white control is replaced by black control.

In conclusion, there are various mechanisms which can be applied in models or structures in order to comply with the above-mentioned requirements or conditions. A test which we should set for the acceptability of a system must always be: What will be in our interests in the event that we end up in the opposition seat? Furthermore, we must also realize that, humanly speaking, there simply are no guarantees. We must think in terms of probabilities, of calculated risks. The will to survive as Afrikaner, and our faith and energy, will serve as our greatest guarantee. Should the Afrikaner not succeed through its own creative power to bring about negotiated structures which are strong and flexible enough to accommodate the conflicting powers in the country, it is inevitable that structures will be forced upon him in which he has no share at all. This will make self-determination impossible.

As at so many junctures in South African history, multi-racialism and non-racialism were counterposed. Even as it groped for a way out of the deepening crisis, the ruling white minority clutched at 'group rights' in an effort to counter 'group domination'. In stark contrast, the ANC pledged its commitment to safeguarding the social, cultural and religious rights of all individuals. In an effort to convert the Freedom Charter 'from a vision of the future into a constitutional reality', the ANC submitted its guidelines for a future non-racial state.

ANC Constitutional Guidelines for a Democratic South Africa, released in 1988:

THE STATE

(a) South Africa shall be an independent, unitary, democratic and non-racial state.

(b) Sovereignty shall belong to the people as a whole and shall be exercised through one central legislature, executive, judiciary and administration. Provision shall be made for delegation of the powers of the central authority to subordinate administrative units for purposes of more efficient administration and democratic participation.

(c) The institution of hereditary rulers and chiefs shall be transformed to serve the interests of the people as a whole in conformity with the democratic principles embodied in the constitution.

(d) All organs of government, including justice, security and armed forces, shall be representative of the people as a whole, democratic in their structure and functioning, and dedicated to defending the principles of the constitution.

FRANCHISE

(e) In the exercise of their sovereignty, the people shall have the right to vote under a system of universal suffrage based on the principles of one person/one vote.

(f) Every voter shall have the right to stand for election and to be elected to all legislative bodies.

NATIONAL IDENTITY

(g) It shall be state policy to promote the growth of a single national identity and loyalty binding on all South Africans. At the same time, the state shall recognize the linguistic and cultural diversity of the people and provide facilities for free linguistic and cultural development.

BILL OF RIGHTS AND AFFIRMATIVE ACTION

(h) The constitution shall include a Bill of Rights based on the Freedom Charter. Such a Bill of Rights shall guarantee the fundamental human rights of all citizens, irrespective of race, colour, sex or creed, and shall provide appropriate mechanisms for their protection and enforcement.

(i) The state and all social institutions shall be under constitutional duty to eradicate racial discrimination in all its forms.

(j) The state and all social institutions shall be under a constitutional duty to take active steps to eradicate, speedily, the economic and social inequalities produced by racial discrimination.

(k) The advocacy or practice of racism, fascism, nazism or the incitement of ethnic or regional exclusiveness or hatred shall be outlawed.

(l) Subject to clauses (i) and (k) above, the democratic state shall guarantee the basic rights and freedoms, such as freedom of association, thought, worship and the press. Furthermore, the state shall have the duty to protect the right to work and guarantee the right to education and social security.

(m) All parties which conform to the provision of (i) to (k) above shall have the legal right to exist and to take part in the political life of the country.

ECONOMY

(n) The state shall ensure that the entire economy serves the interests and well-being of the entire population.

(o) The state shall have the right to determine the general context in which economic life takes place and define and limit the rights and obligations attaching to the ownership and use of productive capacity.

(p) The private sector of the economy shall be obliged to cooperate with the state in realizing the objectives of the Freedom Charter in promoting social well-being.

(q) The economy shall be a mixed one, with a public sector, a private sector, a cooperative sector and a small-scale family sector.

(r) Cooperative forms of economic enterprise, village industries and small-scale family activities shall be supported by the state.

(s) The state shall promote the acquisition of management, technical and scientific skills among all sections of the population, especially the blacks.

(t) Property for personal use and consumption shall be constitutionally protected.

LAND

(u) The state shall devise and implement a land reform programme that will include and address the following issues: abolition of all racial restrictions on ownership and use of land, and implementation of land reform in conformity with the principle of affirmative action, taking into account the status of victims of forced removals.[17]

WORKERS

(v) A charter protecting workers' trade union rights, especially the right to strike and collective bargaining, shall be incorporated into the constitution.

WOMEN

(w) Women shall have equal rights in all spheres of public and private life and the state shall take affirmative action to eliminate inequalities and discrimination between the sexes.

THE FAMILY

(x) The family, parenthood and children's rights shall be protected.

INTERNATIONAL

(y) South Africa shall be a non-aligned state committed to the principles of the Charter of the OAU and the Charter of the UN and to the achievement of national liberation, world peace and disarmament.

Notes

1. The non-Africans elected were Reg September, James Stuart, Aziz Pahad, Mac Maharaj and Joe Slovo. In 1988, another white (Umkhonto we Sizwe strategist Ronnie Kasrils) was elected to the NEC.
2. The SABC broadcast of the funeral of Matthew Goniwe, Fort Calata, Sparrow Mkhonto and Sicelo Mhlauli conveyed the false impression that eminent clerics

such as Beyers Naude and Bishop Desmond Tutu were marching under the flag of, and were thus in support of, the SACP.

3. In October 1989, on the eve of the Commonwealth conference that was to consider strengthening sanctions against Pretoria, President F. W. de Klerk released the prisoners: five who had been arrested at Rivonia in 1963 (Walter Sisulu, Ahmed Kathrada, Andrew Mlangeni, Elias Motsoaledi and Raymond Mhlaba) plus Wilton Mkwayi, who had been caught a year later. Also released was Oscar Mpetha, a UDF and trade union leader who was South Africa's oldest political prisoner, jailed since 1985, and PAC leader Jafta Masemola, who had been the country's longest-serving political prisoner after Nelson Mandela (who remained in prison at that stage). Kathrada, Mkwayi, Motsoaledi, Mhlaba and Mpetha had also been members of the CPSA before it was banned.

4. According to the jargon of activists inside South Africa, 'the alliance' was often code for the SACP itself. Thus members of a COSATU delegation visiting Harare in 1989 asked if, in addition to holding talks with the ANC and SACTU, they could also 'meet the alliance'.

5. At the SACP's seventh congress in 1989 it reported a 90 per cent growth in membership since its 1984 conference, with a racial breakdown of members as follows: 70 per cent African, 16 per cent white, 10 per cent Indian and 4 per cent coloured.

6. The translation is in keeping with the militant spirit of the song; hence *bafana* is translated as guys rather than boys, and *amajoni*, usually understood to mean the virile young rural men who go to work on the mines, is taken to mean young freedom fighters.

7. The claimed black support of a vociferous anti-communist organization, Victims Against Terrorism, was exposed as spurious when the few blacks demonstrating against the ANC on the fifth anniversary of the May 1983 bombing of the Pretoria military headquarters admitted to journalists that they had all been bussed into Pretoria and paid for their services by the VAT's white leaders. A black figure frequently cited as an opponent of 'the communists' and a proponent of sanctions, by the South African government as well as Ronald Reagan, was the right-wing Bishop Isaac Mokoena. The African Spiritual Churches Association publicly dissociated itself from him, charging that his claim to lead 4.5 million members is unfounded and that 'Mokoena is opposed to all progressive organizations and frequently flies abroad for the purpose of portraying the false image that the South African Indigenous Churches support the government's policy of apartheid. The funding of his trips is questionable.'

8. This text contains a number of inaccuracies: striking miners in the Rand Revolt were not members of the CPSA; the CPSA did not reject the Black Republic thesis; and the disbanded CPSA reorganized underground as the SACP.

9. Marion Sparg, sentenced to 25 years in prison in 1987.

10. The media focussed on white trialist Jennifer Schreiner, an academic and a descendant of the feminist writer, Olive Schreiner. It emerged in court testimony that she had been the target of unsuccessful Security Police efforts to turn her into a spy, so as to create the impression that she had been 'planted' in the struggle and to make the point that whites could not be trusted.

11. SACC president Bishop Manas Buthelezi, testifying at the trial of Damian de Lange, Ian Robertson and Susan Westcott, 26 October 1989. The next week newly released ANC leaders Walter Sisulu, Ahmed Kathrada, Elias Motsoaledi and Andrew Mlangeni attended the trial as a show of support for the 'Broederstroom Three', who were sentenced to 25 years, 20 years and 18 years in prison, respectively.

12. The list of foreigners who have engaged in South African resistance politics includes the founder of the ICU, Clements Kadalie, a Malawian, and several people who served prison terms for Umkhonto we Sizwe activities, including Alex Moumbaris, a French citizen; David and Sue Rabkin, both British passport-

holders; Sean Hosey, an Irish citizen; and Helene Passtoors, of dual Dutch/Belgian nationality. The list of clerics who have been actively involved in South African politics includes Anglican Bishop Trevor Huddleston, who now leads the British Anti-Apartheid Movement; Michael Lapsley and John Osmers, New Zealand Anglican priests active with the ANC's Department of Religious Affairs, who were both seriously injured in parcel bomb attacks; and Casimir Paulson, an American Catholic priest who was detained and tortured for three months in Transkei in 1987 and then went to Zimbabwe to work with South African exiles.

13. Albertini's self-effacing account obscures the fact that it was his decision to do an alternative to French military service that resulted in his posting as a civil servant teaching French at Fort Hare (declared by the South African government to be part of the homeland or bantustan of Ciskei). He chose to accept the posting, believing that the journalistic work he could do (under a pseudonym) would make the experience worthwhile.

14. In September 1987, De Jonge, Albertini and 133 Cubans held by the South Africans were exchanged for a South African prisoner-of-war captured by the Angolans, Wynand du Toit.

15. Since 1980, Pretoria has invaded Angola, Mozambique, Zimbabwe, Zambia, Lesotho, Botswana and Swaziland; supported dissident groups in neighbouring states; and attacked their transport and communications links. These actions all represented efforts to 'destabilize' the economies of South Africa's majority-ruled neighbours.

16. The document notes that 'the survival of the Afrikaner is coupled with the survival of the white man, and therefore many of these conditions are also applicable to the survival of the white man'.

17. Those who have been moved out of 'white areas' and forcibly relocated to segregated black living areas or bantustans.

24 The Future in the Present

By the beginning of the 1990s, the broad front had never been broader. Sections of society that had long been firmly anchored within the ruling bloc were dislodged and engaged in mass actions against the state. In this period the struggle for a non-racial, democratic South Africa entered a new phase.

These gains came at a cost: half a decade of unprecedented warfare between the people and the state. Yet the commitment to a non-racial democratic future is now even more deeply embedded in South African history. The fervent defence of non-racialism by the latest generation of activists is a powerful sign that non-racialism will flourish in the future.

The largest and most potent new UDF affiliate was launched in early 1987, in total secrecy at the height of the State of Emergency — the first national youth movement since the ANC Youth League. Recalling the Youth League 'Class of '44', which included Mandela, Tambo and Sisulu, the South African Youth Congress leadership was dubbed the 'Class of '87'. Four decades after the Youth Leaguers opened the debate on non-racialism, SAYCO closed it, by pledging its two million supporters[1] to uphold the non-racial principles of the Freedom Charter.

Freedom march, Durban, September 1989.

'SAYCO speaks on the Charter', SASPU National[2] *publication on the Freedom Charter, 1987:*

How and why did SAYCO adopt the Freedom Charter? SAYCO was formed on the basis of the existence of youth organizations in local townships and villages. Many of these local youth congresses had already adopted the Freedom Charter. The youth have always been in the forefront, the most radical elements within the UDF.

The other factor is that SAYCO arose after COSAS, which adopted the Freedom Charter and non-racialism from its inception. This idea of non-racialism was implanted in the youth congresses and taken up by our youth. When COSAS was formed, non-racialism and the non-racial approach to the struggle made a breakthrough. This was similar to the breakthrough in 1955 when the Freedom Charter was adopted. In 1956, when the Charter was adopted – not by the Congress Alliance, but by the ANC in particular – non-racialism won over what we call narrow nationalism.

But the banning of organizations suppressed the idea of non-racialism and brought up racial approaches again – until non-racialism made another breakthrough. So this informed the formation of SAYCO, as it did the youth congresses throughout the country. Every campaign, every action we take, is guided by our understanding of the Freedom Charter. All other documents, like the so-called Azanian Manifesto, could not compete with the Freedom Charter. Non-racialism triumphed over the racial point of view.

The Charter refers to the coloured people, the Indian people, the African community and the white community as 'national groups'. National groups have nothing to do with races, but they have everything to do with the divisions which exist in South Africa today, created by apartheid. They are the building blocks of the future South African nation that will be neither coloured, Indian, African or white – it will be one South African nation. We need to understand how each of these apartheid-differentiated national groups have come to lose their rights in history. This helps us not to gloss over these apartheid-created divisions by simply ignoring them in quasi-revolutionary sloganeering.

It is this understanding that has actually helped us to formulate clearly and unambiguously the only solution to these divisions, which is unity of our people as a people, irrespective of race, colour, creed and sex: non-racialism. In this respect, non-racialism is the only possible South African liberation scenario which calls for the complete destruction of racism and ethnicity, and which is derived from the realities of the South African situation itself.

Within a year of its founding, SAYCO became one of seventeen anti-apartheid organizations banned by the government.[3] Much of SAYCO's leadership was either detained or forced into exile, and youths accounted for 80 per cent of the thousands detained under the Emergency regulations.

Buras Nhlabati, student activist from Tembisa township, north of Johannesburg:

I was arrested at 3.30 in the morning. There were four whites and two black police and South African Defence Force personnel surrounding the house. When they came inside the house they asked me my name, and then I was beaten up for something like 45 minutes. I was beaten with fists, kicked, and hit with the butt of a gun.

I was then taken to an interrogation room at Tembisa Police Station and they started interrogating me, beating me up for something like five hours. They asked me if I know something about the African National Congress, and about the campaign which maybe the students' congress is planning, and again about others whom they can't find. When I refused to answer I was beaten and given electric shocks from handcuffs. All my comrades were released. I stood firm, preferring to die.

On the second day I was again given electric shocks. I was stripped and put in a rubber suit from head to foot. A dummy was put in my mouth so I could not scream. There was no air. They switched the plug on, my muscles pumping hard. I couldn't see anything. When they switched the plug off, they took the dummy out and said I should speak. When I refused, they put the dummy back and switched on again. After a long time they stopped. I was stripped and put into a refrigerated room, naked, for something like thirty minutes. Then they put me back in the electric shock suit and I was taken into another interrogation room. My hands, feet and head were tied around a pole, and bright searchlights turned on. I felt my mind go dead. I couldn't see. I was dizzy. I was beaten again for the whole day. I have scars on my right hip, in my head, and on my back. I cannot even read at this present juncture.

Did you become at all anti-white as a result of that treatment?[4]

You'll find that even I can be tortured to such an extent that maybe I can be paralyzed, but I don't want to see South Africa only being the blacks there. I want to see South Africa with all races living there in peace and harmony. So that is why I'm not going to change my ideology.

People inside the township, they'll tell you straight that, 'Look, you say you want to drive the whites to the sea — where are our children today? Some are dead, some are in detention, some are in exile, some are in hiding. They are for an ideology of a non-racial democratic South Africa.' I mean, my parents were politicizing me, and what I know now is that I and my parents are following one ideology, which is the ideology of a non-racial society in South Africa.

The ever-broadening struggle for a non-racial future, now known simply as the Mass Democratic Movement (MDM), gathered extraordinary momentum in 1989. A hunger strike organized in the prisons and supported by activists and professionals succeeded in freeing detainees. A Defiance Campaign brought the de facto unbanning of restricted people and organizations. Executions of political prisoners and censorship of the media decreased in response to unrelenting pressure. A local battle to desegregate a whites-only Johannesburg secondary school drew all races into a nation-wide open schools movement. In all these campaigns, non-racialism had never been more manifest, whether in the composition of crowds or the articulation of aims.

Banned individuals and organizations defy the law and declare themselves unbanned in a march through Cape Town in August 1989.

Jay Naidoo, COSATU:[5]

There is a need to clarify what the MDM is: the MDM is a movement, not an organization. At its core is the strategic alliance between COSATU and the UDF. These are mass-based organizations based on sectoral lines: for example, youth, workers, students, women and civics. The core is committed to a unified ideological perspective, namely a commitment to non-racialism, democratic practices and grassroots accountability, the primacy of African leadership and leadership of the working class, and a commitment to the Freedom Charter.

The MDM also recognizes the centrality of the ANC in reaching any solution in the country, and we have a common position on negotiations. We are also united by a programme of mass action aimed at smashing apartheid and rebuilding South Africa along the lines of the Charter, and asserting socialism in the country. The ANC is the primary vehicle for building a non-racial, democratic and unitary South Africa. The releases of ANC leaders have sharpened this perspective and have created the conditions for building non-racialism. The people in this country are ready for a non-racial South Africa and we need to put a lot of energy into building non-racial sectoral organizations.

The wave of mass demonstrations in 1989 took popular protest out of the black townships and into the white city centres. Black and white protesters joined together in 'Open City Campaigns' in Johannesburg, Cape Town and Port Elizabeth, defying apartheid in residential areas, buses, hospitals, schools and beaches.

Steve Tshwete, ANC:

You know, the struggle cannot be fought and won in the black townships. You have to fight in all areas of South Africa, and the white community must be involved in the struggle. You have to take them into the struggle and they must know there's a war going on in South Africa, because they're living a privileged life. They must be involved so that they know that there's a need for change. You know, it's not the African people who are going to fight and die for the liberation of the country alone. It belongs to all of us, and all of us must play a role either to liberate it or to keep it in bondage. But those who like to keep it in bondage must feel the pinch of the position they're taking. Once the struggle's waged across the country and crosses into white residential areas, people become aware. They don't only see it in their own TV screens at night when they're relaxed, you know. That is the point.

Jeremy Cronin, SACP:

The old argument was that if one does try to work in the white areas, one is trying to disorganize whites, to basically demoralize them and that was it. But whites have become much more querying, a lot more aware that the golden life cannot continue for all time. In many ways they are beginning to catch on the rebound some of the effects of the repression that they impose on blacks. Whites are actually feeling the war now. One is seeing the quality of life for whites, ironically, being affected by the privileges which they are being compelled to defend, and it's the price of defending them that's getting high. That's an interesting development, which makes for new possibilities.

Trevor Manuel, UDF:

I think that it's important that whites continue to generate ferment within white ranks, broadly. The kind of work being done by organizations in the white community actually means tremendous gains for our struggle, because democrats are being generated in that process, and unlike the force of events in the black community, it's actually far more difficult for whites in South Africa to come to terms with the reality.

At another level, I also think it is very important for us to take our ideas about current events into the white community. By way of example, I addressed students at Stellenbosch University. The meeting started with a lot of hostility — some forty or fifty rugger-buggers marched into the hall, completely kitted out in their rugby outfits, boots slung over their shoulders, placards, etc. I went there because I thought it was very important to be able to speak to these people. I understand the isolation that Afrikaners, especially, grow up with and live with for their entire lives. I understand the need to break through that. I also understand the counter-revolutionary role that people like that can play — not through any fault of their own, but because they haven't been exposed to any other ideas. My own experience at Stellenbosch illustrated this point very clearly.

You know, I was caught up in discussions there for two hours, long after the meeting had broken up. The people who remained to talk to me were the same rugger-buggers who marched in there intent on disrupting the meeting. They were asking very basic questions like, 'What would happen to us as whites if there were a take-over in this country? Are you going to chase us into the sea? What will happen to our language, Afrikaans?'

It is a difficult situation to read into, but we have to go in there to try and bring them over. We cannot allow an important section of South African society to be written off because of their birth or heritage. We have a political responsibility to present alternatives to them. I think in the longer term this will yield results by giving us the ability to stave off counter-revolution as well.

It's important to try and create as many schisms in the ruling bloc as possible. It's also important to lay the basis for a future non-racial South Africa. I do believe that whites, like everybody else, have made a contribution to South Africa, and that South Africa truly belongs to all who live in it.

Disintegrating alliances within the ruling bloc offered another opportunity for intervention. Big capital was being forced to rethink its strategies, and the traditional alliance with white workers was redundant to its future plans. COSATU saw this as an opportunity to begin implementing a long-term strategy aimed at winning these workers into its ranks.

Themba Nxumalo, COSATU:

I've studied the history of the working class here in South Africa, and I have actually noted periods where the white workers were revolutionary — until they were bought, bribed with privileges, job reservations and things like that, so that they will identify themselves with the ruling class rather than the working class. Now in terms of the national question — that of whites oppressing blacks — you start to understand that actually it's fear that makes the whites react in this way. Because they see themselves as a drop in an ocean, and they have that fear of the day this ocean will swamp them all and their identity will actually be lost. The whites need to be free, they need to be liberated from this fear.

I think the reason why we have actually taken a stand on this question is because we don't see this thing in a short-term period — we see it in the long term. In the long term the working-class struggle cannot be only black workers — it'll be workers in general, whether yellow, green or whatever. If we are really sincere about the working-class struggle, that the worker can only be free when he is the one who controls the political power and then he'll be able to change the economic policies, then of course the white workers come in. That is why we are presently engaged in the national democratic revolution, because before we move to socialism or anything like that, the workers themselves have to unite.

The success of the broad front strategy suggested a tactic unthinkable only a short time ago: recruiting support from within the repressive arm of the state itself. Changing conditions inspired the confidence to venture into enemy territory. In late 1989 a coloured lieutenant won popular acclaim for denouncing police brutality, demonstrating how an enemy of the people could join the people's camp.[6] A black former Security Policeman confessed to his involvement in the assassinations of political activists; then a white former police captain admitted he had commanded a secret military 'death squad', fled the country, and announced that he had joined forces with the ANC.[7]

These unprecedented developments unfolded against a background of rising rural resistance. Demands for the reintegration of the homelands into a unitary non-racial South Africa and the rejection of 'ethnic' separation sparked general strikes and coups throughout the homelands in early 1990.[8] In one striking incident in the Bophuthatswana homeland, police burnt their uniforms to protest the killings of demonstrators at a peaceful rally.

'Black Soldier, Policeman: Stop Killing Your Own People!', ANC pamphlet produced inside South Africa and distributed at the mass march on John Vorster Square Police Headquarters, Johannesburg, September 1989:

You have been told that you are defending the people — but are you not living in shame, rejected and isolated by your own people? Haven't many of your colleagues and family perished at the hands of the oppressed people? You have been told that the racists are superior and invincible. But is the regime not starting to crumble, has it not failed to protect you?

You can liberate yourself from this shameful life and become part of the people once more. Brother soldier, policeman: choose now before it's too late. You can and must join the fight for freedom:

• Refuse to shoot your own people, point your guns at the enemies of freedom.

• Join the mass and armed actions of the people.

- Give information about enemy plans and actions.
- Take action against officers and commanders, sabotage equipment and logistics, disrupt transport, communications and energy.

You can and must become part of the organized fighting contingent. Start now, take a small step forward: pass this leaflet on!

Dissident Police Lieutenant Gregory Rockman leads members of the newly-formed Police and Prisons Civil Rights Union (POPCRU) on a march through Mitchell's Plain, Cape Town, to protest against police brutality (November 1989).

In February 1990, the South African government succumbed to political and economic pressure: President F. W. de Klerk unbanned the ANC, PAC and SACP and released Nelson Mandela. Blacks were jubilant. For whites — aside from the increasingly isolated right wing — initial shock turned to anxious optimism. The South African struggle had entered a new phase, marked by the first talks aimed at negotiating an end to white minority rule. The momentum was clearly irreversible: the long-cherished ideal of a non-racial democracy was shaping a new South Africa.

Celebrating Mandela's release in Soweto, February 1990.

Nelson Mandela, addressing a mass rally in Durban, 25 February 1990:

We are committed to building a single nation in our country. Our new nation will include blacks and whites, Zulus and Afrikaners, and speakers of every other language. ANC President-General Lutuli said, 'I personally believe that here in South Africa, with all of our diversities of colour and race, we will show the world a new pattern for democracy. I think that there is a challenge to us in South Africa, to set a new example for the world.' This is the challenge that we face today.

Murphy Morobe, UDF:

We tend to refrain from engaging in predictions about the future, but what we do believe is that we prepare for the future in the present — and that is one of the big arguments why we believe that the non-racial approach to our struggle is quite important. We believe that the building of a new South Africa does not have to wait for liberation, whenever that will come, but the process has to be begun whilst we are engaged in struggle. The fact that we have white comrades who fight side by side with us, that builds and develops among us that commonness that we hope to see in a future South Africa.

Many whites are withdrawing into their shells precisely because they have a fear of losing whatever privilege they have. And no doubt about it, there is no way an equitable society can come out of South Africa without a relinquishing of some of these privileges which most of the whites have — privileges which nobody could claim they have a legitimate right to be having. Now the question is, how does one do that without being insensitive or inconsiderate of people's views and feelings, or taking things away from people who should be having what they will say belongs to them?

For us to bring a new social system about in South Africa can't be done unless we actually tamper with those privileges. That is why when one looks at the Freedom Charter, on the clause that has to do with economy it talks of the nationalization of monopoly industries. That is something which addresses itself both to the question of imperial domination of foreign capital in the country and also to the fact that we need to develop our own national economy, which would also be able to sustain itself with its own initiative. So I think that, taking that into account, it would be an effort towards streamlining our production relations up to a point where we would be able to distribute equitably the resources that are there. We seek to develop a South Africanism that would, at the point of take-over, not give us problems of having to consider people on the basis of colour. And we have to begin building that now in struggle.

Max Sisulu, ANC:

The point is that we're not simply fighting for non-racialism, because if you fight for non-racialism it becomes simply a civil rights struggle. Ours is a struggle for the seizure of power and its transference to a majority of the people. Non-racialism is a form that the struggle takes, but it is not the content of the struggle, it is not the objective. We're not simply fighting for non-racialism for non-racialism's sake — no, we are fighting to put an end to a situation which prevails where we are foreigners in our own land, where we have no votes and no say, no nothing, and we are simply beasts of burden for the benefit of a minority and the multi-national corporations.

Non-racialism does not mean that the ethnic or the national question disappears. The fact of the matter is that there are these national cultural differences — non-racialism emphasises the fact that these are not fundamental. The fact that you are white or black is simply one of those accidents of history, which should not determine who runs the country or who gets what share of the national cake.

Will there be an effort to ensure black representation in the structures built after apartheid has been dismantled?[9]

Yes, a total lack of discrimination on the basis of race is going to be meaningless if you're not going to do something in order to redress centuries of oppression. To say that the doors of learning will be opened to everybody is meaningless when people have no means of going to school or of buying books. It means you must create those conditions to make the doors really open and enable people to enjoy these benefits. You'd have to do something to redress that imbalance, otherwise apartheid is going to continue in reverse. It will be removed from the statute book, but it will remain if the economy still remains in white hands. So what you need to do in order to destroy apartheid is to destroy it as a political, social and economic system.

Albie Sachs, ANC:

People ask me what is it like being a white working for black freedom: 'What is a nice white person like you doing in a movement like that?' There was something about that question that just jolted me, something all wrong about it. But it made me think, well, what was I doing? I thought about it and thought about it and I thought, no, I had not been fighting for the black people — I had been fighting for myself. I had been fighting for the right to be a free person in a free country, and the only way that could be achieved would be through the liberation of the black people. And the reconstruction of South Africa.

Nobody fights for somebody else. You participate in a cause, and there are lots of cultural problems and questions that have to be handled, and they are not easy and it never ends. It is not something you can say, well, now I am there, it's over.

Non-racialism is not just a bland thing. It is not just an absence of racism — that's empty. In fact, the reality of developing a non-racial culture in South Africa is much richer than that. It is much more active, more dynamic. It includes language, song, it includes dance, movement, it includes laughter, a way of telling a story, a way of making a political point. I enjoy seeing a way of working that maybe takes a little longer, but involves people much more. It has a richness, a strength. It is popular in the sense of being people-oriented, people-participatory.

I feel very enriched. I am gaining, I am not coming into a movement bringing left-wing political ideas which are then imposed on people. The people are grabbing those ideas, they are looking for an explanation of their country in terms of the world. They want to get out of this pure white-black, black-white thing. They want to shatter the limits that apartheid imposes, not simply on what you can do, but on what you can think.

I think a major achievement of the ANC leadership, the source of its great strength in recent years, has been to combine these cultural trends: the culture of resistance and the African culture. It's the talking things through. It's the patient way of involving everybody. It's a respect for every participant. It is looking at the people and knowing they have an immense variety of experiences and backgrounds, and some are Christians and some are anti-Christians and some are non-Christians and some are Moslems, and some have grown up in the ghettos in the cities and others are rural peasants — so all these cultural styles and traditions come in.

It is much more than non-racialism in that bland, neutral sense. Non-racialism doesn't mean that it is a society of 'non'-something. It means you are eliminating all the apartheid barriers, in terms of access to government, in terms of freedom to move, and then you feel that this is your country. But it doesn't describe the quality and personality of the country and people. That is not a non-something — that is a something, and that is a South African personality that is being constructed.

The first white exiles to return home in response to the unbanning of political organizations. ANC and SACP stalwarts Ray and Jack Simons, welcomed by ANC activist Frances Baard in March 1990.

The return of open politics after nearly thirty years.

The PAC maintained its rigid 'non-collaborationist' stance and condemned negotiations with the government at a meeting in Mitchell's Plain

Buras Nhlabati, SAYCO:

What I know is that being blacks alone, we can't reach our goal. The workers alone, they can't liberate our country. Students alone can't liberate our country. Women alone, they can't liberate our country. So you'll find that no party can just lead the struggle alone and liberate the country, but we shall go there to our liberation goal all being united.

Notes

1. At its launch, held clandestinely on 28 March 1987 in Cape Town after three last-minute changes of the venue, SAYCO claimed a signed-up membership of 600–700,000, with a support base of three times that, in 500 youth organizations all over the country. Its potential power was amplified through an alliance with COSATU, whose leadership welcomed the organization of the militant youth as the 'strongest, best and most reliable allies of the working class'. In a new departure for legal opposition politics, from its inception SAYCO operated underground. Nevertheless, its support and status in the townships continued to grow, participation of coloured and Indian youth was greater than ever before, and some of its affiliates even attracted white members.

2. The South African Students Press Union (SASPU) is a NUSAS project to which the English-language universities' official student newspapers are affiliated; *SASPU National* is the national student publication.

3. All but two of the organizations banned on 24 February 1988 (AZAPO and the Azanian Youth Organization, AZAYO) were UDF affiliates.

4. The first part of Nhlabati's comments is excerpted from his testimony to the International Conference on Children, Repression and the Law in Apartheid South Africa, 25 September 1987, Harare, Zimbabwe. With this question, the interview with the author begins.

5. From 'Forward to Freedom: The Tasks After Victory', an interview in *New Nation*, 20–26 October 1989.

6. Lieutenant Gregory Rockman of the Mitchell's Plain police station founded the Police and Prisons Civil Rights Union (POPCRU) and laid a complaint that led to two senior riot control policemen being charged with assault. They were acquitted and Rockman was suspended, then fired from the police force in early 1990, while POPCRU led the first police and prison warders' protest strike in more than 70 years.

7. Butana Nofomela was a death row prisoner when he made his confession in late 1989, naming Dirk Coetzee as the field commander of the secret unit responsible for the assassinations of, among others, Durban human rights lawyer Griffiths Mxenge in 1981, and Ruth First in 1982. Coetzee then confessed to the progressive Afrikaans newspaper, *Vrye Weekblad*, before fleeing the country. A judicial inquiry revealed that an elite military unit tasked with assassinations had been responsible for some 200 operations aimed at anti-apartheid figures outside South Africa.

8. The homeland governments of Ciskei and Venda were toppled in coups, while Gazankulu was paralyzed by a general strike.

9. Efforts to ensure this goal are often known as 'affirmative action', a term coined in the US in reference to policies implemented by government and other employers to hire certain quotas of ethnic 'minorities', i.e., African-Americans, Hispanics, Asians, Native Americans, etc., as well as women and disabled people.

The first ANC delegation to meet the South African government for 'talks about talks' in May 1990.

An evening at a Johannesburg recreation centre.

Biographical Updates

Biographical notes on all those interviewed in this book are provided in this section. These brief updates concentrate on political activities subsequent to the period under focus in the interview. All interviews were conducted by the author, except for two which are noted below.

RAY ALEXANDER wrote *Class and Colour in SA: 1850–1950* with her husband, Professor H. J. (Jack) Simons. She is still known to many by her maiden name, so that is how she is referred to here. She helped found the Food and Canning Workers Union in 1941, and was elected to represent Africans in parliament in 1954, but the government passed a law to prevent her from taking her seat. She also served as the first FedSAW national secretary. In 1964 government bannings forced her into exile in Zambia, where she worked for SACTU, the ANC and the SACP. Alexander and her husband became the first exiles to return home after the unbanning of the ANC and SACP.
Born: 1914 in Varkliam, Latvia. Interviewed: 1986 in Harare, and 1987 in Lusaka, Zambia (*page 10*)

SALEEM BADAT left *Grassroots* after serving as an organizer for three years. He is People's Education Convener of the Western Cape Executive of the NECC.
Born: 1957 in Asherville, Durban. Interviewed: 1987 in York, England (*page 177*)

ESTHER BARSEL was detained in 1964 and launched a hunger strike with fellow women prisoners, which she continued for 35 days. She was charged with twelve others, including Bram Fischer, with reconstituting the CP underground, and was sentenced to three years in prison. On her release she was house arrested for six years. She was 'unlisted' with the unbanning of the SACP, and immediately re-entered public political activity.
Born: 1924 in Lithuania. Interviewed: 1985 in Johannesburg (*page 46*)

FRANCOIS BILL left Federal Theological Seminary when the government took it over, and helped reestablish it near Pietermaritzburg. In 1981 he was elected moderator of the Evangelical Presbyterian Church of Southern Africa and secretary of the Alliance of Black Reformed Churches in South Africa (ABRECSA). He was detained under Emergency regulations in 1987 and held in solitary confinement while the state threatened to charge him for promulgating 'liberation theology'. He was released without charge after eight months, when his wife instigated legal action against the state.
Born: 1934 at Elim Mission, Shiluvane, Transvaal. Interviewed: 1985 in Harare (*page 110*)

MOLLY BLACKBURN was killed in a car accident in 1985, along with Civil Rights League leader Brian Bishop. They had been travelling from Oudtshoorn's Bongolethu township after collecting affidavits from residents regarding army and police raids on their community. Her funeral drew an unprecedented 20,000 people of all colours, and ANC President Oliver Tambo said that 'the name of Molly Blackburn will also be inscribed on our roll of honour'.
Born: 1930 in Port Elizabeth. Interviewed: 1985 in Port Elizabeth (*page 217*)

ANDREW BORAINE was elected to the UDF national executive in 1983, and in 1985 was co-opted onto the shadow Western Cape UDF executive after the entire new executive was detained under Emergency regulations. In 1986 he began conducting research into 'people's power' in street committees and in 1989 joined Planact, a service group which conducts research into urban issues commissioned by unions and civic associations.
Born: 1959 in Pietermaritzburg. Interviewed: 1986 in Harare (*page 172*)

BREYTEN BREYTENBACH was released from prison after serving five years of his seven-year sentence and returned to Paris. In 1986 he went back to South Africa to receive the *Rapport* (Afrikaans newspaper) award, one of the country's most prestigious literary prizes, and donated part of it towards aid to political prisoners. In 1987 he helped

coordinate the historic meeting between Afrikaans writers and intellectuals and the ANC in Dakar, Senegal.
Born: 1939 in Bonnyvale, Cape. Interviewed: 1985 in Harare (*page 147*)

DENNIS BRUTUS helped found the anti-apartheid South African Sports Association in 1958. In 1961 he helped organize a national convention of coloured activists at Malmesbury in the Western Cape, which led to his banning and arrest. He was re-arrested after fleeing to Mozambique and sentenced to eighteen months on Robben Island. After leaving South Africa he re-established the renamed South African Non-racial Olympic Committee (SANROC) in London, and then went to the US, where he is a professor and noted poet.
Born: 1924 in Salisbury (now Harare), Southern Rhodesia (now Zimbabwe). Interviewed: 1987 in Washington, DC (*page 37*)

FRED CARNESON was elected to the CPSA national executive and was among those charged in the 1946 sedition trial following the miners' strike. In 1965 he was convicted of being a member of the underground SACP, but was acquitted of Umkhonto we Sizwe activities on a technicality and thus was sentenced to six years in prison instead of life. Upon his release the government gave him a choice of 24-hour house arrest or an exit permit, so he went to England and worked for the ANC.
Born: 1920, Goodwood, Cape Province. Interviewed: 1986 in London (*page 43*)

CHERYL CAROLUS served as a UDF Western Cape executive member from 1983 to 1985, and was then co-opted onto the interim national executive. A founding member of UWO (now the United Women's Congress, UWCO), she was elected FedSAW general-secretary. In 1986 she was detained after a trip overseas to represent the UDF, and was detained again in 1989 when she challenged police who followed her home from an MDM meeting. In 1990 she was named by the ANC to the first delegation to meet with the South African government for formal talks about a negotiated settlement. She was also named as a member of the SACP's Interim Leadership Group.
Born: 1957 in Silvertown, Cape Town. Interviewed: 1985 in Johannesburg (*pages 176, 222*)

JANET CHERRY helped found branches of UDF and ECC in Port Elizabeth while working at the Eastern Cape Adult Literacy Project. She has endured continual harassment and physical attacks on her home, office, car and person, and has been detained five times since 1985. She was held without charge, mainly in solitary confinement, for nearly a year in 1986–87. In 1988 she went to work for the Port Elizabeth IDASA office, was detained again, then released under restriction. She was awarded the Reebok International Human Rights Award for Young Activists in December 1988, though her restrictions prevented her from personally accepting the prize in New York.
Born: 1961 in Cape Town. Interviewed: 1985 in Port Elizabeth (*page 214*)

REVD FRANK CHIKANE was charged with treason in 1985, but was acquitted in the marathon Pietermaritzburg trial of top UDF leaders. In 1987 he was named General-Secretary of the SACC. He has been repeatedly detained and harassed by the Security Police, his home petrol-bombed and a bomb sent to his mother. During a tour of the US in mid-1989 with MDM leaders who met President Bush he fell seriously ill, and tests conducted at an American university showed that a toxic phosphate compound had been administered to his clothes and luggage before he left South Africa in an apparent attempt to poison him.
Born: 1951 in Orlando, Johannesburg. Interviewed: 1985 in Johannesburg (*page 218*)

CLIFFIE COLLINGS continued to serve as UCC coordinator, heading the Natal Advice Centres Association. In 1989 he and other UCC members were arrested in a march in support of the Defiance Campaign.
Born: 1957 in Wentworth, Durban. Interviewed: 1987 in Harare (*page 192*)

JEREMY CRONIN published a volume of prison poetry (*Inside*, Ravan Press) upon his release in 1983, and was elected to the UDF Western Cape executive. With fellow former political prisoner Raymond Suttner he co-authored *Thirty Years of the Freedom Charter* (Ravan Press, first banned and then unbanned in 1986), which played an important role in popularizing the document for younger activists. In 1987, after spending more than a year in hiding during the State of Emergency, he fled South Africa and worked for the ANC in both political and cultural structures in Lusaka. In 1990 he returned to South Africa and began working in the

Johannesburg office of the SACP.
Born: 1949 in Durban. Interviewed: 1985 in Cape Town (*pages 126, 262*)

KLAAS DE JONGE continues to be active in the Dutch Anti-Apartheid Movement.
Born: 1937 in Groningen, Holland. Interviewed: 1987 in Arusha, Tanzania (*page 250*)

CHRIS DLAMINI was elected vice-president of COSATU at its founding in 1985, and was
elected president of the Food and Allied Workers Union (FAWU) when the COSATU affiliate
was formed in 1986. At the public launch of the SACP in Johannesburg in 1990, he was named
as a member of the party's Interim Leadership Group.
Born: 1944 in Benoni. Interviewed: 1985 in Springs (*page 141*)

NKOSAZANA DLAMINI left South Africa when police uncovered her ANC cell, and joined
the ANC in Botswana in 1978. She qualified as a medical doctor in England and then went to
Swaziland for the ANC from 1980 to 1985. She returned to the UK for further studies in
pediatrics, worked in the ANC office in London, then moved to the ANC's Department of
Health in Lusaka.
Born: 1949 in Polela, near Pietermaritzburg, Natal. Interviewed: 1987 in London (*page 114*)

JESSIE DUARTE continued her work for FedTraw and as an assistant to Revd Beyers Naude.
She was detained for most of 1988, then released under restrictions. When the ANC was
unbanned she began work in its Johannesburg office.
Born: 1953 in Newclare, Johannesburg. Interviewed: 1986 in Harare (*page 201*)

SHEENA DUNCAN was Black Sash president 1975–85 and continued to work in the advice
office. A member of the board of the South African Council of Churches, she was a major
force behind the launch of the Five Freedoms Forum.
Born: 1932 in Johannesburg. Interviewed: 1985 in Johannesburg (*page 95*)

EBRAHIM ISMAIL EBRAHIM worked underground for the ANC following his release from
prison in early 1979 (despite his banning order) until the end of 1980, when he fled to
neighbouring Swaziland, from where he supervised ANC underground work in the Transvaal
and Natal, infiltrating back into South Africa for ten months. At the end of 1986 he was
kidnapped from his Swazi home by men who identified themselves as employees of the South
African Police, and driven across the border to Security Police headquarters in Pretoria.
Ebrahim managed to smuggle a message out of prison detailing his illegal abduction as well as
his interrogation and torture, but the South African government ignored the international
outcry and tried him for treason, sentencing him to 20 years on Robben Island in 1989.
Born: 1937 in Durban. Interviewed: 1986 in Lusaka[1] (*page 133*)

ALEC ERWIN was elected general-secretary of FOSATU in 1979, and education secretary in
1982. With the formation of COSATU in 1985 he was elected national education officer, and
in 1988 he assumed that post in the National Union of Metalworkers of South Africa (NUMSA,
formerly MAWU). He was named a COSATU representative on the ANC's Southern Natal
convening committee in 1990.
Born: 1948 in River Valley, Cape Town. Interviewed: 1985 in Durban (*page 136*)

FARID ESACK had his passport withdrawn by the government in 1989, following his active
campaigning for the MDM inside the country and on overseas tours. He resigned from the Call
of Islam executive in a dispute over organizational issues in late 1989.
Born: 1957 in Wynberg. Interviewed: 1987 in Harare (*page 187*)

PATRICK FLUSK joined the Anti-PC in 1984 and was elected president of the Riverlea Youth
Congress in 1985. He was detained in 1988 and released under restriction in 1989 after going
on hunger strike. He was presented with the Nelson Mandela Award for Courage and Hope in
the Swedish parliament.
Born: 1964 in Riverlea, Johannesburg. Interviewed: 1987 in Harare (*page 185*)

PRESTON GESWINT remained in Port Elizabeth, teaching in the township of New Brighton.
Born: 1963 in Calvandale, Port Elizabeth. Interviewed: 1986 in Harare (*page 190*)

FRENE GINWALA was about to join chambers with advocate Bram Fischer when the ANC
asked her to help get Oliver Tambo out of South Africa and assist in setting up the ANC's
external mission in 1960. She stayed on in Tanzania after the banning of the ANC, completed a
doctorate at Oxford University, and then worked in the ANC's London office.

Born: 1932 in Johannesburg. Interviewed: 1987 in London (*page 101*)

DENIS GOLDBERG was sentenced to life imprisonment with Nelson Mandela and the rest of the Rivonia trialists in 1964. Elected a patron of the UDF at its founding in 1983, he was released from Pretoria Central Prison in 1985 after a lengthy campaign for his release by his daughter (who had moved to Israel) and her fellow kibbutz members. After consultations with the ANC leadership, he began work in the ANC's London office.
Born: 1933 in Cape Town. Interviewed: 1986 in London (*page 85*)

DR GOONAM helped organize opposition to the government-created South African Indian Council in the mid-1970s, until Security Police harassment prompted her to leave South Africa for England in 1977. She settled in Zimbabwe soon after independence, then returned to South Africa after the ANC was unbanned.
Born: 1905 (approximately) in Durban. Interviewed: 1987 in Harare (*page 29*)

REVD FUMANEKILE GQIBA finished his theological degree at the University of Cape Town in 1985, then fled to Lesotho when he learned that police were planning to arrest him for underground ANC activities. He was deported from Lesotho when ANC members were rounded up following the 1986 coup. He then helped form the ANC's Department of Religious Affairs.
Born: 1951 in Cape Town. Interviewed: 1987 in Arusha (*page 128*)

MASTERPIECE GUMEDE (a pseudonym adopted in 1977 when he left South Africa) worked for the ANC's Radio Freedom in Tanzania, then moved to ANC headquarters in Zambia.
Born: 1952 in Durban. Interviewed: 1986 in Dar es Salaam (*page 110*)

FINK HAYSOM completed his law degree and went to work for the Centre for Applied Legal Studies at the University of the Witwatersrand in 1981. That same year he was detained in a nation-wide swoop on white activists and banned upon his release in 1982. His work monitoring repression in Ciskei from 1983 was published in 1986 as *Mabangalala: The Rise of Right-wing Vigilantes in South Africa*. In 1987 he helped set up a public interest law practice in Johannesburg.
Born: 1952 in Johannesburg. Interviewed: 1985 in Johannesburg (*page 149*)

WILLIE HOFMEYR was elected to the Western Cape UDF executive in 1986, and in 1988 was detained and issued with a restriction order upon his release. He attained his law degree despite being barred from attending lectures, then began practising as a human rights lawyer. In 1989 he was one of a group of 22 restricted leaders who declared themselves unbanned as part of the MDM's Defiance Campaign. Detained, he won his release by staging a 28-day hunger strike, but was again severely restricted.
Born: 1954 in Pinelands, Cape Town. Interviewed: 1985 in Cape Town (*page 139*)

TONY HOLIDAY was sentenced to six years in prison in 1976 for producing ANC and SACP material underground, and earned his BA Hons *cum laude* during his prison term. He left South Africa after his release, completed a PhD in philosophy at Oxford, then began lecturing at Thames Polytechnic.
Born: 1940 in Cape Town. Interviewed: 1986 in London (*page 121*)

ZELDA HOLTZMAN helped launch the ANC's Athlone branch.
Born: 1958 in Maitland, Cape. Interviewed: 1985 in Nairobi (*page 191*)

HENRY ISAACS moved to Zimbabwe in 1983, then went back to the US, where he works as a politically non-aligned consultant on southern African affairs. He wrote a book on the PAC, *Struggle within the Struggle*, which fell victim to British libel laws before its planned publication in 1986.
Born: 1949 in Raisethorpe, Pietermaritzburg. Interviewed: 1987 in Washington DC (*page 131*)

MKHUSELI JACK helped form the Port Elizabeth Youth Congress (PEYCO) in 1982 and the UDF in 1983. He served on the UDF's Eastern Cape regional executive and as spokesperson for the Eastern Cape Consumer Boycott Committee until his detention in 1985, when he was severely assaulted and tortured. His ban upon his release in 1986 was overturned after white business leaders joined with black township activists in protest. After an anti-apartheid campaign trip to Europe later that year, he was detained again — his ninth detention in ten years — and held until 1989, when he was released under restriction.
Born: 1958 in Humansdorp, Eastern Cape. Interviewed: 1985 in Port Elizabeth (*page 170*)

JACKIE JOLOBE left South Africa in 1980, then worked for the ANC in Botswana. Her

husband, Rogers Mevi Nkadimeng (the son of SACTU General-Secretary John Nkadimeng), was killed in a car bomb explosion in Gaborone in 1985. She then studied in Harare while working with the ANC.
Born: 1959 in Soweto. Interviewed: 1985 in Nairobi, Kenya (*page 168*)

HELEN JOSEPH helped found FedSAW, participated in the historic march on Pretoria in 1956, and was then prosecuted for the full four years of the Treason Trial. She was banned for the first time in 1957 and detained for five months in 1960. After her ban expired in 1962, she undertook a 7,000-mile journey throughout the country seeking out banished people, and was then served with South Africa's first house arrest order. Her ban was lifted in 1971 when she was suffering from cancer, but was reimposed from 1980 to 1982. She was elected a patron of the UDF and spoke at its 1983 launch, continuing to campaign for the MDM despite failing health.
Born: 1905 in Sussex, England. Interviewed: 1985 in Johannesburg (*page 58*)

ALF KARRIM was elected to the NIC executive at its 1987 conference and is involved in rural development research at the Centre for Community Organizations, Research and Development at the University of Natal, Durban.
Born: 1955 in Durban. Interviewed: 1985 in Durban (*page 198*)

PADDY KEARNEY, director of the Diakonia Ecumenical Church Agency, was detained in 1985 and released in response to an application filed by Archbishop Denis Hurley arguing that the detention violated the provision of the Internal Security Act requiring that there be 'reason to believe' that he was guilty of a security offence. Kearney later successfully sued for wrongful arrest and detention.
Born: 1942 in Pietermaritzburg. Interviewed: 1985 in Durban (*page 217*)

STEPHANIE KEMP served seventeen months of her three-year prison sentence, then left South Africa for London and joined the ANC.
Born: 1941 in Stansburg, Little Karoo. Interviewed: 1986 in London (*page 94*)

HORST KLEINSCHMIDT was detained for three months in 1975 as a result of Breyten Breytenbach's experiment in underground work, and left South Africa upon his release. He went to Holland, where he opened a Christian Institute office, then moved to London and joined the International Defence and Aid Fund for Southern Africa (IDAF), where he is now director. In mid-1990 he returned to South Africa for consultations on the repatriation of exiles.
Born: 1945 in Swakopmund, Namibia. Interviewed: 1986 in London (*page 113*)

WOLFIE KODESH threw up his business interests after the Second World War and began working full-time for the Non-European Railway Workers Union. He was first banned in 1953, and in 1960 was one of the first to be jailed under the 90-day detention law. He accepted the government's offer of an exit permit and spent the next ten years in Lusaka and Luanda as head of the ANC's logistics unit, until ill health prompted him to go to London, where he worked in the ANC office.
Born: 1918 in Benoni, Transvaal. Interviewed: 1986 in London (*page 44*)

PATRICK LEKOTA[2] was released from Robben Island in 1982, and immediately began to work as an organizer for GWU in Natal. Elected the first UDF national publicity secretary, he was detained several times and finally forced 'underground'. While in hiding he appeared at the UDF National General Council and was re-elected to the executive, then arrested in 1985. Repeatedly refused bail, he remained in detention throughout a lengthy treason trial in which 22 prominent leaders and members of the UDF, as well as the SACC and AZAPO, were accused of conspiring with the ANC and SACP to overthrow the state. One of four convicted of treason at the end of 1988, he was sentenced to twelve years' imprisonment but was freed a year later, along with the other UDF leaders, after their convictions were overturned by an appeal court. In 1990 he was named head of the ANC's Southern Natal region.
Born: 1948 in Kroonstad, Orange Free State. Interviewed: 1983 in Johannesburg (*page 133*)

DAVE LEWIS left GWU in 1986 to study in the US for a year and has since resumed his career as an academic at UCT.
Born: 1949 in Klerksdorp, Transvaal. Interviewed: 1985 in Cape Town (*page 143*)

STANLEY MABIZELA was jailed for ANC activities in 1963, worked underground 1964–66,

then fled to Swaziland, where he taught at a Catholic mission school until being named ANC Chief Representative in 1978. In 1982 he moved to Tanzania as ANC Chief Representative, and in 1988 took up that post in Zimbabwe. Elected to the ANC's NEC, he moved to ANC headquarters in Lusaka in 1989, and in mid-1990 he was included in the indemnity for exiled ANC members, which allowed him to return to South Africa.
Born: 1934 in Kirkwood District, Eastern Cape. Interviewed: 1986 in Dar es Salaam (*page 27*)

ILVA MACKAY left South Africa on an exit permit in 1977, after deciding to join the ANC in response to the underground pamphlets she had received by post. She has worked in the London and Lusaka SACTU offices.
Born: 1952 in Kokstad, East Griqualand, Western Cape. Interviewed: 1987 in Lusaka (*page 129*)

SACKY MADI was recruited to an underground ANC cell following the 1976 Soweto uprisings, and left for Botswana at the end of the year. The ANC trained him in radio and he worked for Radio Freedom in Madagascar and Dar es Salaam.
Born: 1958 in Pimville, Johannesburg. Interviewed: 1986 in Dar es Salaam (*page 125*)

NOSIZWE MADLALA served as chairperson of NOW and on the UDF regional executive, despite repeated detentions: she spent almost all of 1987 in solitary confinement.
Born: 1952 in Magok, near Port Shepstone. Interviewed: 1985 in Durban (*page 178*)

PETER MAHLANGU served as SACTU's representative in Canada from 1986 until 1989, when he was named ANC Chief Representative to Canada.
Born: 1951 in Lamontville, Durban. Interviewed: 1987 in Toronto, Canada (*page 142*)

MIKE MAILULA is coordinating youth work for the South African Catholic Bishops Conference, and is active in the Mamelodi ANC branch.
Born: 1963 in Pietersburg. Interviewed: 1986 in Harare (*page 175*)

LESOANA MAKHANDA was arrested in 1963 following the seizure of the PAC's membership lists by the South African police, but charges were dropped and he left for Tanzania. He got a scholarship to study in the US, then worked for General Foods and Gulf Oil as a financial analyst. When PAC representative David Sibeko was murdered in 1979, Makhanda joined the PAC's UN office. In 1986 he was named UN representative.
Born: 1941 in Soutfontein, Orange Free State. Interviewed: 1987 in Arusha (*page 73*)

NISE MALANGE was sent by her parents to Durban in 1982 in an effort to remove her from the disruptive student boycotts in the Cape. She worked for FOSATU 1982–85, becoming an organizer for the Transport and General Workers Union. She coordinated the COSATU Culture and Working Life Project, and her poems were published in *Black Mamba Rising: South African Worker Poets in Struggle.*
Born: 1960 in Clovelly, Western Cape. Interviewed: 1985 in Durban (*page 162*)

TREVOR MANUEL was detained soon after his election to the UDF national executive in 1985, then issued with a virtual house arrest order upon his release. Following several court cases in which such stringent banning orders were overturned, his ban was lifted. He was detained again in 1986 under Emergency regulations and held without charge or trial until 1988. Re-detained again in 1989 and then released with restrictions that confined him to his home from 6 a.m. to 6 p.m. daily, he joined in the MDM's Defiance Campaign and was again detained. He was released after waging a hunger strike, once more under severe restrictions. He was named Western Cape convener of the ANC regional structures announced following the ANC's unbanning.
Born: 1956 in Windermere (now Kensington). Interviewed: 1985 in Cape Town (*pages 184, 262*)

GERHARD MARÉ helped found *Work in Progress* (1977), a periodical devoted to analysis of South African political developments. In 1988 he published a book on Chief Buthelezi and Inkatha, *An Appetite for Power* (Ravan Press, 1988), with Georgina Hamilton.
Born: 1946 in Estcourt, Natal. Interviewed: 1985 in Durban (*page 148*)

ZORA MEHLOMAKHULU works for the Skills Development Project in Langa.
Born: 1940 in Langa, Cape Town. Interviewed: 1985 in Cape Town (*page 138*)

FRANCIS MELI joined the ANC-supporting African Students Association at Fort Hare University when it was formed in 1961, and worked underground for the ANC until he was instructed to leave the country in 1963. He then studied at Leipzig University in the German

Democratic Republic. In 1975 he went to work for the ANC in Morogoro, Tanzania, and then in Zambia until in 1977 he took over the editorship of the ANC journal, *Sechaba*, in London. In mid-1990 he was included in the indemnity for exiled ANC members, thus allowing him to attend the first NEC meeting inside the country in three decades.
Born: 1942 in East London. Interviewed: 1986 in London (*page 79*)

SHASHA MEREYOTLHE works as the Transvaal Education Officer for SADWU.
Born: 1949 in Newclare, Johannesburg. Interviewed: 1987 in Harare (*page 230*)

NOMA-INDIA MFEKETO spent most of 1987 in prison, and was released under restrictions — which she defied in the 1989 demonstrations. She is UWCO chairperson and a member of the Zakhe Cooperative Agency.
Born: 1953 in Elsie's River, Cape Town. Interviewed: 1985 in Nairobi (*page 191*)

SIMPIWE MGODUSO continued to be active in SANSCO at the University of Natal, Durban, where he studied law. He has been involved in the UDF-COSATU Joint Working Committee on Natal Violence, the Society for the Abolition of the Death Penalty, and Lawyers for Human Rights.
Born: 1959 in Appelsbosch Mission, near Pietermaritzburg. Interviewed: 1985 in Durban (*page 171*)

DILIZA MJI was detained for six months in 1976, then continued his work with SASO until its banning, when he was detained for fourteen months. He was released without charge and banned for five years. When he re-entered public politics he helped found the UDF-affiliated Clermont Youth League and the Durban branch of the Release Mandela Committee. He served as general-secretary of the National Medical and Dental Association from its inception in 1982, and in 1985 was elected NAMDA president. A key Natal MDM leader, he was a UDF/COSATU delegate to the 1989 peace talks with Inkatha. In 1990 he was named to the ANC's Southern Natal convening committee.
Born: 1953 in Orlando West. Interviewed: 1985 in Durban (*page 116*)

IAN MKHIZE was politically inactive following the dissolution of the Liberal Party in 1968, until he joined Inkatha in 1979 and also tried to work for change through the Hambanathi Community Council. He quit both organizations and joined JORAC in 1982, and was elected to its executive. He was detained in 1988–89 and was released only after staging a hunger strike. He works for Diakonia as the educational programme organizer.
Born: 1941 in Pietermaritzburg. Interviewed: 1985 in Durban (*page 93*)

JAMES MNDAWENI continues to serve as president of NACTU.
Born: 1953 in Nqutu District, Vryheid, Natal. Interviewed: 1986 in Harare (*page 231*)

PAPI MOKOENA (a pseudonym) participated in a series of SASO meetings in 1974 on the 'second phase' (armed struggle) and then left the country in 1975 after police began arresting and interrogating people who had been involved in those discussions. He went to Botswana and by 1976 had joined the ANC, then worked with the ANC's Department of Manpower Development in Lusaka.
Born: 1945 in Everton, Transvaal. Interviewed: 1987 in Lusaka (*page 113*)

KAY MOONSAMY was a defendant in the 1956 Treason Trial, then worked for the NIC until his banning in 1963. He left South Africa for Botswana in 1965, went to Tanzania in 1968, and in 1972 went to Zambia to work as a member of the SACTU executive. He served as SACTU National Treasurer 1983–87, then was Head of Finance in the ANC's Office of the Treasurer-General, and in 1989 was elected President of SACTU, until the phasing out of SACTU and its merger with COSATU in 1990.
Born: 1926 in Overpoort, Durban. Interviewed: 1987 in Lusaka (*page 33*)

MOHAMMED VALLI MOOSA helped revive the TIC and was elected to the UDF Transvaal executive in 1983. He became UDF acting national general-secretary in 1985, following the detentions of UDF leaders. He was detained in 1986 and then again in 1987–88, after which he and fellow UDF leader Murphy Morobe travelled overseas on behalf of the MDM. While serving as convener of the Conference for a Democratic Future in 1989, he was again detained, then released under restriction. With the ANC's unbanning he began work in the Johannesburg office.
Born: 1957 in Johannesburg. Interviewed: 1985 in Johannesburg (*page 196*)

MURPHY MOROBE worked as an organizer for GAWU upon his release from Robben Island in 1982, helped found the Soweto Youth Congress (SOYCO), and was active in UDF from its inception. Detained in 1984 following an overseas speaking tour, he was elected to the UDF executive after his release in 1985 and then detained again under Emergency regulations in 1986. After his release he went into hiding, continuing his UDF work until his detention in 1987. He escaped from detention with fellow UDF leader Mohammed Valli Moosa during a visit to hospital in 1988, took refuge in the US Consulate for six weeks, and then walked out after receiving government assurances that he would not be re-detained. With the ANC's unbanning he began work in the Johannesburg office.
Born: 1956 in Orlando East. Interviewed: 1985 in Johannesburg (*pages 161, 266*)

GRAHAM MORODI was detained in 1963, banned in 1964, then left South Africa for Tanzania and Zambia. He received military training in Egypt and the Soviet Union in 1965–66, then fought in Umkhonto we Sizwe's joint campaign with ZIPRA in Rhodesia in 1967, was arrested after retreating into Botswana, and served a year in prison. After working for the ANC in Zambia and Tanzania he was posted to Swaziland, where he did 'political reconstruction' work until 1982. He served as ANC Chief Representative in Zambia until 1988, when he was named to that post in Tanzania.
Born: 1923 in Lydenburg, Transvaal. Interviewed: 1987 in Lusaka (*page 26*)

MZALA has been active in the ANC's Research Department, writing frequently for *Sechaba* and the *African Communist.* In 1988 he published a book, *Gatsha Buthelezi: Chief With a Double Agenda* (Zed Books).
Born: 1955 in Zululand. Interviewed: 1987 in Lusaka (*page 243*)

RALPH MZAMO was captured by the Rhodesian Security Forces during the joint ANC-ZAPU military offensive and sentenced to death in 1968 – a sentence commuted to life imprisonment during a round of negotiations with the British to end white minority rule in Rhodesia. He was released when Zimbabwe won its independence in 1980, spent three years in Bulawayo, and then went to England and worked for the ANC in York and Newcastle.
Born: 1940 in New Brighton, Port Elizabeth. Interviewed: 1987 in London (*page 97*)

INDRES NAIDOO[3] immediately got involved in politics again despite being banned upon his release from Robben Island, where he served a prison term 1963–73. He helped organize the Human Rights Committee in Johannesburg, one of the only political bodies to openly support the Freedom Charter in the 1970s. He fled to Mozambique in 1977, serving as chairperson of the ANC's Regional Political Committee until he was forced to leave Mozambique as a result of the Nkomati Accord. In 1988 he was named Deputy Chief Representative to the German Democratic Republic.
Born: 1937 in Johannesburg. Interviewed: 1987 in Lusaka (*page 84*)

JAY NAIDOO continues to serve as COSATU General-Secretary. He travelled with the MDM delegation that accompanied Mandela on his first trip to Lusaka following his release from prison.
Born: 1954 in Greenwood Park, Durban. Interviewed: 1985 in Durban (*pages 233, 261*)

KUMI NAIDOO went into hiding after police arrested students on the University of Durban-Westville campus during the 1986 State of Emergency. In 1987 he became South Africa's first black political activist Rhodes scholar, and got involved in UK anti-apartheid activities, returning home in 1990.
Born: 1965 in Chatsworth, Durban. Interviewed: 1987 in Harare (*page 200*)

M. D. NAIDOO was banned in 1962, house arrested and detained in 1963, convicted of supporting the Communist Party in 1966 and sentenced to five years on Robben Island. Re-banned upon his release, he was prevented from practising law, and after his home was raided in 1977 he fled South Africa. He has worked in the ANC London office since then.
Born: 1919 in Durban. Interviewed: 1987 in London, England (*page 31*)

R .D. NAIDOO died in 1990, while addressing students at the University of Durban-Westville. An active trade unionist and Communist Party member, he was 'listed' in 1953, detained during the 1960 State of Emergency, and continued to work behind the scenes, despite being convicted of breaking his restrictions.
Born: 1914 in Durban, South Africa. Interviewed: 1985 in Durban (*page 34*)

BILLY NAIR was detained four months after his release from Robben Island, and released after a Supreme Court ruling that his detention had been unlawful. When police attempted to re-detain him and five other activists, they sought refuge in the British Consulate in Durban, but were detained again after leaving the consulate. Nair subsequently sued the Security Police for assaulting him and damaging his eardrum. In 1989, he and three of the other leaders who sheltered in the consulate were awarded damages from the government. Nair is on the UDF national executive and worked with the Labour and Education Research Project in Durban, assisting COSATU affiliates. In 1990 he became a member of the ANC's Southern Natal convening committee. He was detained, as was ANC NEC member Mac Maharaj, shortly before the launch of the SACP in Johannesburg, where he was publicly named as a member of the SACP's Interim Leadership Group and its Central Committee.
Born: 1929 in Sydenham, Durban. Interviewed: 1985 in Durban (*page 229*)

LAURIE NATHAN co-edited (with Jacklyn Cock) *War and Society: The Militarization of South Africa* (David Philip, 1989), and wrote a history of ECC. Also on the executive of Cape Democrats, he was among the 143 war resisters who publicly refused to serve in the SADF in 1988.
Born: 1959 in Cape Town. Interviewed: 1985 in Johannesburg (*page 216*)

REVD BEYERS NAUDE helped found the Ecumenical Advice Centre after leaving the SACC, and has travelled overseas with other MDM leaders to explain the movement's position to Western policy-makers. In 1990 he was named by the ANC to the first delegation to meet with the South African government for formal talks about a negotiated settlement.
Born: 1915 in Roodepoort. Interviewed: 1985 in Johannesburg (*page 223*)

PANDELANI NEFOLOVHODWE was president of the SASO executive which took the decision to hold the 1974 pro-Frelimo rallies, and served six years on Robben Island as a result. After his release he helped found the Black Allied Mining and Construction Workers Union (BAMCWU) and the Azanian Council of Trade Unions (AZACTU). He left the unions but continued his work in the AZAPO national executive.
Born: 1947 in Folovhodwe, Venda. Interviewed: 1985 in Johannesburg (*page 108*)

A. B. NGCOBO was prosecuted in the 1956 Treason Trial and detained during the State of Emergency, then confined to Durban by government order. In 1961 he was sentenced to two years in prison for PAC activities, but skipped bail and fled to Swaziland, where he joined the PAC's external mission. He entered the University of Zambia in 1968, but was deported along with other PAC members and has since been teaching in England. He claimed to hold the post of PAC Treasurer-General, but conceded there are other 'pretenders' to that position.
Born: 1931 in Umtomjaneni, Natal. Interviewed: 1987 in London (*page 71*)

BURAS NHLABATI was detained in 1986, went into hiding after his release, then left the country in 1987 and joined the ANC, studying at the Solomon Mahlangu Freedom College (SOMAFCO).
Born: 1970 in Alexandra township, Johannesburg. Interviewed: 1987 in Harare (*pages 260, 270*)

JOHN NKADIMENG was a SACTU founding member who was prosecuted for the full length of the Treason Trial, then banned in 1963 and sentenced to two years in prison for ANC activities. In 1976 he left for Swaziland, headed the ANC's top coordinating body in Mozambique, then moved to Lusaka in 1982 and was elected chairperson of the Political Military Committee. He was SACTU General-Secretary from 1983 until SACTU's 1990 merger with COSATU. He was included in the indemnity for exiled ANC members, thus allowing him to return to South Africa.
Born: 1925 in Sekhukhuneland. Interviewed: 1987 in Lusaka (*page 72*)

FATHER ALBERT NOLAN helped found the Institute for Contextual Theology in 1981 and researches and writes for both the ICT and the Justice and Peace Commission of the Catholic Church. His books, *Jesus Before Christianity* and *God in South Africa*, are known in liberation theology circles world-wide.
Born: 1934 in Johannesburg. Interviewed: 1985 in Johannesburg (*page 175*)

THEMBA NXUMALO was sentenced to five years on Robben Island for Umkhonto we Sizwe activities. Upon his release in 1984 he joined the UDF-affiliated National Federation of Workers and JORAC, and was elected to the Natal UDF executive. He worked as regional secretary of the COSATU-affiliated National Education, Health and Allied Workers Union in Durban.
Born: 1952 in Port Shepstone. Interviewed: 1985 in Durban (*pages 122, 263*)

DOROTHY NYEMBE was a FedSAW leader who was prosecuted in the 1956 Treason Trial. She was sentenced to three years in prison for ANC activities in 1963 and banned upon her release. She was arrested again in 1968 and convicted of 'harbouring terrorists' on the evidence of KwaZulu Chief Buthelezi. After her release from prison in 1984 she was acclaimed as South Africa's most senior female political prisoner, but hounded out of her KwaMashu home by Inkatha supporters. She was detained in 1987–88 and then helped found an Umlazi women's self-help group.
Born: 1931 in Mlambokazi Mission, Dundee district, Natal. Interviewed: 1985 and 1988 in Durban[4] (*page 53*)

REGGIE OLIPHANT was issued with a restriction order in 1988, part of the government's effort to silence *Saamstaan* community newspaper. In keeping with his vow to ignore his stringent restrictions, he joined in a march in Oudtshoorn in late 1989 under the banner of the ANC that was (proportionately, for the small rural community) the largest of the Defiance Campaign protests. He was later arrested.
Born: 1948 in Oudtshoorn, in the Southern Cape. Interviewed: 1987 in Harare (*page 193*)

AZIZ PAHAD was a member of the first delegation of ANC members to return to South Africa for talks with the government, following Mandela's release.
Born: 1940, Schwartze Reinecke, Transvaal. Interviewed: 1986 in London (*page 242*)

JAMES PHILLIPS fled South Africa in 1954 after he was banned from all political and trade union activities, and went to London, where he continued to work for the ANC. Known as 'the South African Paul Robeson' for his singing talent, he trained European choirs to sing South African freedom songs and led ANC singing groups. He died in London in 1987.
Born: 1919 in Sophiatown, Johannesburg. Interviewed: 1986 in London (*page 11*)

DEVAN PILLAY was released from prison in 1982 and went to Cape Town, where he was the representative to the UDF General Council for Woodstock, then the city's only non-racial area committee. In 1985 he went to study South African politics in England. He returned home in 1989 and worked for the *South African Labour Bulletin.*
Born: 1959 in East London. Interviewed: 1986 in London (*page 201*)

BARNEY PITYANA was detained in 1977-78 (during the time that Steve Biko was killed), then fled South Africa for Lesotho and went on to England. After a brief involvement in an association of BC-supporting exiles, he publicly threw his support behind the ANC and then concentrated on his theological studies, becoming parish priest of an Anglican church in Birmingham in 1985. In 1988 he was appointed Director of the Programme to Combat Racism of the World Council of Churches in Geneva.
Born: 1945 in Uitenhage, Eastern Cape. Interviewed: 1986 in Birmingham (*page 129*)

ALFRED TEMBA QABULA was a NUMSA shop steward in the Dunlop factory in Durban. In 1986 he was elected chairperson of the Durban Workers Cultural Local, and his poems were published in *Black Mamba Rising.* In 1988 he began working for COSATU's Culture and Working Life Project.
Born: 1942 in Flagstaff, Pondoland. Interviewed: 1985 in Durban (*page 142*)

MONGEZI RADEBE helped found the Sharpeville Civic Association, served as CCAWUSA branch secretary in the Vaal Triangle until 1986 and then became the Free State organizer for NUMSA.
Born: 1957 in Heilbron, Orange Free State. Interviewed: 1985 in Johannesburg (*page 157*)

CYRIL RAMAPHOSA continues to serve as NUM General-Secretary. In 1986 he was part of a COSATU delegation which met the ANC and SACTU in Zambia. A member of the National Reception Committee that organized the mass response to the release of the ANC leaders in late 1989, he helped coordinate events following the release of Nelson Mandela in early 1990.
Born: 1952 in Johannesburg. Interviewed: 1985 in Johannesburg (*page 230*)

REHANA ROSSOUW was detained in 1987. As coordinator of the Save the Press Campaign she travelled overseas to publicize the government's attacks on the media under the State of Emergency. She also serves on the executive of *Grassroots.*
Born: 1964 in Landsdowne, Cape Town. Interviewed: 1987 in Harare (*page 202*)

MIKE ROUSSOS left SARWHU in 1989 and helped set up a Human Resources Development Project for the MDM. In 1990 he went to work for the ANC in Johannesburg.

Born: 1956 in Johannesburg. Interviewed: 1986 in Harare (*page 236*)

ALBIE SACHS was banned 1955–60, earned his law degree and devoted his legal career to political cases. In 1963 he was detained in solitary confinement for five months, then was re-detained again for three months in 1964, an experience he documented in a book, *Jail Diary* (Harvill Press, 1966). He left South Africa for England in 1966, then in 1977 moved to newly independent Mozambique to teach law and work for the ANC. In 1988 he lost his right arm in a car bomb attack. He returned to South Africa in 1990 to work in the ANC's Cape Town office.
Born: 1935 in Johannesburg. Interviewed: 1985 in Harare (*pages 54, 268*)

MARIUS SCHOON taught and worked for the ANC in Botswana from 1977 to 1983, until UK government officials warned him that the South Africans were planning action against him and his wife. He left Gaborone for the University of Angola, where he taught and worked for the ANC. In 1984 his wife, Jeanette Curtis, and his six-year-old daughter, Katryn, were killed in a parcel bomb explosion in Lubango. He worked at SOMAFCO until 1987, then moved to Ireland, where he worked for the ANC.
Born: 1937 in Johannesburg. Interviewed: 1986 in Harare (*page 151*)

REG SEPTEMBER was detained during the 1960 State of Emergency, was banned and worked underground until his arrest in 1963. He skipped bail and fled the country, then worked for the ANC in Tanzania. He served as ANC Chief Representative in the UK 1969–78, then went to Zambia where he headed the ANC's Department of Political Education. In 1990 he was named as an ANC Western Cape leader and a member of the Interim Leadership Group and central committee of the SACP.
Born: 1923 in Wynberg, Cape Town. Interviewed: 1986 in London (*page 60*)

JOE SEREMANE was arrested in 1963 and sentenced to six years on Robben Island for PAC activities. He was banned upon his release to Bophuthatswana, where he works for the South African Council of Churches and professes political non-alignment.
Born: 1938 in Randfontein, Transvaal. Interviewed: 1987 in Harare (*page 76*)

JACK SIMONS fled South Africa in 1964, after the government banned him from the University of Cape Town, where he had been teaching African Government and Law since 1937. After his retirement as Professor of Sociology at the University of Zambia he continued working for the ANC and the SACP, playing a key role in formulating the ANC's Constitutional Guidelines for a Democratic South Africa. He returned to Cape Town in 1990.
Born: 1907 in Riversdale, Cape Province, South Africa. Interviewed: 1987 in Harare. (*page 8*)

MAX SISULU, the youngest detainee in South Africa in 1963, fled the country after his father (ANC Secretary-General Walter Sisulu) was arrested at Rivonia. He joined the ANC's external mission in Tanzania, studied for a Master's degree in the Soviet Union, and then served as ANC representative to the World Federation of Democratic Youth in Hungary. He researched the role of transnational corporations in South Africa under a Dutch fellowship, and founded the ANC's Department of Economic Planning in Lusaka. Included in the indemnity for exiled ANC members, he was allowed to return home for the NEC meeting in Johannesburg.
Born: 1945 in Soweto. Interviewed: 1987 in Lusaka (*pages 78, 267*)

JOE SLOVO published a widely-read booklet in *1990, Has Socialism failed?* in response to the upheaval in Eastern Europe. He was named by the ANC to the team that met President de Klerk for the first round of 'talks about talks', and stayed on the team despite the government's complaints. He presided over the launch of the SACP inside the country, marking the party's 69th anniversary.
Born: 1926 in Lithuania. Interviewed: 1988 in Harare (*page 246*)

JAMES STUART was administrative secretary in the ANC Secretary-General's office in Lusaka. The 1990 ANC indemnity enabled him to return home.
Born: 1936 in Maitland, Cape. Interviewed: 1987 in Harare (*page 242*)

RAYMOND SUTTNER was elected to the UDF Transvaal regional executive in 1985. He was detained when the government declared a State of Emergency in 1986 and remained in prison, mainly in solitary confinement, for more than two years — the longest-serving white political detainee in the country. Upon his release he was effectively house arrested, but in 1989 he defied his restrictions to join the MDM's delegation to the Organization of African Unity

conference in Harare. He returned home early in 1990 and was named Political Education Department head of the ANC National Interim Leadership Committee.
Born: 1945 in Durban. Interviewed: 1985 in Johannesburg (*page 164*)

I. B. TABATA was banned in 1956 and after the order expired in 1961 he helped found a new organization, the African People's Democratic Union of South Africa (APDUSA). In 1963 he left South Africa for Zambia, and he moved to Zimbabwe after its independence, continuing to hold the position of president of both the Unity Movement and APDUSA.
Born: 1909 in Queenstown district in the Eastern Cape. Interviewed: 1986 in Harare (*page 39*)

PULE THATE is a member of the FAWU and treasurer of COSATU's National Education Committee.
Born: 1950 in Western Native Township, Johannesburg. Interviewed: 1987 in Harare (*page 231*)

JOE THLOLOE continued on the MWASA executive while working for the *Sowetan* newspaper. In 1988 he was awarded a Nieman journalism fellowship to study at Harvard University in the US.
Born: 1942 in Johannesburg. Interviewed: 1987 in Harare (*page 207*)

AMY THORNTON (known in the 1950s by her maiden name of Rietsteen) began working at the Woodstock Advice Office in 1986 and helped run Community House, the headquarters for a range of mass-based organizations in Cape Town. She was elected chairperson of Cape Democrats at its 1988 launch, then was detained and served with a restriction order. In 1989 she joined with other ex-detainees in defying their restrictions as part of the MDM's Defiance Campaign. In 1990 she helped launch the ANC in Cape Town.
Born: 1932 in Cape Town. Interviewed: 1985 in Cape Town (*page 163*)

DAN TLOOME was banned in 1953, then became publisher of *Liberation* magazine. When he was house arrested in 1963 he fled to Botswana. He moved to Lusaka in 1980, where he served as a member of the SACP central committee and the SACTU executive. In 1987 he was elected chairman of the SACP. The 1990 amnesty allowed him to return home.
Born: 1919 in Bloemfontein. Interviewed: 1987 in Lusaka (*page 24*)

LECHESA TSENOLI was elected to the Natal regional executive at the UDF's founding in 1983, and served as chairperson of the Natal International Youth Year (IYY) committee in 1985. In 1987 his Emergency detention was challenged in a landmark court case that led to his release and that of several other detainees. In 1989 he started work at the Natal regional newspaper, *New African.*
Born: 1955 in Bultfontein, Orange Free State. Interviewed: 1985 in Durban (*page 178*)

STEVE TSHWETE was banished to the Ciskei homeland upon his release from Robben Island in 1979. With the formation of the UDF in 1983 he was elected Border region president, was detained, and upon his release banned from entering South Africa from Ciskei. He went underground and continued to operate politically until he was nearly arrested in 1985, and fled to Lesotho and then Lusaka. He coordinated the ANC's 75th anniversary celebrations in Lusaka, and in 1987 was named Umkhonto we Sizwe Political Commissar and elected to the NEC. With the 1990 amnesty he returned home and began organizing ANC structures in the Eastern Cape.
Born: 1938 in Springs. Interviewed: 1987 in Harare (*pages 159, 262*)

TOM WASPE was detained in 1986–87, and one of the reasons cited by the court in denying an application for his release was that the constitution of JODAC (which he chaired) endorsed non-racialism, and that he was involved in the mobilization of the white community against apartheid. He teaches at a non-racial secondary school and is active in the All Schools for All People campaign.
Born: 1953 in Johannesburg. Interviewed: 1986 in Harare (*page 219*)

DAVID WEBSTER helped found the Five Freedoms Forum in 1987. He helped set up the Detainees' Education and Welfare Committee and the Human Rights Commission when DPSC was banned in 1988, and led the organizing of public 'tea parties' for detainees' relatives. Shortly after writing a report on political assassinations in 1989, he was assassinated in front of his Johannesburg home by gunmen who sped away in a car. Later in the year police arrested a suspect also connected to the assassination of Namibian civil rights lawyer Anton Lubowski. Police inquiries into the two murders uncovered a top-secret army hit squad, the 'Civil

Cooperation Bureau' (CCB), tasked with 'eliminating activists from the political scene'. Government commissions of inquiry into the CCB revealed that Webster was the target of spying and then murder because of his political activities.
Born: 1945 in Luanshaya, Zambia. Interviewed: 1985 in Johannesburg (*page 212*)

ROLAND WHITE lived in hiding in Grahamstown from 1986–87, then moved to Johannesburg to work as a political analyst for the Urban Foundation. A government inquiry into the CCB revealed that he had been one of the activists targeted for 'elimination' and was put under surveillance shortly after the assassination of David Webster.
Born: 1962 in Durban. Interviewed: 1985 in Grahamstown (*page 221*)

PETER WILLIAMS was detained in 1986, wrote his matriculation exams in detention, and began studying law upon his release. He was a delegate to the 1987 Harare Conference on the detention of children, and is active in CAYCO.
Born: 1967 in Athlone, Cape Town. Interviewed: 1987 in Harare (*page 190*)

M. B. YENGWA was banned in 1953, prosecuted in the 1956 Treason Trial, arrested again in 1963 and imprisoned for his underground ANC work, and banished to his home village in Zululand upon his release. In 1966 he fled to Swaziland, then went to England in 1970, where he served as chairman of the ANC's London region. He continued his political work, despite suffering a debilitating stroke in 1971, until his death in London in 1987.
Born: 1923 in Mapumulo village near Stanger, Natal. Interviewed: 1986 in London (*page 52*)

ZOLA ZEMBE (the assumed name of Archie Sibeko) was banned in 1956 and prosecuted in the Treason Trial. He went underground during the 1960 State of Emergency and then fled South Africa and went to work for SACTU. He served as SACTU's Western Europe representative from 1983 until SACTU's merger with COSATU in 1990.
Born: 1928 on the Tyumi River near Alice in the Eastern Cape. Interviewed: 1986 in London (*page 40*)

WANTU ZENZILE was detained six times while he was leading COSAS in the early 1980s, and was so severely tortured that he suffered permanent damage to his ears. His last detention was with fellow student leader Siphiwe Mtimkhulu, who was hospitalized upon his release and eventually paralyzed — his system poisoned by thallium, an illegal substance administered in prison. After Mtimkhulu mysteriously vanished in 1982, Zenzile fled South Africa. He then studied at SOMAFCO until 1987, when he received a scholarship for university study in the US.
Born: 1957 in Port Elizabeth. Interviewed: 1987 in Dar es Salaam (*page 166*)

JACOB ZUMA worked underground for SACTU and the ANC upon his release from Robben Island, then left in 1975 for Swaziland, where he worked for the ANC and was elected onto the NEC. He then moved to Mozambique, where he served as ANC Chief Representative until 1987. In early 1990 he became the first member of the ANC's NEC to return to South Africa in preparation for talks with the government.
Born: 1942 in Mapumolo, Natal. Interviewed: 1987 in Harare (*page 123*)

Notes

1. The interview with Ebrahim was conducted by Dutch journalist and author Rudi Boon and is excerpted in *Beyond Fear: Ebrahim Ismail Ebrahim versus the Apartheid State*, Anti-Apartheid Movement, Netherlands.
2. Part of the interview with Lekota was excerpted in Julie Frederikse, *South Africa: A Different Kind of War*, James Currey, Ravan Press and Mambo Press, 1986, and Beacon Press, 1987. He is also known by his nickname, 'Terror', earned on the football field, not in the political arena.
3. Naidoo is a very common Indian name in South Africa; none of the Naidoos interviewed for this book are directly related to each other.
4. This interview, the only one in the collection in a language other than English, was also conducted in Zulu by Rafora Rangongo.

Index